Jessica Ayesha Northey is a researcher at the Centre for Trust, Peace and Social Relations, Coventry University and Algerian country expert for the Bertelsmann Foundation. She has carried out numerous assignments for international organisations and completed her PHD in Social & Political Sciences at the European University Institute, Florence.

'A breath of fresh air has entered the polarised debates about associational life. After interviewing civil society actors in Algeria for more than ten years, Jessica Northey confidently takes us beyond facile generalisations about the value of associations. She shows – in detail and with subtlety – how citizens in this turbulent and authoritarian country have been staking claims to be legitimate political actors. She uses her trove of local insights to suggest sometimes surprising answers to weighty social scientific questions: can associations inculcate democratic behaviour? Do external donors like the EU help or hinder the development of this democratic process, as fragile as it is precious?'
Diana Wylie, Professor of History, African Studies Center,
Boston University

'Based on months of in-depth fieldwork, this highly original book explores the internal dynamics of Algerian society, its attempts to take advantage of any vacuum inadvertently provided by the bureaucracy and its pragmatic use of European support, without adopting the conceptual framework of European institutions. It will be of great interest to those working on the evolution of civil society and national identity and on the future of political participation in Algeria and the region.'
Professor Olivier Roy, Joint Chair of the Robert Schuman Centre for Advanced Studies at the European University Institute, Florence

'This is an important and welcome publication for scholars seeking to understand the relationship between civil society and state not only in Algeria but across MENA. Jessica Northey offers engaging insights into a range of grass roots organisations in Algeria based on her extensive fieldwork and knowledge of the political, historical and social issues at play. Her focus is on the construction of civil society in Algeria over the past three decades, examining the effects of the post-1988 reforms, the role of European Union funding and the link between such forms of funding for associations and the EU's strategic aims and objectives in the Southern Mediterranean. But it is her astute use of empirical data gathered from an impressive range of interviews carried out during extensive field-work trips to Algeria that gives the reader such a real insight into the resilience and agency of ordinary Algerians – those who have worked for social and cultural change through associations that allow communities to shape change. This book is marked by methodological rigour, enriched by Northey's linguistic and listening skills and informed by human empathy. *Civil Society in Algeria* brings us into the heart of everyday Algeria in a way that few books do and is essential reading for those of us who seek to understand civil society in North Africa.'

Patrick Crowley, Head of Department of French and Senior Lecturer, School of Languages, Literatures and Cultures, University College Cork

'This fascinating book identifies some of the key dynamics of socio-political change in contemporary Algeria. Drawing on personal experience and wide-ranging research in the country, including impressive fieldwork, Northey's analysis of the emergence and behaviour of numerous voluntary associations, active particularly in the fields of heritage preservation and social welfare, charts an extremely interesting and positive evolution in the relationship between state and society and argues persuasively that earlier pessimistic assessments of the role of associations in Algeria are now seriously out-of-date. A crucial feature of these dynamics is the way the associations she describes have eschewed contestation of the state and instead have developed strategies of constructive engagement and persuasion that tend to prompt new, equally constructive, responses on the part of Algerian officialdom. The associations demonstrated how their independent initiatives and activities, while advancing particular concerns and projects, have also been contributing to the commonweal, thus inducing the state to adopt a new and positive attitude towards them. Now, association activists and government agencies and office holders have begun to move along vital learning curves into new and hopeful territory. Northey's lucid and judicious analysis authorises us at last to speak of the emergence of civil society in Algeria without debasing that venerable concept. This is an original and important book and a most welcome contribution to the study of contemporary Algeria.'

Hugh Roberts, Edward Keller Professor of North African and Middle Eastern History, Department of History, Tufts University and author of *Berber Government* (I.B.Tauris, 2017)

CIVIL SOCIETY IN ALGERIA

Activism, Identity and the Democratic Process

JESSICA AYESHA NORTHEY

I.B. TAURIS
LONDON • NEW YORK • OXFORD • NEW DELHI • SYDNEY

I.B. TAURIS
Bloomsbury Publishing Plc
50 Bedford Square, London, WC1B 3DP, UK
1385 Broadway, New York, NY 10018, USA
29 Earlsfort Terrace, Dublin 2, Ireland

BLOOMSBURY, I.B. TAURIS and the I.B. Tauris logo
are trademarks of Bloomsbury Publishing Plc

First published in 2018
Reprinted 2019
Paperback edition published 2023

Copyright © Jessica Ayesha Northey, 2018, 2023

Jessica Ayesha Northey has asserted her right under the Copyright,
Designs and Patents Act, 1988, to be identified as Author of this work.

For legal purposes the Acknowledgements on p. xii constitute
an extension of this copyright page.

All rights reserved. No part of this publication may be reproduced or
transmitted in any form or by any means, electronic or mechanical,
including photocopying, recording, or any information storage or
retrieval system, without prior permission in writing from the publishers.

Bloomsbury Publishing Plc does not have any control over, or responsibility for,
any third-party websites referred to or in this book. All internet addresses given
in this book were correct at the time of going to press. The author and publisher
regret any inconvenience caused if addresses have changed or sites have
ceased to exist, but can accept no responsibility for any such changes.

A catalogue record for this book is available from the British Library.

A catalog record for this book is available from the Library of Congress.

ISBN: HB: 978-1-7883-1159-5
PB: 978-0-7556-4774-3
ePDF: 978-1-7867-3535-5
eBook: 978-1-7867-2535-6

Typeset by OKS Prepress Services, Chennai, India

To find out more about our authors and books visit
www.bloomsbury.com and sign up for our newsletters.

In memory of our friend and colleague Ahmed Bouchetata, Allah yerhmou, *and for all the associations*

CONTENTS

List of Illustrations   x
Preface   xii
Acknowledgements   xviii

Introduction   1
   Data Gathering   8
   Scope and Structure of the Book   11

Part I   Civil Society and Democracy Promotion in the Arab World

1. **Civil Society in the Arab World and Algeria**   17
   Associations in the Arab World   18
   Civil Society and Democracy   24
   Perceptions of Civil Society in Algeria   31
   Associative Activism in a Post-Conflict Environment   34
   Conclusion   37

2. **International Donors and Democracy Promotion**   39
   Development Paradigms and the Language of Donors   41
   Regional Variations in EU Support to Civil Society   45
   Civil Society Support in the MENA Region: Algeria,
      Palestine and Lebanon   50
   Conclusion   58

Part II Algerian Civil Society and Relations with the State

3. Historical Perspectives on Civil Society in Algeria — 63
   Traditional Civil Society and the Impact of Colonialism — 65
   Civil Society in an Independent Algeria — 72
   Democratic Opening and the Black Decade — 78
   Conclusion — 80

4. Civil Society and the State — 82
   State–Society Relations and the Failure of Dialogue — 84
   The Arab Spring, Associative Action and State Responses — 87
   Civil Society and the 2012 Law on Associations — 91
   Conclusion — 100

5. Associations in Algeria — 103
   A New Typology of Associations — 104
   The Regional Focus of Algerian Associations — 108
   The Sector Focus of Algerian Associations — 112
   Conclusion — 116

6. Algerian Associations Protecting the Past — 119
   Heritage Associations in Algeria — 120
   Associations and Urban History — 124
   Preserving Roman History in Algeria — 127
   Algeria's Archaeological Past — 130
   Religious Heritage and Traditions — 133
   Conclusion — 136

7. Algerian Associations and Social Welfare — 138
   Social Sector Associations in Algeria — 139
   Social Work, Disability and New Voices in Oran — 143
   Contesting State Provision in Kabylia — 147
   Associations, Faith and Health Care in El Oued — 149
   Dealing with Trauma — 151
   Conclusion — 155

Part III Donors, Democracy and the Language of Others

8. Europe, Civil Society and Democracy in Algeria — 159
   European Diplomacy in Algeria — 161
   European Union Programmes in Algeria — 166

	European Support to Algerian Civil Society	169
	Conclusion	175
9.	**Language and the Construction of Civil Society**	177
	The Performative Effect of Language	180
	Historical Narratives	184
	Language Policies and the Public Sphere	188
	Conclusion	193
10.	**Imagining a New Future**	195
	The Hirak Revolution	199
	Pandemic Activism	205
	New Tools, Space and a Revolutionary Consciousness	211
	Conclusion	216
Conclusion		219
Notes		227
Bibliography		252
Index		267

LIST OF ILLUSTRATIONS

Figures

Figure 1.1 Numbers of registered associations in MENA countries.	19
Figure 1.2 Registered associations by population in MENA countries.	20
Figure 1.3 Civil society and democratisation in academic journals.	25
Figure 2.1 EU development spending in Algeria.	52
Figure 2.2 EU development spending in Palestine.	54
Figure 2.3 EU development spending in Lebanon.	55
Figure 2.4 EU spending on NGOs in three MENA countries.	56
Figure 5.1 Typology of associations, reasons for creation and levels of autonomy.	108
Figure 5.2 Density of associations by *wilaya*.	109
Figure 5.3 Association density map of Algeria by *wilaya* and population.	111
Figure 5.4 Map of EU-financed NGO projects in Algeria.	112
Figure 5.5 Local associations in Algeria and their sector focus.	114
Figure 5.6 National associations in Algeria and their sector focus.	115
Figure 6.1 Regions with most cultural associations per capita.	122

Figure 7.1 Social associations in Algeria. 141

Figure 7.2 Regions with most social associations per capita. 143

Tables

Table 1.1 Associations in the MENA countries. 21

Table 2.1 EU development spending on NGOs in three MENA countries. 57

Table 6.1 Association density – cultural associations per 100,000 inhabitants (ten densest regions). 121

Table 7.1 Local social sector associations. 140

Table 7.2 National social sector associations. 141

Table 7.3 Association density – social associations per 100,000 inhabitants (ten densest regions). 142

Table 8.1 History of the EU delegation in Algiers. 164

Table 8.2 EU support to Algeria between 1976 and 1996. 166

Table 8.3 EU support to Algeria between 1995 and 1999 (MEDA I). 168

Table 8.4 EU support to Algeria between 2000 and 2006 (MEDA II). 168

Table 8.5 Sectors of the EU's second Support to Algerian Associations Programme (ONG2). 173

PREFACE

Algerian history, as well as the contemporary political life of the country, particularly since 2019, offer us important insights into how societies could seek to achieve revolutionary transformation. The preface to this new edition of *Civil Society in Algeria* is written in July 2022. This is 60 years exactly from Algeria's declaration of independence, after 132 years of brutal colonial rule. In 1962, after eight years of bloody war, Algerians defeated France, one of the world's most significant military powers. They had almost no means, only a total determination that right was on their side and the conviction that they must leave a fairer, democratic and just society for their children. Though leading powers such as the UK and the United States continued to supply weapons to France, by the end of the war, the world order had transformed. With support from South America to Asia, Algeria led its combat against colonialism, for not only Algeria and the Maghreb, but also the entire African continent. The importance of this revolution is still recognised today, even in those Western capitals that had sided with the colonial power and who generally opted for amnesia as a means to process this painful history.[1] Throughout 2022, at conferences from the Sorbonne in Paris to Harvard in the United States and SOAS in London, Algerian scholars at home and in the diaspora have been invited to speak and reflect on the politics and history of Algeria.

An enhanced interest in the Algerian Revolution, politics and history is fuelled also by the more recent mobilisation of young Algerians, in the massive, peaceful, political demonstrations of 2019. Known as the *hirak*, the 'movement', this brought millions of Algerians onto the streets demanding democracy and an end to president Abdelaziz Bouteflika's twenty-year rule, to corruption and to mismanagement. In the years following the publication of the first edition of this book, pressure and tensions have mounted. While civil society associations continued to mobilise within the constraints of the system, the question was becoming increasingly urgent as to who would succeed Bouteflika: a president who could no longer speak in public and who was replaced by a framed picture at his electoral rallies. By December 2018, frustrations were high. Something had to happen. The humiliation of poor governance and lack of leadership – policymaking or action – had become unbearable. As it became clear that no successor had been found, the decision for Bouteflika to stand yet again in a fifth presidential mandate sparked, in February 2019, the most impressive mobilisation and marches the region, if not the world, has seen. Beginning in the east of Algeria, on 16 February 2019, then in the capital Algiers on 22 February, millions of ordinary Algerians took to the streets to demand the president stand down. Following Friday prayers on 22 February, Algerians, led by young people, demonstrated peacefully in the streets of every city of the country.

Largely overlooked or ignored by Western media, perhaps due to the difficulty of conducting research or journalism in Algeria; perhaps, more cynically, due to their lack of violence, these marches continued over 54 weeks, from 2019 into 2020. The president stood down in April 2019. Business leaders and politicians were charged with corruption and imprisoned. Gradually, General Gaid Salah, now the de facto leader of the country, accepted the collective demands and the crowds became bolder in their demands. As well as marches on Fridays and Tuesdays, Algerians held forums on the steps of the theatre, in Algiers, conducted concerts in public squares, held debates in universities, produced films and artwork and songs to accompany the protests. For the vast majority, the marches became an opportunity for reconnection, not only to the public space, but equally to one another, as they marched side by side, despite the divisions and traumas of the past. Rather than demonstrating anger against Bouteflika himself, Algerians called out a system plagued with corruption and nepotism, which needed to change. With humour and art, they called out Western imperialism, including the extractivism of international petrol companies and risks presented by fracking in the Algerian south. Connecting to multiple ongoing protest movements, from the unemployed to environmentalists, they marched together for social justice, fairness and equality. Benalycherif, in his photojournalism, quotes one participant who explained the importance of the demonstrations in uniting against the previous divisions and false, divisive narratives, stating that, 'Algerians did not speak to each other. They didn't trust each other. This *hirak* has made it possible to recreate bonds, to bring people together.'[2] Others held placards, thanking Bouteflika for having united the population: '*Merci Boutef de nous avoir uni*'. As well as uniting Algerians, the *hirak*, it is argued, has progressively re-politicised Algerian society.[3] Prior to the 2019 protests, many considered 'that the national trauma of civil war made the Algerian people apolitical'.[4] Whereas the trauma and 'legacy of the unresolved conflicts of the 1990s' did make unity difficult to achieve, and divisions did emerge,[5] it is important nevertheless to understand the significance of this year-long peaceful protest movement, in terms of citizenship, identity, civil society and democracy, for Algeria and the wider region.

In many ways, the developments described in this book anticipated this explosion of civil society activism in 2019. The grassroots mobilisation, organising and activism of thousands of Algerian associations following legal reforms in 1990, meant the space for civil society was more open. With more associations than any other in the region by the early 2000s, such developments may well have contributed to the longevity of the Algerian *hirak*. What is significant in the *hirak* is not only the duration and sheer numbers – way beyond the 3 per cent the Harvard scholar Erica Chenoworth argues to be necessary for a social movement to be successful – but also the way in which they organised.[6] The absolute commitment to the Algerian term *silmiya* (meaning peaceful), as a form of protest, meant that whatever attempts were made to destabilise the movement, and the protesters' resolve, these failed. Acutely aware that the extremely well-equipped

Algerian army and security services would automatically win in any violent confrontation, the protesters explicitly chanted their commitment to peace. They chanted that the army and the people were brothers, *'jeich, chaab, khawa khawa'*, offered flowers to the soldiers and formed rings around police officers to protect them. Following the marches, groups of young people would clean the cities. Other groups organised first aid, and collective dinners were prepared for anyone visiting from outside the capital. The social solidarity displayed on the streets of Algiers, and in the diaspora, where similar marches and demonstrations took place, was phenomenal. As Professor Zahia Salhi argued during the Harvard conference on the Independence anniversary in June 2022, this was completely different from the Arab Spring movements. Whilst drawing on Algeria's recent history of civil society development and collective organisation, it was an entirely new form of mobilisation, worthy of analysis in its own right.[7]

After fifty-four weeks of marching, the Covid-19 pandemic hit in March 2020. Algerians chose to end the marches and moved the mobilisation predominantly online. Organisations still continued to clean the cities, collect food for affected families and support the health services with protective and medical equipment. In the diaspora, fundraising continued and collective solidarity flourished. The Algerian economy suffered from the micro- to the macro level, as people lost their jobs and businesses closed. Falling oil prices left the new government in a vulnerable position and the challenges seemed overwhelming. Yet Algerians continued to mobilise. Protests against the imprisonment of political activists continued online. Universities in particular took advantage of the move online to connect with the diaspora and international scholars to continue debates about the future of Algeria.

In March 2020, with a network of Algerian and international scholars, I was awarded a large grant by the British Academy to investigate how young Algerians imagine the future. Our focus was on environmental livelihoods and the green economy. Forced to rewrite our methodology entirely, face-to-face interviews went online, and focus groups were conducted by Zoom, now also including the diaspora. With our network of Algerian researchers from Jijel University, PhD students from across Algeria and Algerian postgraduate students in the UK, we conducted multiple training programmes, as well as interviews from Adrar to Algiers, and Skikda to Tlemcen. We engaged with young environmental activists, associations and academics interested in youth politics, the environment and sustainability. We documented new forms of activism and engagement emerging in Algeria since 2019 and the continuation of grassroots mobilisation as discussed throughout *Civil Society in Algeria*.

The data collected during this time inspires the new and final chapter of this book. It confirms my own conviction that Algerian civil society, youth politics and activism have hugely significant lessons for us all. This comes at a time when we all need radical transformation of our societies and economies to face new and urgent global challenges. The effects of climate change, species extinction, biodiversity loss and pandemics will respect no borders. The extensive forest fires experienced across northern Algeria and the entire Mediterranean in the summer of 2021 underlined this. It is essential that we look to our civil societies in new ways and explore different modes of collective organisation and revolutionary transformation to tackle these crises and respond in time. The Algerian experience, I argue, can once again offer new tools and models, not only of mobilisation, but also of the collective organisation and solidarity we will need in the twenty-first century.

The psychologist and Algerian nationalist Franz Fanon wrote during the War of Independence of the importance of individual liberation, for the Algerian Revolution. He described how 'the Algerian has brought into existence a new, positive, efficient personality, whose richness is provided less by the trial of strength that he engages in than by his certainty that he embodies a decisive moment of the national consciousness'.[8] Fanon described how FLN (*Front de Libération Nationale*) fighters not only combatted 'the torturing parachutists' but were deeply concerned with the challenges 'of building, of organising, of inventing the new society that must come into being'.[9] He writes, 'Many colonized peoples have demanded the end of colonialism, but rarely like the Algerian people.'[10] Algerians experienced not only the interdependent processes of liberation, but also the domino effect of their struggle across continents and the world, and the disintegration of the colonial system. They also witnessed and themselves achieved the construction of a nation in what seemed impossible conditions.

Preface

As Fanon himself predicted, the postcolonial period in Algeria was not easy. The challenges discussed throughout *Civil Society in Algeria* were in many ways foreseen. There are no panaceas to the collective struggles for democracy, environmental and social justice that so many aspire to, in Algeria and beyond. Yet, the collective will, solidarity, personal engagement and confidence of the hundreds of Algerian youths, activists and associational members interviewed over the course of writing this book, who benefit from this historical legacy of radical revolutionary potential, inspire hope. The new final chapter seeks to assess whether the popular energies apparent in the community associations, engaged in heritage and social welfare, contributed to and shaped the political contestation and its peaceful nature in 2019. What range of possibilities for public and political life now exists in Algeria? In learning from the Algerian experience, of the grassroots mobilisation in associations over the last three decades, and of the mass peaceful mobilisations of 2019, we can begin to imagine how a better future might look.

Notes

1. The historian Benjamin Stora, speaking at the Sorbonne University, Paris, on 25 June 2022 argues that France opted for total amnesia, whereas Algeria thoroughly examined its history of the war.
2. Sabri Benalycherif, '"Nothing Will Fall from the Sky": Algeria's Revolution Marches On' – Photo Essay (18 December 2019), *African Arguments*, 2019.
3. Benalycherif, '"Nothing Will Fall from the Sky"'; Yahia Zoubir, 'The Algerian Crisis: Origins and Prospects for a "Second Republic"', 21 May 2019. *Aljazeera Centre for Studies Report*, p. 12.
4. Faouzia Zeraoulia, 'The Memory of the Civil War in Algeria: Lessons from the Past with Reference to the Algerian Hirak', *Contemporary Review of the Middle East* 7/1 (2020), pp. 1–29, p. 2.
5. Latefa Guemar, *Algerian Women: Experiences of Exile from the Black Decade to the Hirak* (Exeter, forthcoming in 2023), p. 159.
6. Erica Chenoweth and Maria Stephan, *Why Civil Resistance Works: The Strategic Logic of Nonviolent Conflict* (New York, 2011).
7. Professor Zahia Salhi, speaking at Harvard University, 30 June 2022, argued that due its numbers and methods, the *hirak* represented an entirely new form of mobilisation.
8. Frantz Fanon, *Toward the African Revolution: Political Essays* (New York: Grove Press, 1988), pp. 102–3.
9. Ibid., p. 103.
10. Ibid.

ACKNOWLEDGEMENTS

This book is a result of support from the European University Institute in Florence, from the Centre for Trust, Peace and Social Relations in Coventry University and from hundreds of Algerian associations who participated in this project to understand more about civil society in Algeria. I extend heartfelt thanks to Olivier Roy, Lahouari Addi, Pascal Vennesson and Patrick Crowley who offered their expertise, as did Bahar Baser, Leila Hadj-Abdou, Tamirace Fakhoury and Benoit Challand. Exceptional colleagues in Algeria – Assia Harbi, Téric Boucebci, Ahmed Bouchetata, Youcef Rahmi, Ahmed Djebara, Mohamed Hadj Hammouda, Ferial Assia Selhab, Belkacem Messaoudi, Faycel Hattab, Zoubida Kouti, Tarik Loumassine, Karima Slimani and Madjid Azzoug (and their families) – invested much time supporting the fieldwork over the last decade. It was a privilege to have spoken with Abdelmadjid Harbi, Youcef Hadj Ali, Francis Ghilès, Robert Parks, Omar Derras, Brahim Salhi, Anouar Benmalek, Yahia Belaskri and Maissa Bey, who all gave useful feedback and encouragement. Annette Boucebci's friendship, and her endless optimism and love for Algeria, made the fieldwork so much more inspiring. From the associations, many people gave their precious time, on top of their dedication to improving conditions, in social, cultural and environmental aspects of Algerian life. Ahmed Daoud, Houaria Djebarri, Djamila Hamitou, Mohamed Ider, Cherifa Kheddar, Kouider Metair, Khelil Moussaoui and Saleh Tirichine are a few of the inspirational people who are behind the case studies and interviews discussed throughout this book. Earlier versions of some of the material in Chapter 6 appear in 'Algerian Heritage Associations:

National Identity and Rediscovering the Past', in Patrick Crowley (ed.) *Algeria: Nation, Culture and Tansnationalism, 1988–2016,* reprinted by permission of Liverpool University Press. I am grateful to I.B.Tauris, to Sophie Rudland the editor, and to the excellent anonymous reviewers, for taking on this manuscript and these different perspectives on Algerian civil society. Finally, Matthew, my family and my mother Julie in particular, have all provided moral and editorial support to ensure these stories can be told with the minimum of eloquence they deserve.

INTRODUCTION

On 24 June 1996, Cherifa Kheddar lost both her brother Mohamed Reda and her sister Leila. Both were assassinated by Islamist terrorists in an attack witnessed by their mother, who survived her injuries. This happened in their home in Blida, in the Mitidja region of Algeria, an area which came to be known as the 'triangle of death' during Algeria's 'black decade' (a period of appalling violence) at the hands of Islamist insurgents, with often equally violent responses from the state. During the 1990s the rise of extreme Islamist ideology, and the subsequent conflict which engulfed Algeria, saw almost all categories of society targeted. Journalists, teachers, artists, lawyers and public sector workers were classed as traitors if they did not carry the Islamist project in their hearts, in their behaviour or visibly on their bodies. Catholic priests, such as those of the Tibhirine Monastery, were kidnapped and killed. Many imams who refused to issue deadly *fatwas* condemning their fellow Algerian citizens were murdered. Women in particular were targeted. Not wearing the veil, going to work, teaching in a school and even carrying a briefcase could result in a death sentence.

After the assassinations of her sister and brother, Cherifa Kheddar refused to give in. That same year she created an association, *Djazairouna* (Our Algeria). Through this association, she and other families of the victims set up support networks. They bravely accompanied the families of victims to their funerals, knowing this could put them on a death list. Women stood against tradition and went to the cemeteries, despite the first day of mourning usually being reserved for men. They offered counselling, financial support, legal advice and comfort to those who had lost everything. Faced with such violence and intolerance, women in Blida, and across Algeria, did not succumb. They went to work and many, despite often being devout and practising Muslims, chose not to wear the veil. They joined together – in the darkest of conditions – and formed associations, forged support networks and stood up for the values of peace, non-violence, solidarity and tolerance. Twenty years later, *Djazairouna* continues to fight for human rights, women's equality and for the right of Algerian civil society to have a place in the public sphere.[1]

Despite the violence of the 1990s, this example of grassroots organising and support to vulnerable people was replicated in towns and cities across Algeria. This was not a new phenomenon. Indeed, such collective action drew upon a long history of activism and struggles for freedom and justice in Algerian society. Pre-colonial traditions of community-based activism and decision-making in Algeria have been clearly documented by authors such as Hugh Roberts.[2] In the nineteenth century, however, the brutality of French colonial rule over 132 years decimated many of these traditional foundations of society. Under colonialism, Algerians had to find ways to re-structure, both in the everyday politics of non-political associations[3] and in the anti-colonial struggle of the twentieth century. In the period of independence, the challenges of rebuilding the nation also dampened the spirits of autonomous civil society organisations. In an attempt to bring about a unified 'collective sense of nationhood',[4] while under the stress of rolling back the colonial state, the new government struggled with the existence of independent organisations.[5] From the 1960s, the government officially allowed only the Soviet-style *organisations de masse*, until these became too critical, whilst tolerating others that operated semi-clandestinely. This period of rupture for associative life was, as Sarah Ben Nefissa writes, characteristic of 'the construction of modern states after independence' in many Arab countries.[6] In Algeria, the need to unify the nation after the bitter War of Independence with France from 1954 to 1962 meant there was a 'refusal to accept politics and conflict', and a denial of plurality.[7] As such, the 1970s and 1980s were dominated by state-controlled organisations with little freedom of association. The state set up organisations to create unconditional support structures in order to frame, control and manage society.[8] This unsuccessful policy, along with declining socio-economic conditions, led to riots in 1988.

These country-wide riots resulted, quite surprisingly however, in a remarkable democratisation project in Algeria. Legal reforms allowed for political pluralism, freedom of the press and freedom of association. Under the new law of 1990,[9] which drew significantly on the French law of 1901, Algerian associations were now free to register without prior authorisation or vetting and be recognised by the government. Anna Bozzo writes that October 1988 in Algiers was, despite its ultimate failure, the protest movement which 'opened the way for this new series of demonstrations' two decades on with the so-called Arab Spring of 2011.[10] The cancellation of the elections in 1992, and the *coup d'état* by the military, brought to a tragic close this ambitious democratic reform programme in Algeria. The decade-long conflict which followed, between Islamist insurgents and the military regime, resulted in the deaths of over 200,000 people, including the family of Cherifa Kheddar. Worse than the War of Independence in some ways, as the enemy was far more difficult to define, this conflict caused a complete breakdown in trust across society and an escalation of violence to an extent that no one could have predicted. In such difficult conditions, one might have expected decreased levels of civic engagement. Yet the previous reforms, notably the 1990 Law on Associations, along with the sheer determination and bravery of the Algerian population, brought a significant increase in the number of registered associations in the towns and cities of Algeria. During the conflict of the 1990s, despite the violence and severe restrictions on public spaces, certain sectors of civil society flourished. Algeria had more associations than any other country in the region and their astonishing growth initially led to great optimism amongst Algerian commentators. In the early 1990s, many felt that associations were part of a growing civil society and as such could contribute to democratisation of the Algerian political system.[11] This perception continued, despite the ongoing turmoil of the violent conflict throughout the 1990s which consumed the Algerian state.

By the early 2000s, however, with the absence of any significant political transformation in Algeria and across the region, the role of these new associative actors became highly contested. Prior to the Arab Spring uprisings of 2011, Western scholars increasingly questioned the assumption that civil society actors in Algeria, and in the Arab world more generally, were capable of contributing to democratisation as had been predicted in the 1990s. For some commentators such as Liverani, it was worse; the growth of associations seemed to support the conservation of an authoritarian order.[12] Under such an authoritarian regime, associations simply could not be democratic. For other scholars, associations were categorised as merely too weak or too divided to be able to enact real change.[13] Questioning the role of associations as a force for political renewal, some challenged the independence of Algerian civil society from the state, arguing that 'associational life has hindered – rather than boosted – Algeria's democratization process'.[14] Equally, the intervention of international donors, in supporting such civil society organisations, was claimed to further impede Algerian democracy. Such external support could, according to some, legitimise the state internationally, whilst conserving an authoritarian order within Algeria.[15]

The risks of external donors imposing their vision on local societies, using Western concepts about civil society and democratisation, have been highlighted by different authors. In his analysis of civil society in the Middle East and Central Asia, Olivier Roy, for example, warns of the damaging impacts of donors ignoring the traditional, indigenous and real actors for change.[16] This creates a mirror effect in which projects and organisations simply mimic donor guidelines. For Roy, political legitimacy of the state and of traditional actors is central to prospects for democracy. Such organisations – the press, cafes, musical societies, theatres, sports clubs, trade unions, religious associations, local political structures or charitable organisations – rooted in Algerian traditions drawn from pre-colonial structures, as well as from the movements born under the colonial legislation of 1901, all constitute a significant part of Algerian civil society and, it is argued, are the real actors who merit further attention.

The role of associations and civil society actors in the political landscape of Algeria is still evolving. The uprisings that occurred across North Africa, in neighbouring Tunisia and Libya in 2011, inevitably affected Algerian society. Regional instability, the risks of a return to terrorism, the turmoil in Libya, the rise of Islamic State and tensions across the Sahel all impacted on the political environment in Algeria. Following the 2011 uprisings, a public consultation and constitutional revision process led to a new constitution in 2016. This new constitution reinstated presidential term limits, made Berber an official language and strengthened the legislature. It went some way to meeting societal demands. However, there remains a deep scepticism among the population concerning the need for more serious reforms to strengthen the justice system, improve political participation and strive for real socio-economic equality in Algeria. Political and legal reforms in 2012 for associations, political parties, elections and the media opened up some of the political and public spheres but increased restrictions in other parts. Journalists and associations still face repression and barriers if they challenge the government. The re-elections of President Bouteflika, despite his failing health and age, have caused deep frustration in the increasingly young population. Opposition parties have been numerous since the 2012 law, but their fragmentation means there is little combined and strategic opposition to the FLN (*Front de Libération Nationale*), the party that has ruled Algeria since 1962.

Civil society organisations, social movements and new networks have nevertheless brought new voices to the political sphere across the region. In Algeria, since 2011, networks of associations have been challenging legislative proposals. They have fought to increase female participation in the Algerian Parliament, have struggled for reform to laws on domestic violence and have campaigned for the recognition of Berber as an official language. External actors, such as the European Union and other donors, had already been funding some of these civil society organisations over the last two decades, but their role has been controversial and much-criticised. The majority of these associational networks are, however, national ones, developed internally within Algeria and with little, if any, international development funding. International donors have a limited space, as do researchers. Access to both associations and their members depends on a degree of trust and acceptance. The weight of colonial history, the sense of abandonment during the 1990s conflict and the general feeling that Europeans have little understanding of Algeria make it hard for outsiders to grapple with the complexity of the societal challenges facing the country.[17]

A further obstacle to understanding these new voices within Algerian society is that most investigations are based on studies of organisations made at a fragile point in Algerian history – at the end of a decade of violent conflict. The tendency to view negatively any possibilities for social or political reform in such a period is understandable. From this comes a risk, however, of creating a 'failure complex', a self-fulfilling prophecy of defeat, through the categorisation of any political and social reform as unsuccessful. This can be highly damaging and, as Albert Hirschman writes, 'may itself lead to real failures'.[18] The language of internal and external actors arguably shapes the perceptions of and possibilities for future action and reform, in Algeria and beyond. Performative words have the power to create reality and the language of failure can impact on the actors at the grassroots level.[19]

There is a more positive strand in analytical discussions about Algerian civil society. In *Civil Society and Democratization in the Arab World, The Dynamics of Activism*, Cavatorta and Durac argue that, although often divided, in the absence of political parties Algerian associations do indeed now form a powerful framework within which politics happens.[20] In order for associations or civil society organisations to have an impact, with a voice of their own, they need to have had time and appropriate support to stabilise and flourish. Algeria has now experienced over a decade without armed conflict. Equally, with the political revolutions that transformed countries across the Arab world in 2011, the language and perceptions about the capacity for mobilisation and the desire for democracy are gradually changing across the region as a whole.

As well as these political changes, international donors have now slowly returned to Algeria. Since 2001, two significant programmes to support civil society have been implemented by the European Union, now the largest external donor in Algeria. These programmes have supported over 1,000 local Algerian associations through small grants and training. The EU's global budget for civil society in Algeria is one of the lowest in the region. The majority of the organisations involved were created in Algeria during the period of conflict, independent of any external support. The trauma of conflict not only prevented the proper functioning of Algeria's numerous associations, but also meant that associational life in the 1990s grew in a vacuum. Away from donors and funding calls, activities were often directly linked to the immediate needs of the population and arose from abuses and tragedies, the consequences of one of the most painful conflicts in recent history, as was the case for *Djazairouna*. It is the huge surge in associational life, in these isolated and difficult conditions, that makes Algerian associations an interesting and inspiring area to explore.

At the same time, it is important to avoid extreme visions of the potential of these structures. As Abu-Sada and Challand argue in their recent research into civil society in the Arab world, associations are neither a panacea for all political problems, nor simply a privileged instrument manipulated by states and donors. They write:

> Associations are, depending on the case, seen as places of innovation, free from the bureaucracy of administrations which have for years claimed the monopoly on development, as a place of dissent, a counter-power, a laboratory for an alternative society, for democratization of Arab regimes and societies, a place of local and political mobilization. Almost inversely, they have also been considered a privileged instrument at the service of development policies, to be mobilized by the authorities as by donors, to promote their policies: as key institutions, new development policies, even as 'Governmental NGOs.' It is in-between of these two visions, the real effects they produce, that needs to be examined.[21]

Civil Society in Algeria: Activism, Identity and the Democratic Process aims to examine these real effects at the micro level and to challenge some of the critiques and the scepticism about civil society as a force for political change in the region. The following chapters will explore grassroots associations across Algeria and their relations with local communities and political institutions. To do this, the book uses the concept of civil society to understand the place of these associations within the Algerian political system. It raises the questions posed by Antonio Gramsci as to whether civil society represents a sphere of hegemony, creating consent in the subordinated classes, or whether civil society can be a counter-hegemonic force, challenging the authoritarian tendencies of the state. Is civil society, as Alexis de Tocqueville argued in the nineteenth century, an essential component to the functioning of democracy? Or, as Robert Putnam found in Italy, is it an important indicator in the performance of political institutions? And if so, under which conditions can civil society organisations contribute to political change and democracy?

Overall, the book explores and questions certain assumptions found in recent discussions about civil society in the Middle East and North Africa. First, it challenges the assertion that the associational movement in the Arab world has, in the main, proved to be a conservative force that simply serves to legitimise and reinforce authoritarian regimes. Second, it questions to what extent donors have really supported this process. To challenge these assumptions, by exploring the case of Algeria, the book will discuss the nature of activism, the implications in terms of identity and the impact of associational engagement on the democratic process in the country. In seeking to avoid extreme visions of civil society, the book aims to analyse the reality experienced on the ground by the leaders and members of local associations. It hopes to assess the roles of associations in the lives of their communities, as well as their impact upon the larger political institutions of the country.

Data Gathering

This research focuses its investigation on over 200 Algerian civil society organisations, many of which I had the privilege of working with between 2007 and 2009 through my role in an EU-funded civil society support programme. Employed by this programme, I was based in the National Ministry of Solidarity and the Social Development Agency in Algiers, where I spent over two years with the national technical team responsible for assisting the Ministry. It was the exceptional energy and commitment of my Algerian colleagues, and of the associations, in successfully implementing this programme that inspired me to return many times to Algeria in the following years to research their work further. Outside of the Ministry, as an independent researcher, I wanted to explore the impact of these Algerian associations – which had successfully run so many small projects at the grassroots level – upon their wider political environment and local democracy. I also wanted to understand how their activism might influence debates about national or transnational identities and about historical representations, and I further wanted to consider whether external actors actually had any real influence on Algerian civil society at all.

Returning for two month-long trips and several shorter trips, colleagues, friends and networks of associations helped me to organise meetings in different cities and towns across Algeria. I spoke mainly with regional associations, and sometimes officials and academics, in Algiers, Annaba, Blida, Oran, Sidi Bel Abbes, Tiaret, Tizi Ouzou, Bou Saada, Ghardaia, Djelfa, Medea, Tenes, Naama, Timimoun, Bechar and in other diverse towns in the different regions of the vast territory. These organisations were working in many different areas: environmental protection, cultural projects, health care, sport, archaeological preservation and the protection of vulnerable populations such as disabled children. The themes of heritage protection and social welfare emerged as particularly significant in the different towns. As such, during the second trip, I focused more specifically on those sectors, asking members of thematic networks to recommend similar associations in other towns.

As a female researcher, I was welcomed into the families of some of the associations. I was helped by former colleagues to take buses and trains, or given lifts to the next destination and colleagues recommended particularly active associations. Algerian friends accompanied me for some of the meetings and were often surprised to learn what was apparently happening on the ground within small, often remote associations. They were also concerned for my safety and potential risks I could face or cause. Ten years earlier, it would have been highly inadvisable for a foreigner to travel to many of the places I visited. Nonnationals had been prime targets of Islamist violence or kidnappings. I tried to always listen carefully, to follow their advice and to ensure that my actions should not add to the anxieties and traumas that all Algerians had suffered when friends or family travelled during the ten years of violence and insecurity in the 1990s.

As an outsider in Algeria, a non-Algerian with only basic Arabic, most of the interviews and group discussions were conducted in French. Having worked with many of the organisations integral to this investigation, I was also not entirely an outsider. I felt much sympathy with the goals, challenges and ambitions of many of the respondents. I *wanted* them to succeed. I wanted to challenge the negative discourse around Algerian and Middle Eastern civil society generally. As such, questions of my own position in the research were sometimes problematic. It was not always easy to maintain a neutral position, to acknowledge in some cases the failures, the weaknesses or even the desperation of some of the organisations. Associations could be effectively disrupted, silenced or, in rare cases, even criminalised by the state or local competitors. Occasionally, this might be rightly done for, say, mismanagement, but more often it was due to a misplaced prejudice. Conflicts were a main topic of discussion and these sometimes involved organisations or officials with whom I had previously worked. It was not always easy to remain calmly objective, but I have tried as much as possible to honestly reflect the voices from all sides. There were also risks that, by highlighting the successes of certain organisations, I was potentially putting them in danger of becoming a target for malice or jealousy. In a post-conflict context, in which state–society relations were slowly recovering after a complete breakdown in the 1990s, the need for discretion, humility and understanding weighed heavily throughout the fieldwork.

Looking beyond Algeria, this book also draws on previous personal experiences working with EU development programmes which targeted civil society in the Maghreb and in Africa. This convinced me of the importance of understanding Algerian civil society within the context of the Arab world, with which Algeria has so many cultural and political links, and with which it also faces similar funding programmes and pressures from its main donors such as the EU. Between 2010 and 2012, I travelled as an independent researcher to neighbouring Mauritania and to Lebanon, where I was able to exchange views with civil society organisations and donors in similar contexts. In both countries, at least on the surface, there did not appear to be the same dynamism, resilience or selfless hard work by so many volunteers within such small, grassroots associations that I had witnessed in Algeria.

In total, I visited associations from 23 of the 48 provincial governorates (*wilayas*) of Algeria. Interviews were conducted with associations across different sectors, many of which had never received any funding from an international donor. I also participated in a number of regional forums and activities of the associations and followed their work via the internet and social media. Data come from interviews with the Algerian Ministry of National Solidarity, and the Social Development Agency and its regional offices, the European Union office in Algiers, the French and British Embassies and various European cooperation projects. In Algiers, the Ministry of Solidarity gave me access to financial and technical data from over 200 associations funded by the different support programmes. These data included the statutes, financial and technical reports and evaluations from the different monitoring processes. Similar data from non-funded associations within Algeria were obtained directly from the organisations. A more in-depth study was made of 25 associations from the different regions, which emerged in two central sectoral themes of cultural heritage and social welfare. Semi-structured interviews and discussion groups enabled me to interact with the presidents, boards and members. Significant time was

INTRODUCTION   11

spent in the field with these associations and with the populations identified as the beneficiaries of their actions. This was complemented by interviews with the partners with whom they work, in formal or informal networks, either from the state ministries or agencies, from other civil society organisations or from donors.

Interviews and field visits involved discussions about the independence of associations from the state and from the private sphere, and about their effectiveness both individually and as a movement. Interviewees discussed the role of religious associations, religion in politics, the conflict of the 1990s and the impact on associations and their members. They were often very critical of state policies, of the living conditions of the populations they sought to serve, of the protection of Algerian heritage, and the role of the state and other associations in promoting a better future for Algerians. They were also optimistic, on many occasions, about the potential of associations to bring about change, reflecting on their own roles in challenging past narratives and in improving the life chances and the cultural and social welfare of all Algerians. The members acknowledged the difficulties in working together within the associational movement and within associations themselves. Conflicts within different networks and individual associations often limited their potential to cooperate with each other or with state institutions. The fieldwork in Algeria examined the work and diverse experiences of these different associations and of the associational movement itself, exploring their role, their relations with the state and their influence in local and national politics. It enquired about their impressions of working with external actors such as the EU, by far the most significant donor within Algeria today, and also investigated how the staff of international donors experienced their work with civil society in Algeria.

Scope and Structure of the Book

The book is divided into three parts. Part I explores civil society, politics and democratisation programmes in Algeria and in neighbouring countries in the Arab world. Part II introduces Algerian civil society more specifically, focusing on its historical roots, relations with the state and associational activism in the heritage and social sectors. Part III examines the relationship between associations, donors and the democratic process in Algeria and how the language of different narratives has impacted upon this. Within Part I, Chapter 1, 'Civil Society in the Arab World and Algeria', examines current debates about civil society in the Middle East and North Africa (MENA) in general and in Algeria in particular. It begins by exploring deliberations about the potential of civil society to contribute to political change and democratisation. Examining the recent growth in the numbers of associations across the Arab world, it assesses how such developments have been perceived and represented. Chapter 1 also introduces the role of civil society in peace and reconciliation, indeed as a fundamental part of that process. Subsequently, Chapter 2, 'Internal Donors and Democracy Promotion', examines models of support for civil society and democratisation that international donors have attempted to implement in Algeria and in the MENA region. The chapter identifies the point at which the concepts of civil society and democratisation enter into development policy literature, showing how these paradigms have influenced donor models of development. A comparative approach looks at the different levels of funding international donors provide to civil society actors and the large disparities between countries. Three different cases of donor funding to Algeria, Palestine and Lebanon are examined; three seemingly comparable cases on the surface, but with surprising differences.

Part II examines Algerian civil society in more detail. Chapter 3, 'Historical Perspectives on Civil Society in Algeria', presents the historical background of Algerian civil society, from traditional consensual structures to the near-decimation of Algerian culture under colonial rule. A detailed analysis of the more recent evolution of Algerian state–society relations is presented in Chapter 4, 'Civil Society and the State'. This chapter explores how the difficulties in constructing the nation itself, and an Algerian identity, contributed to difficulties in achieving plural opposition in post-independence Algerian politics. The chapter discusses the evolution of the legislative framework and examines the impact of the Arab revolutions on Algeria, with the political and legal reforms launched in 2011. It assesses the associative responses to these reforms and analyses a number of particular cases that highlight changing state–society relations. Chapter 5, 'Associations in Algeria', continues by developing a new typology of Algerian associations. This challenges previous conceptions that have influenced our understanding about Algerian civil society and offers a broader range of identities and aims which associations might take on. The chapter also examines the role of external financing, or the lack of it, within certain areas of particularly dense associative life across Algeria. It explores questions of why people create associations, where they are concentrated and what they seek to achieve. It also identifies different sectors in which associations are particularly active, in order to guide case study selection for the following chapters. Two main sectors that emerged as important to Algerian activism are those of cultural heritage and social welfare.

Chapter 6, 'Algerian Associations Protecting the Past', explores heritage associations and examines how they respond to the challenges of redefining national and regional identity, through protecting historical monuments and sites and by going beyond the previous boundaries established or promoted by the state. It explores state–society relations and contested identities within Algeria through the lenses of urban history and archaeology, examining faith and heritage organisations. Chapter 7, 'Algerian Associations and Social Welfare', explores associational activism, barriers and reforms in the social sector across Algeria. It examines the different ways in which associations protest and propose new ideas. A number of cases highlight how associations challenge or interact with the state and how the social sector is intricately linked to the memory of victims of Algeria's recent conflict.

Part III focuses on associations, donors and language in recent and current developments within the political life of Algeria. Chapter 8, 'Europe, Civil Society and Democracy in Algeria', examines the role of donors and civil society support in Algeria and their impact upon democracy. It examines the place of the European Union, arguably one of the most powerful donors and external political actors in Algeria, and the EU's relations with the government and civil society. Chapter 9, 'Language and the Construction of Civil Society', seeks to draw together the different elements concerning performative language, political life and civil society in Algeria. The chapter considers the role of associations in challenging the language of donors, as well as the historical narratives of the state, and what impact this has on their place in the public sphere. Finally, language policy itself is examined, exploring how this may have impeded attempts to construct civil society from within. The chapter examines how associations have challenged the previous stigmatisation of the vernacular languages of Algeria, of Berber and Arabic (but also that of French), and how they have defined new needs and lobbied for change in the education system, the media and the cultural sphere. The book concludes by reflecting on the future of political participation in Algeria and the role of associations and civil society within this.

PART I

CIVIL SOCIETY AND DEMOCRACY PROMOTION IN THE ARAB WORLD

CHAPTER 1

CIVIL SOCIETY IN THE ARAB WORLD AND ALGERIA

Political concepts such as civil society can travel across cultures, but they are only meaningful if rooted in the historical experiences which shape the collective memory of the societies to which they are applied. Recurrent violent confrontations, experienced in almost all post-colonial regimes, have undermined the potential for building sustainable civil society. Such confrontations, experienced across the Middle East and North Africa, were described by Mohammed Arkoun as 'politically-programmed collective tragedies'.[1] With the challenges of deconstructing the colonial state, nation-building in the Maghreb has not always permitted the existence of autonomous spaces.[2] Today, faced with contemporary realities of rapid urbanisation, growing social exclusion and the precarious position of the middle classes, the difficult task of building civic culture is left to citizens, under the control of often unaccountable institutions. Across the Middle East and North Africa, societies have had similar political trajectories. Many have undergone liberalisation processes, whilst witnessing a strong military dominance over the state. Longevity of their rulers, violent internal conflict, failed democratic transition and incomplete reconciliation processes characterise many states. High unemployment and rural poverty exacerbate frustrations with state institutions. Lack of accountability in political life is a grievance for citizens in Algeria and across the Arab world. Although Algeria was heavily influenced by over a century of French colonial laws, and Algerians have ongoing cultural, personal and political ties with France, today the challenges facing Algerian citizens are far closer to those facing citizens elsewhere in the Arab world. Despite challenging conditions across the Arab world, citizen activism and political engagement have increased. Reasons for this include advances in modern technology, communications and transportation, leading to increased awareness of governance failures and human rights abuses.[3] Non-state actors have come to the fore, as 'a motor for, as well as a consequence of, social and political transformation' and this trend has been particularly prominent in the Middle East and North Africa.[4] So how did this new associational phenomenon develop across the Arab world and what does it mean for political life? What role did these organisations and their members have in the Arab revolutions? How did civil society grow in a context of violence and how have these societal transformations been interpreted? This chapter will explore such questions, including the nature of civil society and the expectations, theories and assumptions about its role in political change and democracy. It will, first, present recent figures about the number of associations in different countries across the Arab world. Second, it will explore assumptions about civil society and democracy in the Middle East and North Africa, questioning their purported limitations in authoritarian settings and the assumptions made about the Algerian context in particular. Finally, it will explore the role of associations in post-conflict Algeria, in terms of reconciliation and rebuilding the peace.

Associations in the Arab World

Across the Middle East and North Africa (MENA) there has been a surge in registered associations since the 1990s. Nowhere has this been quite as pronounced as in Algeria, where, in 2017, the Ministry of Interior reported the existence of 109,000 associations, even though half of these were described as 'not conforming' to regulatory requirements. In 2012, there were over 93,000 officially registered Algerian associations, compared to 10,000 in the late 1980s and to almost none under the single-party system of the 1970s.[5] This surge made Algeria the most association-dense country in the region. However, since 2012 there has also been a massive increase in associations in Morocco, going from an estimated 40,000 to over 130,000 in a very short space of time due to specific government initiatives. The following diagrams illustrate the numbers of associations registered in MENA countries based on information from recent studies,[6] interviews and government websites.

Even taking into account the considerable differences in population, there are significantly more associations officially registered in Algeria and Morocco than in neighbouring countries, as shown below.

Table 1.1 provides the numbers of associations in each country and indicates the reliability of the data, as well as the most recent increases. It is difficult to obtain the number of members across the different countries. In Algeria, given that the previous 1990 Law on Associations required 15 founding members, it can be estimated that at least 1.4 million people are members of an association. This represents around 7 per cent of the adult population. As many associations indicate a much higher membership, the figures are likely to be greater. Similar figures for across the region would provide an even stronger indicator of associative life. The data enable us to gain an insight into the facility with which an association can be created in each context, and the will of the population to do so. Apart from Palestine, there have generally been increases in the number of associations officially registered in most of the MENA countries.

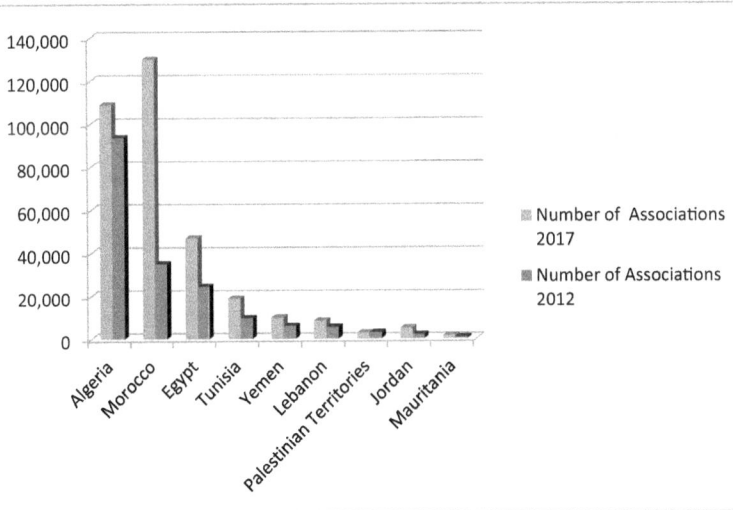

Figure 1.1 Numbers of registered associations in MENA countries.

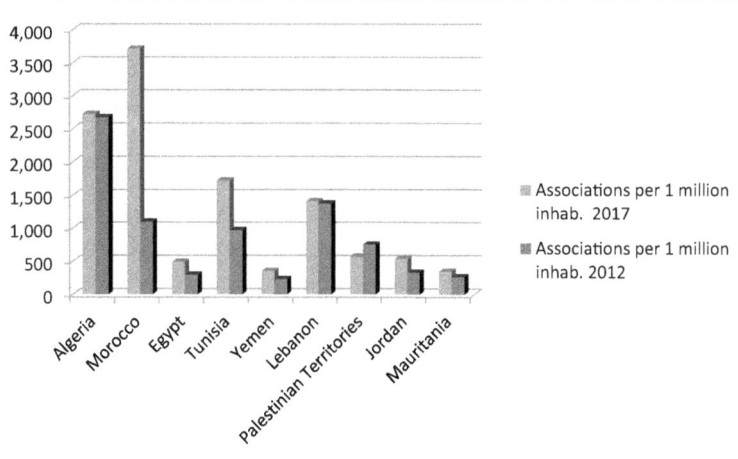

Figure 1.2   Registered associations by population in MENA countries.

These sources, including Ministry data, NGO monitoring programmes and academic research, show significant increases in registered associations across the region. They also indicate important legislative reforms which have enabled these developments in countries such as Algeria, Lebanon and Yemen. Algeria represents an exception in the region, with consistently high numbers of associations since the mid-1990s, despite the violent conflict. International NGO monitoring websites such as ICNL have criticised the lack of freedom to register organisations in Algeria, yet figures show that Algerian authorities have registered huge numbers, particularly of local associations, across the country. Algeria has roughly the same number of registered associations, per capita, as England and Wales have registered charities.[7] It is important to now shed light on what they actually do, how they interact with or challenge the state, whether they constitute a new public sphere or have an influence on local democracy or civic institutions. If so, do they then impact on policy making? Do they have contacts with external actors, or have transnational or trans-regional networks? Do they constitute part of an active civil society? Or, rather, are they co-opted by the state or by external donors? What changes in state–society relations have arisen through this increasing associational activity?

Table 1.1 Associations in the MENA countries.

Country	Population in millions 2016	No. of registered associations	No. of associations / 1 million inhabitants	Sources
Algeria	40	109,000	2,725	Ministry of Interior statistics in 2017 show 109,000 associations – of which 56% are indicated as 'not conform', http://www.interieur.gov.dz/images/pdf/Thematiquedesassociations.pdf. ICNL (the International Center for not-for-profit Law) show figures from 2012 with 94,000 registered associations, http://www.icnl.org/research/monitor/algeria.html. Figures for 2007 showed 78,000 according to the Ministry of Interior.
Morocco	35	130,000	3,714	Figures from the first governmental report on civil society in Morocco 2016 indicate a sharp increase to 130,000, www.medias24.com/SOCIETE/162411-Le-Maroc-compte-130.000-associations-en-2016.html. There are only 223 associations with the statute of 'public utility' in Morocco. Previously, Human Rights Watch indicated between 30,000 and 80,000, p. 3, www.hrw.org/sites/default/files/reports/morocco1009frsumandrecs.pdf. An interview with the PCPA programme in Rabat (Oct. 2011) indicated 35,000 but that it is 'very difficult to have correct figures'. ICNL previously indicated the figure was unknown for Morocco.

Table 1.1 Continued

Country	Population in millions 2016	No. of registered associations	No. of associations / 1 million inhabitants	Sources
Egypt	95	47,000	495	2017 estimates from the Ministry of Social Solidarity are 40,000, see ICNL, www.icnl.org/research/monitor/egypt.html. ICNL previously noted 24,500 in 2007.
Tunisia	11	19,000	1,727	There are 19,000 Tunisian associations according to ICNL 2016 figures, www.icnl.org/research/monitor/Tunisia.html. IFEDA, a Tunisian Association, indicated 9,600 in early 2011, www.tunivisions.net/28266/152/149/plus-de-9700-associations-en-tunisie.html.
Yemen	28	10,000	357	2016 figures are set at 10,000 according to ICNL, www.icnl.org/research/monitor/yemen.html. Cavatorta, 2011, quotes USAID figures in 2007, of 5,632. ICNL indicated 6,000 associations registered with the Ministry of Labour and Social Affairs in 2012, following the new Law on Associations of 2001.
Lebanon	6	8,500	1,417	In 2016 there were 8,500 associations according to ICNL, www.icnl.org/research/monitor/lebanon.html. Cavatorta, 2011, gives figures for 1999 which indicated only 1,100. Recent increases (following a Ministerial Circular in 2006 to improve practices) were reported by ICNL, which indicated 5,523 associations in 2012.

Palestinian Territories	5	2,793	570	In 2015, in Ministry of Interior figures the number of Palestinian NGOs had fallen to 2,793 from 2,999 associations previously registered with the Ministry of Interior (2009 est.), www.icnl.org/research/monitor/palestine.html.
Jordan	10	5,108	538	Ministry of Social Development figures quoted by ICNL indicate 5,108 associations registered, www.icnl.org/research/monitor/jordan.html, Cavatorta, 2011. A study by Kassim in 2006 indicated 1,000 NGOs. ICNL indicate 2,000 in 2012, registered with the Ministry of Social Development.
Mauritania	4	1,400	350	Figures given by Hamoud Ould T'Feil, the Director of Civil Society in the Ministry in Nouakchott, 2017. Previous figures were taken in discussions with the European Union delegation in Nouakchott, 2010.

During the Arab Spring uprisings in 2011, the role of associations in Algeria was limited. They were criticised within the country by state institutions and parliamentarians as not having prevented trouble.[8] External actors, on the contrary, complained that they were not real actors capable of providing a coherent platform of opposition.[9] More recently, in 2014, Charity Butcher challenges these perceptions, describing how the Arab Spring protests did in fact provide an opportunity for associations, as seen with the creation by opposition actors of the National Coordination for Change and Democracy (CNCD).[10] On this platform, civil society groups and political parties from across the secular and religious divide came together to peacefully challenge the government and demand reform. Before exploring these developments in more detail in the following chapters, it is important to first explore basic assumptions and theories about civil society, political life and democracy.

Civil Society and Democracy

The concepts of civil society and democratisation entered into academic language over the course of the 1980s and 1990s. Previously, both concepts had been generally absent from scholarly debate, particularly about development policy. In international development journals, the concept of civil society started to appear in titles in the late 1980s and democratisation was increasingly included in the period around 1992. Figure 1.3 represents the number of times either concept appears in a selection of six major development policy journals over a period of 30 years.

The diagram shows a recent reduction in the use of the terms in the journal titles, particularly the concept of civil society. After the period of 'civil society romanticism', there appeared to be less interest from the academic community and an increasing scepticism regarding theories linking civil society and democratisation. Why was there this renewed interest in the historical concept of civil society, how did scholars define it and what did this mean?

In his discussion of civil society in the Arab world, the Egyptian American sociologist Saad Eddin Ibrahim defines civil society as the 'freedom of human beings to associate'. In his 1998 article 'The troubled triangle: Populism, Islam and civil society in the Arab world', he describes civil society as:

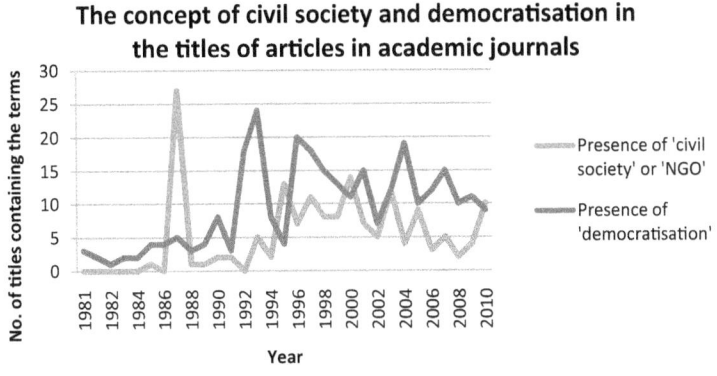

Figure 1.3 Civil society and democratisation in academic journals.[11]

the totality of self-initiating and self-regulating volitional social formations, peacefully pursuing a common interest, advocating a common cause, or expressing a common passion; respecting the right of others to do the same, and maintain their relative autonomy vis-à-vis the state, the family, the temple and the market.[12]

Civil society includes the press, trade unions, teachers, academia, intellectuals, artists and charitable associations. It incorporates the media and religious groups, all of which are regulated either by charities law or by a similar legislative framework. The arena of civil society is an independent one, primarily from the state and the market, to which Ibrahim adds the temple and the family. The associational movement, made up of formal and registered associations, represents an important part of this civil society. Charity Butcher points out that 'political parties are not generally part of this definition of civil society',[13] though she recognises that the link between associations and political parties is important, particularly in Algeria, where new, mainly Islamist political parties have developed since the early 1990s.

Civil society as a concept remains ambiguous in all contexts and has been discussed over the centuries by philosophers. Hegel, in particular, discussed the relations between civil society, the macro level of the state and the micro level of the family. He stressed the necessity for the state, as a separate entity, to foster civil society, giving it a sense of community and regulating it. Civil society represented the space of differentiation where individuals sought interests within the framework of the law.[14] On the left, building on Hegel's work, Marx challenged this separation, categorising civil society as the space where the bourgeoisie dominated over the working classes. Rejecting the presumed legitimacy and autonomy inferred by previous thinkers, civil society was now seen as an expression of capitalist forces deprived of political value and independence. Further developing the discussion from the leftist perspective, Antonio Gramsci challenged the Marxist view that civil society was coterminous with the economic base of the state. Gramsci considered that civil society was located within the political superstructure, representing the cultural ideological capital for the survival of the hegemony of capitalism. Whilst Gramsci saw civil society as a site for solving problems and a potential realm of contention, in reality it was part of the state and as such was responsible for creating consent in the subordinated class.

In contrast, democratisation theorists have argued that civil society and associational life can be a way of promoting democratic socialisation and increasing freedom in the political sphere through local empowerment and popular participation in functioning organisations.[15] Scholars have long debated whether there is a 'functional role played by the associative sphere', as a precondition of democracy.[16] From the liberal perspective, Alexis de Tocqueville's findings about associations in America in the nineteenth century highlighted them as 'schools for civic virtue' and a fundamental part of American democracy.[17] Tocqueville's commitment to democratic freedom was sadly less robust with regards to Algeria, where, during the colonial conquest, he saw France's subjection of rights and brutal oppression of the population as a mere necessity of France avoiding humiliation.[18] Proponents of Tocqueville's thinking continue to argue that through associative engagement, citizens gain skills in political representation, public speaking and democratic governance.[19] Cavatorta and Durac explain how civil society has been regarded as good for democracy in that 'it promotes the interaction of people in a voluntary setting, where differences of opinion have to be taken into account'.[20] In the same vein they quote Robert Putnam, who argues that associational life also contributes to building social capital, as 'civil society activism enhances the internal capacity of communities to generate social wellbeing'.[21] Similar to Asef Bayat's ideas about everyday politics and the importance of what he describes as 'non-movements', or ordinary people, in bringing about change in the Middle East,[22] Putnam argues that even non-political organisations are important for democracy. The generation of social capital, trust, shared norms and values is made possible through the experience of associational activism.[23] In his comparative research into 20 Italian regional governments, Putnam analysed the links between the density of civic life and the quality of regional government in Italy.[24] His findings showed that variations in government performance were related to the intensity of associational life. In the north, where there were far more sports clubs, choirs and cultural associations, governments were more efficient and creative in policy choices. In the south, where associative life was much weaker, so was the quality of government, which tended to be less efficient and prone to corruption. He explains this phenomenon as arising from the trust which grows between members of associations due to their interaction, and the social capital developed through this network of participation and governance.

In *Some Propositions about Civil Society and the Consolidation of Democracy*, Philippe Schmitter outlined five ways in which he felt the work of civil society organisations might consolidate democracy.[25] Schmitter writes that the role of civil society can be positive in that it stabilises expectations and regroups information; it inculcates civic and democratic behaviour; it provides channels for expression; it steers members towards collective commitments; and it provides a source of resistance to tyranny. Civil society, he warned, could also present risks for democracy, depending on the specific characteristics of individual organisations and on the systems in which they function.[26] Civil society can negatively impact on democracy if it makes the formation of majorities difficult; if it biases influence and becomes class-based; and if it gives rise to policies no one wants, each association satisfying its own interests at the expense of the whole. There is also the risk that civil society organisations divide along ethnic, language or cultural grounds, or exclude certain groups. In such cases, Schmitter suggests, civil society groups simply reproduce 'squabbling, self-interested organisations' incapable of agreeing on a common cause. According to Schmitter, the potential success of civil society organisations in their contribution to democratic processes depends on the nature of the organisations.

Ibrahim's normative conception of 'peaceful' and 'respecting' organisations contrasts with the more functional, neo-Toquevillian conception of civil society that has been suggested by other authors. Liverani describes this as the 'functional role played by the associative sphere', which he defines as a 'precondition of democracy'.[27] Associational life can be a way of increasing freedom in the political sphere, through 'empowerment and popular participation'. In contrast to this, Cavatorta and Durac suggest that:

> A positive perception of the pro-democracy role that civil society plays is misplaced [...] [and that it is perhaps more useful for civil society to] be construed as a neutral analytical category.[28]

They seek to go beyond a normative or a functional role for the concept of civil society, to focus on the practical characteristics of associational life in different contexts. In his research on the Middle East and Palestinian NGOs, Benoit Challand also considers it important to define contextually the concept of civil society, in 'spatial' terms. Challand defines civil society as a

> space (as independent as possible from the direct interventions from the state, private business and family realms) for voluntary collective deliberations and actions that function as a source of autonomy.[29]

Civil society actors must be independent of external actors in order then to have the freedom to define a common political project. For Challand, one of the current impediments to this autonomy, particularly in the Middle East and North Africa, is the dominance of external donors. The imposition of external agendas on national actors limits civil society. For him, it is this 'autonomy' of actors to create spaces for dialogue, to define their agendas and objectives, to contribute to policy dialogue, that allows us to define civil society. In his discussion of Arab civil society in 1998, Ibrahim argued that this autonomy had in fact emerged and that civil society in the Arab world had revitalised itself. He argued that new socio-economic formations 'have been growing' and that weakened states have 'less capacity to repress' them. He wrote that, 'despite notable distortion and time lags, the Arab world is currently going through civil society building and democratization'.[30]

Much of the literature up until 2011, however, has presented a rather sceptical view as to the autonomy of these organisations and their capacity to bring about change or act as a counter-hegemonic force. Some authors have gone as far as to suggest that there cannot be any Arab-Muslim civil society, and that this absence implies that Arab society and culture are inimical to democratisation.[31] Within the Maghreb, Filali-Ansary writes that,

> Most scholars have offered negative judgements on this particular strain of nascent civil society. In their view it is artificial, its role marginal and often manipulated by state (secret) services. It is, for them, either an elite operation, a kind of fashion, or an outcome, a product of foreign influence. Elite strata are seen to continue manipulating society to serve their interests. Even if most of these accusations are exaggerated, or lack foundation, the 'outburst' of civil society activity does not appear to have imparted durable and dependable strength, or meaningful autonomy to society.[32]

For other scholars, civil society in closed political systems is often more likely to ensure the durability of authoritarian regimes, rather than lead to a more open society.[33] Vickie Langhor develops Thomas Carothers' strong critique on NGOs – questioning the capacity of NGOs as opposition actors – in the title to her article, claiming there is 'too much civil society, too little politics'.[34] The focus on specific interests such as human rights makes them 'ill equipped to mobilize a much broader set of constituencies' for goals such as regime change. Their dependence on foreign aid reduces their legitimacy at home and she recommends focusing policy and academic analysis on political parties rather than on NGOs.

Three competing visions of Arab civil society, as seen by external commentators, are identified by Cavatorta and Durac.[35] These are, first, civil society as an exclusively liberal, secular model, and thus very weak and unable to challenge regimes. Second, civil society has been categorised as strong and uncivil, not necessarily adhering to liberal values and predominantly Islamist in its outlook. Finally, civil society has been viewed as massively increasing, but, as the co-opted product of regimes, it is therefore entirely artificial. In both Islamist and secular models described, civil society organisations are seen to have only a marginal role, providing social services, responding to the secular state's inability to do so. The authors reject these three visions as inaccurate, including the assumption of an artificially 'created civil society', to appease foreign donors and to tame society. They write that it is:

> misleading to consider that all civil society groups lack autonomy and independence from the regime. It might be argued on the contrary that the increased number of civil society organisations throughout the Arab world truly constitutes an attempt from sectors of society to reclaim the public sphere and to introduce changes in the ways in which governance is implemented. While the outcome of their work and activism might not have been translated into significant political change at the institutional macro level, the picture of a society which is held hostage by the regime may be misleading.[36]

This, they argue, is for three reasons. First, a strong repressive apparatus indicates that there is a real opposition. Second, globalisation and the internet make it hard for any regime to control all of society and all information. And finally, state-sponsored civil society has been far more reactive than proactive. The associations created by the state are usually in response to real and effective autonomous ones in society, rather than the other way round.

The authors go on, however, to quote Jamal, who argues that under authoritarian regimes, associations are obliged to play by the rules of the game and work within corrupt systems, ones which do not encourage democratic practices. Despite recognising the existence of a real opposition, which is difficult for any regime to control, Cavatorta and Durac ultimately agree with Jamal, that under authoritarian regimes civil society is ineffective in supporting any real form of democratic development. Jamal argues that where associations function in political environments that are not conducive to their development and free functioning, the link between civic associations and democracy 'is a circular and self-reinforcing relationship'.[37] For Jamal, there need to be pre-existing political institutions. Otherwise, she suggests, 'ineffective democratic institutions promote levels of civic engagement, including social capital, supportive of non-democratic procedures'.[38] Associations supporting non-democratic regimes 'enjoy rights and privileges not guaranteed to associations in opposition'.[39] Cavatorta and Durac equally argue that though a vibrant civil society can exist, authoritarian contexts create divisions among civil society actors that prevent them from challenging incumbent regimes.[40]

Other scholars, however, point to the capacity of civil society organisations to promote non-violent political revolution. Referring to the role of Eastern European cultural institutions that facilitated peaceful transitions, it is argued that civil society actors can frame change as desirable. Glenn writes that in Eastern Europe, civil society was able to 'engage in active construction of the messages', and became 'a framing strategy to mobilise support' for political reform.[41] In the Middle East and North Africa, Abu Sada and Challand describe the 'repoliticisation' of associations in many countries following the Arab Spring. As the state in these countries has been losing its monopoly over public action in recent years, they argue that new forms of contestation are occurring. In Palestine, the context Jamal explores in most detail, they argue that a new form of repoliticisation is now emerging through associational life. It was essentially excessive donor interventions in the 1990s, they suggest, that had depoliticised many associative actors there.[42] This contrasts particularly with Algeria, where there have been very low levels of external donor funding and a particularly active associational movement.

Perceptions of Civil Society in Algeria

In the case of Algeria, there was great optimism in the early 1990s as to the potential for these new associations to bring about political change. In the 1990s, according to Kazemi and Norton, Algerian associations constituted, an 'impressive array of rights oriented groups'.[43] Others went further to claim that 'the indisputable existence of an increasingly resolute civil society provides the potential for genuine democratization'.[44] In her 2002 book, *Pouvoirs et Associations dans le Monde Arabe*, Sarah Ben Nefissa recognised that:

> Algeria seems to be the only Arab country which, in its legal system, has the system of declaration and not authorisation

[for registering associations]. Today, it is possible to speak of a real explosion of associations. The social categories that feel most threatened by Islamist extremism and by the Algerian state have been the first to organise. This is mainly women and Berbers. Currently, it is possible to say that the associative form, more than political parties or the press, constitutes one of the main modes of expression for Algerian society that seeks to avoid being imprisoned between the state and the Islamists.[45]

An increasingly sceptical view of Algerian civil society, however, did develop in the following years. In the conclusion of their book *Algeria: Anger of the Dispossessed*, Evans and Phillips quote the national newspaper *Liberté* in 2006, which argued that electoral apathy, directionless violence, juvenile delinquency and the ongoing riots across the country were 'a telling comment on the lack of a civil society'.[46] Hugh Roberts, the British academic and North Africa expert, stated in 2005:

> I personally do not think that this development [of the huge increase in associations] for the time being translates into something that is politically significant other than a factor that helps to stabilize the State and defend and reproduce it.[47]

Andrea Liverani's in-depth research into Algerian associations, published in 2008, also presents one of the strongest critiques of Algerian civil society, which, he argues, is strongly controlled by the state. Liverani questions both the capacity for change and the degree of independence of Algerian civil society. Many of the associations are still inherently weak – tied to the state for funding and for access to opportunities. In turn, he writes, they support the state politically, at key moments, such as electoral campaigns, representing state corporatism over the associative sector.

Cavatorta and Elananza have argued that civil society can be an agent for change in Algeria. They suggest that in the absence of effective political parties, the civic arena has become the space in which politics often takes place. It is within an increasingly politicised civil society, they argue, that 'demands for radical change to the political, economic and social structures are articulated'.[48] The the internal divisions in Algerian civil society, between secular and religious organisations, continue to prevent it from being a real actor for regime change. The radically divergent demands concerning the status of women and the family code, for example, are expressed in the associative movement, but are irreconcilable. Cavatorta and Durac further argue that:

> the divisions within civil society dating back to the conflicts of the 1990s and [...] relations between different sectors of civil society, namely the Islamist camp and the secular one, are fraught with tensions and suspicions which allow the regime to divide and conquer the opposition through a careful process of co-optation and marginalization.[49]

For such authors, civil society in Algeria is vibrant and autonomous, but the inability to build effective coalitions allows the state to 'divide and rule', thus ensuring its own survival. Civil society replaces active politics, but its efficacy in this role is questionable due to the fragmented nature of the organisations and, arguably, of society as a whole.

Pre-existing divisions in Algeria, often rooted in its traumatic colonial past, were exacerbated by the conflict of the 1990s. However, despite 'the problematic relationship between the secular and Islamist opposition'[50] there are also many cases of cooperation.[51] Algerian associations have arguably overcome many divides. One important example is the cooperation between Islamist and secular associations which collectively challenge the state policy of reconciliation brought about with the 2005 Reconciliation Charter. This provided amnesty for Islamist insurgents in exchange for laying down arms, whilst criminalising any criticism of the state's role in ending the violence. Across the political spectrum associations work together to argue that state policy does not provide justice for the families of the victims of the 1990s violence. Despite tensions, it is in the associative sector that difficult political claims are debated and formulated. Conflicts exist not only between religious and secular organisations, but within secular movements and Islamist movements. The trauma of ten years of bitter conflict has scarred Algerian society. Yet this does not mean that civil society organisations cannot be agents of change, challenge state policies or propose new forms of activism. Many associations do vocally challenge state policies, both in the press and online, taking risks as they do so.

Benramdane, in his 2015 study on Algerian associations, documents this emergence of autonomous, trained, professional associations which are effectively involved in structured projects working for the development of the country.[52] He notes their increasingly effective role in the realms of human rights, women and children's rights and the health sector. Yet he also notes the stigmatisation of associations, reinforced by a speech by the Minister of Interior in 2006, and widely repeated by the press. He further quotes the Algerian sociologist Brahmi Salhi, who describes the delegitmisation of associations, the refusal to listen, the explicit critique by state actors and the media, in contrast to the clear development and increasing autonomy of many of the organisations.

The explosion in the number of associations in Algeria, the fragmentation and lack of autonomy, raises interesting questions about civil society for political analysts and for Algerians themselves. Over the last two centuries Algeria has experienced significant repression. The country is still under *Front de Libération Nationale* (FLN) rule. This is the political party which has governed since independence. How does a population of increasingly active citizens interact with the political system in such a tense, post-conflict environment? Algeria's problems have not been resolved. Algerians still want to be 'treated as citizens', they demand 'good government, the rule of law and use of oil and gas wealth for the benefit of the majority'.[53] Civil society, whilst vibrant, still operates in a difficult environment. Most Algerians seek peace and stability rather than upheaval. Many fear a return to the insecurity and violence of the 1990s. In such a context, civil society is heavily constrained.

Associative Activism in a Post-Conflict Environment

The role of associations in the post-conflict period – in the reconciliation process and in the consolidation of peace in Algeria – has become increasingly important but also increasingly contested. Since the 1990s, many associations have shaped their role in response to the needs of the victims during and after the conflict. Although sometimes limited by the state of emergency imposed on Algerians or by the Reconciliation Charter, associations were consistently at the forefront in responding to the conflict. The 1990s was a defining period in the evolution of the

Algerian associative movement and of its autonomy from state structures. The intensity of the suffering of the Algerian population generated a more fearful, strained and cautious social culture, one in which trust was severely damaged. Fragility caused by violence in any context creates a difficult environment in which civil society can develop. Yet, at the same time, the rapid growth of civil society organisations in many countries which have experienced painful conflict, such as Uganda, Lebanon and Algeria, perhaps also signals the potential of endogenous forces for recovery. In the cases of Uganda and Lebanon, Hadenius and Uggla write that:

> If the situation is one in which the central power has been virtually absent as in Uganda during the civil war, a great number of organisations tend to emerge in its stead. Under such conditions, the population must turn to non-state institutions for support. In Uganda and in Lebanon, the result was that the emerging regime faced an array of independent organisations. Not all these qualified as democratic and they were certainly not of an integrative bent, even so they could not be disregarded politically.[54]

In the Algerian context, there was no absence of state power during the conflict of the 1990s, nor in the following years. Despite claims by certain authors, such as Liverani, that Algeria has a weak state, most commentators agree that the Algerian state is particularly powerful. Nevertheless, in the eyes of the population there was a loss of state legitimacy, both during and after the period of violence. There was also a common experience of injustice. This injustice in many cases formed the basis for collective action (either in social movements or, more commonly, in associations) to stand up to the atrocities committed against individuals or communities by the state or the Islamist insurgents. Hirschman writes that:

> Occasionally it happens then that the common experience of having been taken advantage of, swindled or otherwise hurt will lead to some collective reaction that takes the perpetrators by surprise. This is also true for aggression by powerful individuals or by the State. The poor are used to their poverty which they bear in

silence and isolation, but the fact of being treated with *injustice* can bring out unsuspected capacities for indignation, resistance and common action.[55]

The sense of injustice that Algerians felt throughout the 1990s contributed to the creation of many different kinds of associative initiatives. National and regional organisations such as *Djazairouna* and *SOS Disparus* were created with the aim of seeking information and justice for families of the disappeared. Foundations were created to commemorate politicians, intellectuals and artists who were assassinated. Further charitable associations such as the *SARP* (*Pour l'Aide, la Recherche et le Perfectionnement en Psychologie*), a psychology association, were set up prior to the violence but soon became deeply involved in caring for the victims. These organisations provided psychological care for orphans, youths and families who had suffered. Such associations are important, just by their very existence, in that they commemorate and shape the narrative history of Algeria. They also play a practical role in reconciliation and healing.

From many of the interviews conducted with associations, it became clear that the main motivation of the actors appeared to be that of being involved in a project of importance to Algerian society. Personnel indicated their wish to bring positive and visible changes for the future rather than focusing on the conflict or contestation of the past. One such association is the Boucebci Foundation in Algiers, discussed in more detail in Chapter 7. This association commemorates the life and work of internationally renowned psychiatrist Professor Mahfoud Boucebci, who was assassinated by Islamist insurgents on 15 June 1993 in front of his hospital in Kouba, Algiers. No one was ever brought to justice for this crime. The Islamist leader Anouar Haddam, who claimed the assassination to be the 'execution of a sentence by the mujahideen', was given visas for the UK and the US.[56]

In all the interviews at the foundation, and in similar discussions with the *SARP* association and *Djazairouna*, members referred to the importance of rebuilding Algeria. They wanted to respond to the needs of the victims and deal with the trauma which had been passed on to children due to the experiences of their parents. Whilst still facing many challenges, such organisations provide new, interesting spheres of activism in which motivated and qualified personnel are involved. In the cases examined throughout this book, personnel were often voluntary.

In the Boucebci Foundation, the majority of the psychologists were young graduates or retired professionals. Such associations directly touch the lives of ordinary people and work with the local structures of Algerian society: town halls, education and health authorities, on policies which concern the reconstruction of Algerian society after the conflict. They also create safe spaces in which people can act, exchange, criticise and propose. In his work on cultural representations of trauma, Patrick Crowley discusses the impact and the role of associations, as well as artists, in post-conflict resolution. He writes,

> in a society where justice has been deferred the only escape from trauma's hold is either ethical, as in the case of the Fondation Mahfoud Boucebci, or aesthetic – points of recovery, resistance to the spread of trauma's hold upon the present.[57]

Despite continuing fears that the state may seek to control such autonomous spaces for reconciliation in Algeria, these spaces of activism continue to exist. The personnel of asscocaitions find fulfilment in their new roles, which are not so readily available in the public or private sector. Following the decade of conflict and the deep suffering of the population, collective solutions through civic activism continue to grow and adapt to the evolving needs of the communities they serve.

Conclusion

Associational life in the Middle East and North Africa, and in Algeria in particular, has evolved in a restricted space which is faced with the multiple problems of state-building and violence suffered in the post-colonial context. Countries of the region face many similar challenges, including institutional reform, political transition and ongoing conflicts. It is useful to compare experiences across culturally similar societies, such as Palestine, Lebanon or Algeria, which have different political trajectories, but similar colonial legacies and challenges in terms of their legal frameworks for civil society and in terms of asserting independence from foreign interventions. In light of the Arab Spring revolts, the experience of Algeria, with its uprisings in 1988, is highly relevant beyond its borders. Equally, from a comparison of the figures concerning civil society organisations across the region, Algeria is an important case, with by far the highest number of registered associations since the 1990s. There has been significant development and growth of the associative movement in Algeria, and also across the region, despite a disabling security situation and challenging political, economic and social environments. It is important to understand what this could mean in terms of potential for democratic reforms keenly campaigned for by so many, particularly since 2011 and the Arab Spring.

The concept of civil society and theoretical discussions about its role in democracy are useful to our understanding of the place of associations in Algeria and their potential as agents of change in the wider region. Some Marxist perspectives view civil society primarily as a means for state control. Other liberal theorists argue that civil society can bring about public participation and, as such, contribute to democracy. More recently the ideas of Schmitter, Bayat, Putnam and Challand highlight the importance of examining the micro level, the work of specific organisations, how they act in the public sphere and in political life, if we are to understand their transformative potential. The interference of external donors, authoritarianism or divisions between religious and secular groups, are all said to be factors inhibiting civil society in the region. Yet it appears that there are examples, particularly in Algeria, where associations have overcome such limitations, stood up to the state and bridged divisions. Furthermore, civil society associations have played an important role in post-conflict reconstruction. In light of the recent debates which have been predominantly sceptical about the potential of civil society to contribute to political change globally, but more particularly in the MENA region, this book seeks to understand in far more detail the surprising evolution of associational life in Algeria and the implications this could have for future perspectives of political transformation. With their presence in Algeria fairly limited, in comparison with other MENA countries, it is also important to understand how the role of external donors can either support or inhibit civil society and democracy. This will be the focus of the next chapter.

CHAPTER 2

INTERNATIONAL DONORS AND DEMOCRACY PROMOTION

> Too many meetings and seminars see Europeans peddle their democratic wares and lecture the Maghreb on women's rights while official representatives of the Maghreb ask northern rim countries to atone for their colonial sins and give them more money.[1]

Since the early 1990s, aid donors have increasingly sought to invest resources in ambitious civil society and democracy promotion programmes around the world. The general template for these projects has assumed a sequence of events in which authoritarian controls could be loosened, followed by transformational elections, followed by power shifting to new liberal and democratic forces. Sheila Carapico explains:

> The monitoring of 'breakthrough' elections in a number of Arab countries in the early and mid-90s was followed by a host of projects designed to stimulate 'demand' for democracy from civil society by explaining democratic rights and responsibilities to political opinion-leaders. The premise was that politically active women, parliamentary candidates, judges, law students, journalists, teachers, and non-governmental organisation activists would then lobby governments and rally public support for gradual reform and a liberal agenda.[2]

These policy goals, to promote universal values of democracy and freedom of association in other countries, may be examined chronologically and in context to determine when, where and how the decision to cultivate democracy evolved. The EU is one of the biggest such donors in the world. What has the EU actually done to support civil society and promote democracy abroad, in the Arab world and in Algeria in particular? Were its underlying motivations an altruistic belief that fostering democracy is a 'good in itself', or more covert agendas, such as the promotion of political stability, or the expansion of trade liberalisation? European fears about migration and fundamentalism appear to underpin efforts to promote civil society in many contexts. This was certainly how it felt in Algeria, as reported back by civil society activists in interviews. One activist stated that 'they are supporting us here in Algeria, because they don't want us over there'.[3] Youngs confirms that this was particularly the case in the Mediterranean and in sub-Saharan Africa, despite there being no evidence that the promotion of civil society would necessarily provide any significant counter-balance to either phenomenon of migration or fundamentalism.[4] Federica Bicchi, in 'Our size fits all', describes the EU's desire to diffuse its own political solutions abroad, and believes that European foreign policy can be seen as 'an unreflexive behaviour mirroring the deeply engrained belief that Europe's history is a lesson for everybody'.[5]

Significant differences exist in donor approaches across the world, including inconsistencies in regional partnerships and in democracy promotion strategies. Large-scale donor funding, even if apparently from non-governmental sources, is rarely neutral. Behind noble development objectives lie the political or economic interests of donor states which impact upon development policy interventions.[6] Carapico argues that donor aid programmes are 'an industry heavily reliant on public funds administered through grants and contracts, linked to great powers' foreign policy, and only quasi-non-governmental'.[7] This does not necessarily imply that the actors or actions are rendered ineffective. However, the imposition of donor agendas through large-scale funding can often limit the autonomy of local actors and create confusion if there is a plethora of actors. In light of this, the language and the development paradigms of international donors can take on new layers of meaning in different contexts, particularly in one such as Algeria, which has a powerful state and limitations on the space accorded to external donors.

Development Paradigms and the Language of Donors

The idea of promoting civil society as a means of fostering democracy was part of the post-Cold War democratic paradigm and of the liberal peace theory, which holds that democracies are less likely to engage in war with each other. Civil society re-emerged as a concept in political discourse, along with the democratic transitions in Eastern Europe in the early 1990s. It was quickly integrated into the democracy promotion policies of all major donors. The major assumption was that associational activity automatically brings about democracy. Civil society was seen as a vehicle to pursue common, universal goals which were thought to be 'good in themselves', as civil society organisations provided a space in which to practise values of tolerance, consensus and democracy. The drive for this promotion of civil society came from the highest levels of international policy-making bodies, with publications such as Boutros Boutros-Ghali's *An Agenda for Democratization* in 1996, and the inclusion by the World Bank, USAID (United States Agency for International Development) and the Canadian Development Agency of democracy promotion as part of their portfolios. These were in addition to the EU's new approach in the African, Caribbean and Pacific (ACP) countries, which explicitly included civil society and democracy promotion objectives, and to the Euro-Mediterranean initiative from the Barcelona Conference of 1995, which included a drive for democracy promotion in its aims to provide support in the arts, the environment and academic research.

As a result of this, there was a very substantial growth across Europe and North America of what Carapico terms 'democracy brokers'. These were the think tanks, research groups, NGOs and academic groups which sprang to life during the late 1980s and early 1990s in response to changed global circumstances after the fall of the Berlin Wall. All the major Western players set up such organisations. In Britain, in 1992, Parliament established the Westminster Foundation for Democracy as a non-partisan, independent public entity 'to help developing countries and countries transitioning to democracy'.[8] Similar groups aiming to support civil society and democracy abroad were set up around the world, including in the US, Canada, Germany, France, Austria and Sweden. The ultimate justification for these groups was, according to Stefan Mair, in *The Role of the German 'Stiftungen' in the Process of Democratization*, to:

support partners in developing countries which make a structurally effective contribution towards the realization of social justice, toward the widening of political participation, and toward the framework of goals laid down by the United Nations Declaration of Human Rights.[9]

This drive changed certain models of resource transfer from Western nations to developing nations. Aside from the traditional government-to-government transfer of funds, there was now an alternative model which allowed Western donors, to a certain extent, to bypass the executive arms of foreign governments for small but politically important percentages of development funding. Donor governments often resented this, due to the political importance of the nature of such funding and the perceived breach of sovereignty it implied. Grimm and Leininger point to the challenges of multiple donors and brokers in any one context, explaining how:

> Any target country of democracy promotion will find itself facing a multitude of international actors pursuing divergent interests and goals. Consequently, the objective of democratization is likely to compete with alternative objectives of foreign policy of the various international actors. At times, the same actor can simultaneously attempt to pursue competing objectives.[10]

After a decade of increasing numbers of actors promoting democracy abroad, the assumed link between civil society and democratisation increasingly came to be questioned. The weaknesses and sometimes 'uncivil' nature of organisations being funded were cited as reasons for the failure of civil society to promote democratisation processes in a number of authoritarian regimes, notably in the Middle East and North Africa.[11] Sarah Henderson's research into the external financing of Russian civic organisations provides an insight into the potentially negative impact of donor funding on civil society, placing the responsibility with the donor funding mechanisms.[12] In Russia, she argues, client-patron relations, vertical (donor-dominated) networks, lack of clear constituencies and the divisive, uncivic and corporate nature of funding all limit the potential for civil society to contribute to democracy in any meaningful way. She describes how grants are often 'duplicated', like 'winning the lottery', and how the selection of projects can be corrupted from within the American funding system of USAID.[13] Similarly, Julia Elyachar describes the marketisation of NGOs in Cairo. Her ethnographic investigations show how 'the language of empowering the poor' serves to reinforce systems of dispossession encouraged by neoliberal policies and the financialising of social networks through relations of debt mediated by NGOs.[14]

In his research in Central Asia and the Middle East, Olivier Roy puts forward a more nuanced critique of donor support to civil society, identifying a gap between the 'civil society concept' and real life.[15] He points out that the accepted Western notion of civil society – of networks of free citizens, such as professional associations or unions, that create political space as a prerequisite for building democracy – fails to take into account traditional or religious structures that may exist in the receiving communities. He contrasts this to Islamist and traditionalist notions of civil society. In his assessment of the Central Asian case of Tajikistan, the problem is precisely that of ignoring the indigenous civic associations and their pre-existing structures and potential. He concludes that the Western concept of civil society, perceived as 'an abstract and idealized paradigm that stems from modern Western experiences', has fall-out effects when applied in other contexts by external actors. Donors' creation of material incentives to spark new cooperation initiatives could lead to overlooking already-existing structures on the ground. Such incentives, Roy shows, can create a 'mirror effect', whereby initiatives simply reflect what a donor wishes to see, with no anchorage in society. For certain donors, a focus on 'civil society' is often an excuse to ignore the political constraints and demands of a given society. Taking into account real political actors and addressing what political legitimacy means is a far more difficult but necessary prerequisite for democratisation. Such legitimacy presupposes the rooting of actors in the history and traditions of a society, something which external donors often struggle to understand as outsiders in a foreign environment.

These academic debates on how civil society might or might not contribute to democracy were largely overlooked, or happened too late to influence donor programming and practices in many countries and regions. The existence of grassroots organisations came to be regarded as a precondition for democracy, regardless of their aims, their mission, or any anchoring they may have had in local society. After the successful transitions in Eastern Europe, constructing civil society elsewhere seemed to become an 'end in itself'.[16] For Western policy makers and academics, civil society, according to Thomas Carothers, simply 'became a mantra'.[17] Policy makers in the international donor institutions placed civil society at the centre of democratisation programmes without sufficiently considering how to work with real associations on the ground. In line with these trends, the EU also launched many new regional dialogue initiatives and individual country programmes targeting civil society. Two such programmes were initiated in Algeria from the early 2000s, despite the EU having very little experience in the country and almost no other funding programmes set up due to the conflict of the 1990s.

With these increases in funding and the apparent ignoring of local or traditional organisations, donor language and development paradigms tended to frame civil society as a European concept. Simultaneously, the language of international donors, and of academics, often reinforced negative images of the Arab world, or even diminished the very existence of Arab-Muslim civil society. Challand writes that:

> the over-concentration of much of the literature on 'what went wrong' by spotting the absence of some local prerequisites further contributes to the impoverishment of the theoretical content of civil society in the region.[18]

Questions in the academic literature, such as 'is there an Arab civil society?' or 'can there be a Muslim civil society?' (Gellner clearly implied that there was not)[19] contributed to reinforcing adverse stereotypes and ultimately to the difficulties experienced by civil society organisations on the ground in the Arab world. As Roy found in Central Asia, Western scholars and policy makers denied the variety of Arab civil society and the richness of the Muslim public sphere because it failed to correspond to Western conceptions of the term 'civil society'. Local recipients were regarded as lacking forms of democracy; as such, those norms and values would have to be exported through actions such as the US programme for the Greater Middle East, to bring democracy and to construct civil society from scratch. This not only undermined the real local actors, but fed into self-fulfilling prophecies of failure, limiting the potential for internal processes of political reform. This was in stark contrast to the vocal support from Western governments for revolutions and democratic transitions in Eastern Europe.

Regional Variations in EU Support to Civil Society

At the end of the Cold War, the EU embarked on a series of civil society and democracy promotion policies around the world.[20] The argument in favour of such interventions was supported by several factors, including empirical evidence from the East. The positive role Eastern European civil society organisations had played in the democratic transition encouraged interest in new actors and NGOs in the African, Caribbean and Pacific (ACP) countries, the Middle East and North Africa. In the following years, the EU developed strategies for the promotion of democracy through investment in civil society on the African continent, in Eastern Europe, Latin America and the Middle East, but in quite different ways. Despite aiming to support what are claimed to be universal principles, the EU had very different approaches to its new-found focus on civil society and democracy across the regions.

In the democratic transitions in Eastern Europe in the 1990s, organisations such as the Catholic Church, free trade unions, literary movements and theatre groups had been important agents of change. As a result, after 1990, the EU invested substantial funds in programmes such as TACIS (Technical Aid to the Commonwealth of Independent States) and Poland and Hungary: Assistance for Restructuring their Economies (PHARE) programmes. Through these programmes, they promoted local NGOs in Eastern Europe, often creating new structures from scratch. The promise of the benefits of accession enabled the EU to impose significant structural changes on the institutions and on civil society and its Eastern partners. Güney and Çelenk note how the 'interaction between supranational organisations and nation-states became quite significant in bringing about change in their political systems'.[21] With these processes of democratic transition, the concept of civil society became embedded in political discourse. Through their experiences in the East, the EU and Western donors were comforted that their assumptions were correct. Raik writes that 'the central role of peaceful civic activity in bringing about political change was reaffirmed by the recent transitions in Georgia and Ukraine'.[22] The concept of civil society as a tool or a master frame to promote democratisation was increasingly integrated into the democracy promotion policies of the EU.

As a result, in its relations with other regions and states around the world, the EU increasingly insisted on the importance of civil society in all aspects of its cooperation agreements. The Cotonou Agreement, signed with countries in Africa, the Caribbean and the Pacific (ACP), outlined a role for non-state actors, including civil society 'in all its forms', as long as organisations were prepared to 'address the needs of the population' and were 'managed democratically and transparently'.[23] Article 4 states that these actors would 'be informed and involved in consultation on co-operation policies and strategies' and 'provided with capacity building' and 'financial resources'. Governments were now obliged to consult non-state actors in the adoption of international agreements and programmes signed with the EU. Reference to civil society actors, democratic principles and the rule of law progressively entered into EU–ACP cooperation agreements. The essential role of non-state actors and the *obligation* to consult with civil society in all domains of cooperation, national policy making and political dialogue were enshrined in the legally binding Cotonou Agreement. Article 96 of the agreement is a key example of this obligation, in its provision for the suspension of aid should the basic conditions of democracy, human rights and the rule of law not be respected by one of the parties. According to one EU consultant specialising in civil society support, the very fact of including this obligation within the Cotonou Agreement has had a significant impact on African civil society.

> Twenty years ago the main actors and beneficiaries of this type of EU aid in ACP countries were only European NGOs, primarily the Christian ones. Now there exists an important number of capable African NGOs with ambitions to play a greater role in political life.[24]

Under the 9th European Development Fund, the EU financed 42 programmes that directly supported civil society organisations in 38 ACP countries, at a cost of 200 million euros.[25] Limited successes in the EU's other development programmes in ACP countries led certain commentators to increasingly target the African state as the source of the problem. The Eastern experience, and its model of civil society support for reform, conveniently allowed the EU to progressively target NGOs rather than purely engaging with national governments. This rather prescriptive relationship with the ACP states – concerning civil society and democracy promotion – contrasts, however, with the weaker position taken by the EU as regards the MENA region.

In the revised Mediterranean Policy adopted in 1990, the concepts of civil society and democracy were conspicuously absent. A change of approach seemed to be signalled with the new Euro-Mediterranean Partnership, launched by the Barcelona Process in November 1995. In this, 12 Mediterranean partners were required to sign up to the principles of pluralism. The partnership aimed to 'encourage actions of support for democratic institutions and for strengthening of the rule of law and civil society',[26] yet one had to scroll down to page eight of the declaration to read this first mention of civil society. These political intentions remained vague, compared to the highly detailed parts of the document that dealt with economic liberalisation. The late inclusion of democracy promotion suggested an element of document standardisation, or perhaps an afterthought. In the association agreements, and in the Euro-Mediterranean Partnership, which replaced the Barcelona Process with the Union for the Mediterranean in 2008, there was no mention of civil society and the primary initiatives related mainly to the environment and the business sector. It was designed from an EU perspective, re-affirming that the Union for the Mediterranean would promote economic integration and democratic reform across the 17 neighbours to the EU's south in North Africa and the Middle East. For many, it appeared to be less about a union across the whole region and more about the EU promoting certain policy objectives in the south. No real assessment of the needs of the southern neighbouring region was made and the priorities remained broadly economic and environmental, rather than political reform.

In its relations with the southern Mediterranean countries generally, the EU's European Neighbourhood Policy (ENP) has stood accused of having allowed European interests to override legitimate socio-economic needs. Hakim Darbouche, for one, describes how the EU managed to inculcate 'a form of Euro-Arab dialogue based on reform and governance in response to European fears rather than to address the region's socio-economic preoccupations'.[27] Underpinning this regional dialogue was the fear of Islamism and a preference for stability over real democratic reform. Trade liberalisation, guilt over failed past policies, security interests and the fear of terrorism, the desire for greater immigration controls, as well as national foreign policy interests, were also said to be factors underpinning the ENP. Moreover, a desire for a hub–spoke relationship with its partners meant that standardisation was implicit in many of the EU's programmes. Ironically, the difficulty of engaging in democratic debate within the EU institutions themselves meant that one solution, after difficult internal negotiations, had to be accepted by all external partners.

There are of course legitimate regional variations between the different partnerships in which the EU engages. These respond to the negotiations and political priorities of the different states. Variations in what are argued to be universal moral values promoted by the EU, such as democracy, human rights and freedom of association, would be more difficult to reconcile. Yet, there appear to be significant inconsistencies in EU democracy promotion strategies in geographical terms. Over the last 20 years, the Mediterranean appears to have been exempted from the prioritisation of democracy promotion. This can be seen in the EU discourse, the absence of conditionality measures, such as those with ACP countries, and in the more modest nature of its development funding. Inconsistencies in the EU's discourse about civil society and democracy in the Mediterranean region, and in particular in Algeria, have been noted in academic studies, along with the accusation that the EU never really supported indigenous democracy.

In Algeria, the EU's goals have also been limited by the diminishing level of trust between the two sides due to troubled historical relations, which will be discussed later in this volume. Algeria's conflict created a difficult environment for external actors and their presence was limited for a number of years. The European Commission closed its offices in Algiers between 1993 and 1998. Furthermore, for the Algerian state, the posture of the EU throughout the conflict was 'problematic at best'.[28] There was a lack of cooperation concerning the presence of wanted Islamist terrorists sheltering in European capitals and a failure to support Algeria at key moments when democratic reform was possible. Overall, this meant that, from the perspective of the Algerian state and population, the EU was part of the problem, not the solution. External actors, who displayed little understanding of the realities of Algerian politics, were kept out of it. Like Moscow, and many other neighbouring capitals, Algiers clearly disliked being given lessons in democracy from actors situated in the comfortable environs of the European capitals.[29] Entelis had also earlier pointed to Algeria's unique and brutal history, which had led to a political culture in which there was a sense of an 'Algerian nationalist consciousness and political community' unparalleled within the Arab world, and at the same time a 'distrust of all things foreign'.[30] The overbearing presence of French politics remained deeply problematic for Algerian politicians and academics, leading the Algerian state to be suspicious of any form of European democracy promotion.[31]

So despite the Algerian regime's far-from-exemplary democratic credentials, 'meaningful dialogue on democracy promotion is notably absent from the agenda of any EU-Algeria official interaction'.[32] The strong economic position of Algeria also meant that Algeria now no longer needed financial assistance from external actors. If the EU had indeed become part of the problem, through lack of understanding, then its decision to withdraw backstage could be understood in this context. Standardisation and the logic of its policies meant paying lip service to the ideals it was trying to promote but with no real will to find policy tools to implement them, either in its financial assistance, in its conditionality or in its cooperation agreements in general. Following the 2011 regime changes in the Arab world, the EU was once again obliged to renew its Mediterranean policy. Many pointed here to the EU's sense of failure or embarrassment for not having understood or supported moves for democratic change in the region. The Enlargement and Neighbourhood Policy Commissioner, Füle, at the time stated that:

> Europe was not vocal enough in defending human rights and local democratic forces in the region. Too many of us fell prey to the assumption that authoritarian regimes were a guarantee of stability.[33]

The weaknesses and inconsistencies in the EU's role in the region seemed to have undermined the seriousness of its intentions to support civil society and promote democracy. Yet the more modest approach, in Algeria in particular, does not mean that the EU had been entirely absent. Within the MENA region a comparison of donor programmes for civil society in relatively similar countries such as Algeria, Palestine and Lebanon can help us to understand whether Algeria represents an exceptional case within the region, with its protection from some of the more negative effects linked to excessive donor funding, and, if so, whether this can then be considered to be due to the historical context, the power of the Algerian state or something more inherent in Algerian civil society itself.

Civil Society Support in the MENA Region: Algeria, Palestine and Lebanon

Despite regional variations and increasingly critical evaluations, the EU continues to support civil society and democratisation in the Middle East and North Africa through its European Neighbourhood Policy; indeed, following the Arab Spring, donor support to civil society even increased.[34] The EU model for civil society support includes specific interventions, programmes and legal instruments. In the framework of its Neighbourhood Policy, the EU signs National Indicative Programmes with each country's priority sectors. Within these priority sectors, the EU, together with the national authorities, puts in place individual programmes, technical assistance, grant schemes, or budget support to the state in order to achieve their joint objectives. The EU often develops specific civil society support programmes providing grants, training and institutional support. Equally, within sector programmes, from road building to prisons support, the EU can often include a component targeting civil society. These actions are complemented by other regional or global funding initiatives. They include the European Instrument for Democracy of Human rights and the Non State Actors budget line, which are managed either by Brussels or the delegations. These programmes can support civil society initiatives and finance European or national NGOs. The national allocations of funding are not based on need or population, but rather on a competitive basis, on political negotiations, relationships with different ministries, on the partner country's capacity to absorb funds and the capacity of the EU delegation in place to manage them. It is within these structures that the EU, similar to other donors, provides concrete support to NGOs and other civil society organisations. Although programmes are regional and apply across the Middle East and

North Africa, at country level the support depends on the budget that is negotiated with Brussels. Disparities in these country budgets are significant. Within the MENA region, countries such as Algeria, Palestine and Lebanon negotiate different support programmes, with different budgets, and these will now be explored in more detail.

Algeria

In the Country Strategy and National Indicative Programme for Algeria, elaborated upon with the national authorities for 2002–6, the EU committed to 'improving competition between the peoples of the region and the development of an active civil society'. In the National Programme 2007–10, it committed to supporting three priority axes of justice reform, economic growth and employment and reinforcing basic public services. Within these national programmes, the EU launched in Algeria two significant initiatives to support civil society.[35] The first programme represented 5 million euros over a five-year period, and the second 11 million euros, of which 1 million euros was financed by the Algerian state. The overall EU budget for Algeria for 2007–10 was 220 million euros, an average of 55 million euros per year. The amount reserved for civil society support was a small fraction. These programmes financed, respectively, 76 and 131 local Algerian NGOs with short-term grant contracts for social, heritage, environment, gender, youth, culture and community development projects. The programmes also financed training schemes to accompany the NGOs in the implementation of their projects. Monitoring and coaching visits were financed, as well as exchanges of experience and sectoral training to encourage networking opportunities and forums for dialogue.[36] Under the different budget lines coming directly from Brussels, the EU financed around 25 projects in Algeria with relatively limited budgets. These had a maximum of 1 million euros over three years, with the majority obtaining much lower sums. They were funded by the Non State Actors budget line and the European Initiative for the Defence of Human Rights. The Algerian government initially refused to approve the EU's human rights funding calls amid public and private claims that the EU had 'little moral authority to claim to teach Algerians about human rights'.[37] When relations gradually improved, the funding calls were approved. Grants were won by Algerian and European NGOs working on projects ranging from victims of terrorism to cultural and social issues. It remains difficult to calculate precise yearly allocations to civil society organisations, especially as the EU cooperation programmes have been increasing – particularly since 2011. However, it is estimated that, in recent years, just over 2 million euros per year is allocated to civil society organisations and NGOs in Algeria by the European Union.

Other donor initiatives remain equally humble in Algeria. Despite policy statements, most donors find it difficult to identify partners and to find the appropriate structures with which to contract.[38] Algerian legislation does not encourage foreign involvement in its civil society, perceiving it as interference. Such foreign involvement is also, as British Embassy officials pointed out in interviews, perhaps legitimately seen as a threat in that there is the potential for external financing of extremist groups under the cover of legitimate associations.[39] There is a limited legal framework for foreign NGOs and actions remain sporadic.[40] The main actors working with Algerian civil society organisations are the French, British and German Embassies, the German development foundations, Spanish, Dutch, Canadian and Swiss cooperation agencies, the World Bank and the United Nations. The UN has funded civil society on a very limited scale in recent years following the bombing of its headquarters in 2007 by Islamist extremists.[41] It is estimated that no more than 4 million euros is disbursed to civil society organisations by external donors per year. This figure is strikingly low compared to other countries in the region.

EU Development spending in Algeria (in millions €)	
Overall support to Algeria – MEDA programme/2008 (average per year: 2007–10 NIP is €220 million)	55
Financing for NGOs in Algeria:	
• Support Programme to Algerian NGOs (ave)	1
• ONG/PVD (sust. dev/refugees/disability)	0.6
• Non-state actors/Local authorities	0.0
• EIDHR	0.6
• Human ressources/youth & victims of terrorism	0.2
TOTAL	**2.4**
In millions € – annual averages for 2008, EU delegation Algiers.	

Figure 2.1 EU development spending in Algeria.

Palestine

With many cultural and political links to Algeria, Palestine also has a similar recent history of conflict and a backdrop of colonial repression. The place of external and European donors in particular, however, is hugely different in Palestine than in Algeria. Palestine has only a tenth of the Algerian population, yet the EU's financial commitments towards supporting NGOs in Palestine are considerably higher. The EU funds a significant number of European or international NGOs, which manage large-scale, expensive programmes. These are contracted again through calls for proposals under regional and country-specific programmes for NGOs. These calls are, in the main, aimed at European NGOs with the capacity to manage large grants which may trickle down to national organisations. Benoit Challand's detailed research in 2005 estimated that, in total, aid to NGOs in Palestine could reach between 300 million and 400 million dollars per year.[42] This is 100 times the estimated amount accorded to Algerian NGOs. With the Palestinian population at a tenth of the size of Algeria's, this represents a relationship of 1000:1. The EU's Neighbourhood Action Plan for the Palestinian Authority was all-encompassing and granted more financial assistance per capita than for any of the other neighbourhood states.

Challand's investigations in 2010 brought him to the conclusion that the EU's interventions, motivated by guilt and shaped by a lack of sensitivity, have potentially fed the conflict by supporting civil society in this way. A number of cases of violence against NGOs have been reported in Palestine. Challand writes, 'that people turn violent against their own CSOs trying to promote reconciliation speaks abundantly about the resentment that external aid can generate'.[43] A survey in 1997 revealed that 40 per cent of the population believed that foreign funding had a negative or very negative effect in the territories.[44] In her article 'Missionaries of the new era', Merz quotes Ava Leone, who writes that in Palestine, and particularly in Ramallah, 'virtually no space, physical or imagined has been untouched by some aspect of foreign aid'.[45] The EU's contributions to civil society, democracy and the government of the Palestinian Authority confirm this trend, as demonstrated in Figure 2.2.

The EU dedicates an estimated 22 million euros annually to NGOs in Palestine. This compares dramatically to the estimated 2 million euros to NGOs in Algeria. In Palestine, CARE International's budget alone

EU Development spending in Palestine	
Support programmes to NGOs in Palestine:	
• Non-state actors programme	4
• Food security programme	10
• Partnership for peace	7.5
• Investing in people	0.5
• Culture	0.4
TOTAL	**22.4**

In millions € – based on annual averages for 2008, EU delegation West Bank website & Challand (2010:14)

Figure 2.2   EU development spending in Palestine.

rose from 4 million dollars for 2001, to 'an incredible 15.5 million dollars in 2003'.[46] The presence of multiple international donors contributing up to 400 million euros each year to civil society in Palestine raises questions about the coordination as well as the effectiveness of such funding, particularly given the continued daily challenges of the Palestinian population living under occupation.

Lebanon

In between the two preceding cases lies EU development cooperation in Lebanon. Despite its history of conflict, Lebanon has historically been relatively open in its foreign policies and partnerships with the EU and other actors. Cavatorta and Durac describe the Lebanese context as one where civil society can easily organise, which in turn encourages activity from international donors for whom there are few limitations in terms of foreign funding. Many organisations receive international support and 'the liberal nature of the country and the relative autonomy of civil society actors from the government make it possible for external donors to pursue their agendas of change'.[47] Cavatorta and Durac describe, however, how 'this influx of foreign money creates a very competitive environment for civil society groups, which tend to try to appease donors thereby reinforcing patterns of patronage'.[48] The divisive nature of funding can be seen, for example, in the accepting of UK or US money, at a time when these donors' support of Israel's war against Lebanon made them highly unpopular. Receiving such funds from the West, including the EU, meant accusations from the Islamist sector of civil society of 'doing the West's bidding'. Shiite and Sunni groups must, respectively, look to Iran and the Gulf States for support. All this contributes to further division along sectarian grounds, rather than support of Lebanese citizenship through civic organisations.

Since the end of the civil war in 1990 the EU has been actively supporting reconciliation measures, often through the NGO sector. In the last decade, two important programmes directly targeting civil society have been funded: AFKAR 1 and 2.[49] These programmes have trained NGOs and financed 40 small projects, mainly focusing on the rule of law, human rights and civil society dialogue. NGOs respond to the standard calls for projects from Brussels, and recently two local calls, for human rights and culture, have been launched by the EU delegation. In Lebanon, the European Union commits roughly 10 million euros annually to NGOs; this for a country with a population of just over 4 million inhabitants (Figure 2.3).[50]

Interviews with EU officials in Beirut highlighted awareness within the EU structures (and staff) of the problems identified above. EU officials acknowledged that external financing can have negative impacts on organisations. It can encourage opportunism or create projects which pander to European wishes rather than the real priorities of national civic

EU development spending in Lebanon	
Overall support to Lebanon – ENPI programme/2008 (average per year: 2007–10 NIP is €187 million)	47
Support programmes to NGOs in Lebanon :	
• AFKAR (4 months/4 years)	1
• Estimated commitments for EIDHR	
• Local and central calls to NGOS	9
TOTAL	**10**

In millions € – based on annual averages for 2008, EU delegation Beirut and website.

Figure 2.3   EU development spending in Lebanon.

organisations and local communities. In Lebanon, EU staff noted a tendency for opportunism in the responses to calls for projects, but clearly attributed the blame for this to the donors themselves. As one official stated:

> If the projects proposed by NGOs are mediocre or seem to be opportunistic, as exists everywhere in the world, often they are corrupted by the call itself – and that is our problem. We need to better design the project calls to inspire the NGOs and to respond better to the real needs of civil society so that they contribute and not just seek financial support.[51]

In the three cases discussed, there has been significant criticism of the role of donors insofar as their funding to NGOs can often exacerbate internal problems and conflicts rather than promote development or democratisation. There are also huge disparities in the levels of funding attributed to different countries. Compared to other countries in the region, the figures show that the EU and other donors too have had a very low profiles and budgets for all civil society programmes in Algeria. This is illustrated in the spending levels shown in Figure 2.4 and Table 2.1.

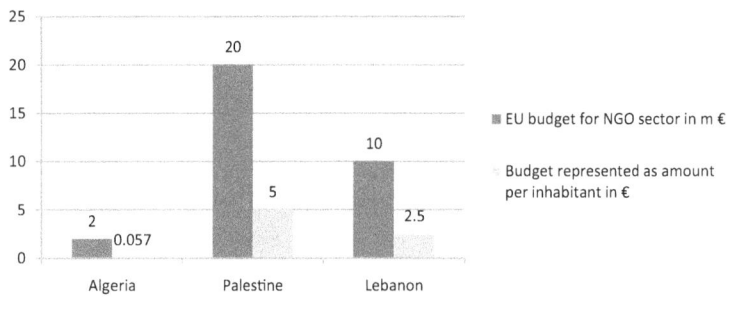

Figure 2.4 EU spending on NGOs in three MENA countries.
Sources: estimates from interviews with EU delegation officials and websites.

Table 2.1 EU development spending on NGOs in three MENA countries.

Figures for 2007–10 period	Annual EU development spending on the NGO sector in three MENA countries		
	Algeria	Palestine	Lebanon
EU budget for NGO sector in m €	2	20	10
Budget represented as amount per inhabitant in €	0.057	5	2.5
Population	35	4	4

Sources: estimates from interviews with EU delegation officials and websites.

This low level of funding has been gradually changing, however, with the EU looking to Algeria as a stable partner in an unstable region. The EU has now significantly increased its commitments to Algeria. The approach of the EU in the country over the last decade has been modest, both in financial and technical terms. It has focused more on national institutions and organisations, human resources and embedding civil society initiatives in national structures. The first EU civil society support programme was managed by an Algerian research centre, and the second by a national ministry. Comparing the figures, it appears that the EU in Algeria supported far more organisations than it has supported in other countries in the region. This has been done with much lower grants, using primarily national structures to implement the programmes in the absence of international or European NGOs. External monitoring and evaluations have been generally positive about the results of the EU's support of Algerian NGOs.[52]

When comparing Algeria to Lebanon and Palestine, another difference is the non-political bias of EU funding in Algeria. Only a few Algerian organisations work on human rights or political campaigns; the majority concentrate on the social sector. In Lebanon and Palestine, project calls published on the delegation websites often target human rights, rule of law and other more politicised objectives, encouraging NGOs to work on those areas. The more reserved approach in Algeria is often criticised by academics as limiting the opportunity to bring about change. However, it also potentially encourages a less divisive approach to funding than that witnessed in Lebanon. Charities coming from an Islamic background, providing social care or educational programmes, are not excluded from the EU's Algerian programmes and work alongside secular associations in all sectors. The greater barrier, as argued by most associations interviewed, would seem to be one of language and their struggles with French rather than political position or religion.

Conclusion

The nature of the EU's more modest approach to supporting civil society in Algeria contrasts hugely with the alternative of flooding it with funds, diminishing the autonomy of local actors and, as seen in Lebanon and Palestine, creating divisions and even violence. The refusal of the Algerian Government to accept certain forms of European interference, or standard models for civil society support, may well have created more effective organisations on the ground. The more limited availability of funds implies that the associations which emerged in Algeria were created in response to the real needs of the population – in a context of violence and societal breakdown – rather than as an opportunistic response to the availability of funds, as had been the case in so many other countries since the 1990s paradigm shift amongst donors. Through their growing experience of implementing such civil society programmes, for their part, donors have nevertheless increasingly reflected on their interventions and how these impact on the local context. As shown in Lebanon, EU officials noted the problems of opportunism in responses to calls for projects and clearly took the blame. Donor interviewees also recognised the problems of achieving a coherent strategy, as well as the problems of dependence on foreign aid, capacity constraints, opportunism and the uncivil nature of some NGOs. There also seems to be increasing awareness that difficulties in intervening in foreign contexts are worsened if there is a plethora of different actors with competing interests – something so far avoided in Algeria, due to the limited number of foreign donors.

There are clearly significant disparities and inconsistencies in the way international donors support civil society and democracy across different regions and countries. Whilst there are standard templates, each donor and each recipient country shapes its programmes differently. The EU negotiates with actors who accept, reject, adopt or, to a certain extent, re-model the approaches. The size of the vastly different donor budgets in the region for civil society, as shown in the above cases, does not seem to be any real indicator of impact. Rather, it seems that more modest approaches potentially have more successful outcomes. If donor interventions adapt to the local context and target existing initiatives, smaller grassroots associations or indigenous structures, as Olivier Roy suggests, donors could avoid creating a mirror effect or an artificial civil society. This, it is argued, is what has happened over the last two decades for Algerian civil society. The combination of historical Algerian nationalism, the devastating conflict and the powerful Algerian state have meant that international donors have been able to play only a very modest role in the country. Algeria is an exception in the region in terms of limited donor support and an exceptional increase in indigenous associations, many of which are implicated in protecting vulnerable populations and rebuilding Algerian society. These recent developments in the associational movement will now be explored in more detail – from the historic backdrop to specific cases – to better understand the role of civil society and activism in contemporary Algeria.

PART II

ALGERIAN CIVIL SOCIETY AND RELATIONS WITH THE STATE

CHAPTER 3

HISTORICAL PERSPECTIVES ON CIVIL SOCIETY IN ALGERIA

Nowhere are the challenges of recurrent violent confrontation and the fragility of civil society as important and as pressing in Algeria. Struggling with the legacy of the most destructive form of colonialism, with religious extremism, with political violence and with increasing economic and social inequalities, the country represents an important case for the post-colonial nation. Algeria has been described as a 'microcosm of the contemporary world'.[1] To understand Algeria's complex, often conflictual, development it is important to explore the evolution of civil society over time, beginning with the traditional structures of the village communities and religious brotherhoods. It is also necessary to question previous interpretations of Algerian society and governance structures, in pre-colonial times in particular, given the predominance of colonial narratives which often seek to justify the 'civilising mission'. In his recent work on *Berber Government, The Kabyle Polity in Pre-colonial Algeria*, Hugh Roberts challenges French sociologist Pierre Bourdieu and British anthropologist Ernest Gellner, who had defined Algerian, particularly Berber, society as divided, disordered, somehow static and underdeveloped, or as a society with no history.[2] Roberts describes how, in pre-colonial Kabylia, the Berber region to the east of Algiers, every village was a political unit and the Arab hillsmen of Algeria had similar governing structures. He writes:

Significant social development was occurring in Kabylia well before the colonial period. The kind of order which prevailed there by the mid-nineteenth century was not that of a society without a history. And central to the history of pre-colonial Kabylia was the establishment of political institutions and a system of self-government based upon these institutions and the development thereby of political traditions which have survived the colonial impact and with which the independent state still has to reckon.[3]

In *A History of Algeria*, James McDougall describes the place of the religious structures developed around the Sufi *zawiyas* during the Ottoman Regency, prior to the French colonial conquest in 1830. Including 'a mosque and centre of learning, sometimes with a library and hospice for students and pilgrims', the *zawiyas* revolved around the mausoleums of particularly important saints, and were considered sanctuaries or 'repositories of spiritual power'.[4] From the late eighteenth century, the custodian families of these local shrines and *zawiyas* affiliated to one of the different Sufi orders of Islam whose networks spanned West Africa and Asia. In Algeria, these included the Rahmaniyya, the Qadiriyya and the Tijaniyya orders or ways (*tariqas*) which institutionalised communities of learning and spirituality. In the early nineteenth century, many of the uprisings in response to failing crop harvests, food shortages and the plague were mobilised by Algerian society as constituted and organised within the *zawiyas*. McDougall writes how these demonstrations of political unrest were 'legitimised by rurally based religious figures associated with the *tariqas*', which were ultimately protesting against the Ottoman Regency as a 'corrupt and unjust government'.[5] The great historical figure of the anti-colonial struggle in the 1830s, the Emir Abd el-Kader, himself drew his faith and spiritual learning from his family's affiliation to the Qadiriyya order.

From the late eighteenth century onwards, the increasingly nepotistic authority of the Ottoman Regency worsened relations with local organisations and heightened their distrust of the central state. However, far worse was to come. The tensions, suspicions and challenges of building a plural political system today are most deeply rooted in the decimation of the indigenous structures of Algerian culture and society under colonialism. The consensual approaches of traditional local governance and religious structures soon came into direct conflict with the increasingly violent forces of nineteenth- and twentieth-century French colonial rule.

The destruction of Algerian society, and the trauma of the liberation war, also set a difficult scene for post-independence governments to engage in nation-building. The desire to unite Algerians under one identity meant state formation was deemed to preclude the development of autonomous organisations that might threaten the newly independent nation. Yet despite these tendencies, and despite the history of violence under colonialism, the War of Independence and even the conflict of the 1990s, Algeria remains one of the most open regimes in the region in terms of freedom of association, political parties and the press. In the most difficult of conditions, civil society in Algeria has undergone significant development. To understand the current context, it is important to study, first, the trajectory which led Algerians to the revolutionary movement for democracy, civil liberties and human rights. This movement, which ultimately brought liberation and the creation of the Algerian nation, finds its roots in a structured and organised tradition of civil society, activism and local governance.

Traditional Civil Society and the Impact of Colonialism

Whereas both Morocco and Tunisia, respectively, had experienced state-building impetus since the eleventh and eighth centuries, Algeria has only truly existed as a unified territory since the sixteenth century. This was when the Ottoman Regency was present in North Africa – at the request of the Muslim populations – to prevent the expansion of the newly united Spanish Kingdom in its re-conquest of the Mediterranean. Prior to this (and subsequently) successions of invasions and migrations, from the Phoenicians, Carthaginians, Romans, Arabs, Almoravids and Almohads to the French invasion of 1830, had made 'Algeria' an unstable area where the small family, the village and the tribe were the basic units of society. The original Berber population was defined by clan, lineage, tribe and family, with a strong emphasis on self-reliance as a response to insecurity and weak government.[6] Under the Ottoman Regency, Algerians continued to follow customary law; the village came together to decide important matters through ancient forms of consultation in the village *thajmaaths* or the *aarouch* councils in Kabylia, and these were naturally egalitarian. Roberts describes how nineteenth-century European observers saw the Kabyle communities they encountered as 'a remarkable society of numerous, unusually large, rigorously ordered' villages.[7] He writes:

> This development was that of a mountain society which was both egalitarian and unusually orderly, fiercely independent and highly integrated but also outward looking, and of an economy characterised by intensive and highly diversified commercial craft manufacture and by an equally diversified pattern of commercial and labour migration. This society was regulated by a remarkable system of self-government which achieved its final form between the early seventeenth century and the middle of the eighteenth century.[8]

Heads of noble families and communities of religious scholars played an important role in local affairs and political life. Traditional Arab civil society was based around a public space shared by the ulama, merchants' guilds, Sufi orders and sects, which ran their collective affairs through elected or appointed leaders. The Sufi brotherhoods and village councils both impacted on collective decision making. These consensual approaches were said to have influenced the type of government later proposed by President Houari Boumediene.[9] Associative life in Algeria began, then, with these egalitarian local structures situated within a multicultural society. The rich cultural diversity under the Ottoman Regency meant that, whilst there was some friction, lines were not drawn between Muslims and Jews, natives and foreigners, Arabs and Berbers. Urban–rural divides may have prevailed, as could linguistic rather than ethnic divisions. Even language, however, could change within a generation. Berbers assimilated to Arabic-speaking society, as did European renegades; language practice, as today, was often multilingual where different populations met.[10] With the decline of the Ottoman Regency, Algerians strengthened their historical distrust of the central state. Some claim that it was the Ottoman Regency which indeed transformed the state into an object for enrichment. Profiteers could gain access to easy wealth through links to the state, a practice which continued under French rule.[11]

Following the French colonial conquest in 1830, the reality throughout much of nineteenth- and twentieth-century Algeria was that of high levels of repression and restriction of any oppositional civic, religious or traditional structures seeking to play a role in the country's development and political life. A centralising, state-led vision of development was imposed upon society by the colonial administration. This was achieved through legislation, harsh repression and intervention in the functioning of any autonomous grouping. It had been a deliberate policy of the French colonial administration to break up traditional Muslim structures and families in Algeria. Malika Rebai Maamri describes how the 'colonial conquest and imposition of European rule shattered the old political and religious orders'.[12] In her book *The State of Algeria*, she goes on to describe the brutality of the colonial conquest. She quotes Tocqueville, who wrote, 'I returned from Africa with the distressing notion that we are now fighting far more barbarously than the Arabs themselves. For the present, it is on their side that one meets with civilisation.'[13] Rebai describes the cruelty of the French Army, the use of concentration camps, mass executions, torture and terrorising of the local population to subdue them. Through land expropriation, famine and enslavement on the colonial farms, they aimed for the complete subjugation of the Algerian people. Rebai writes:

> The French war of pacification unleashed uncontrolled human destructiveness. It inflicted both physical and moral torture on the colonised and involved not only the dismantlement of the existing social structures and economic system but also massive expropriation of land, which deprived most Algerians of their basic means of subsistence.[14]

She continues that, with the French colonisation of Algeria, 'it was not merely economic exploitation or political domination it sought but an extensive annexation aimed at eradicating its culture'.[15] By 1894, Governor General Cambon regretted this strategy of completely 'suppressing the forces of resistance', the result of which meant that the French subsequently had no means of knowing with whom to negotiate. Their success in preventing any form of Muslim opposition body meant that they were left with what Cambon described as 'a sort of human dust on which we have no influence'. When opposition took them by surprise, they had no means of understanding or interacting with it.[16] Reducing Algerian society to a *poussière d'hommes*, anarchic and incapable of self-government, James McDougall describes how the colonial prejudices have continued to feed into perceptions of Algeria as a weak and fragmented society. This is despite, as he points out, the often highly resilient forces within society, beyond state structures, that enabled the Algerian population to keep going despite the incredible brutality and repression they had endured.[17]

Despite such repression and the denial of citizenship under the *Code Algérien de l'Indigénat* from 1865, a politically active civil society did evolve during the colonial period. In the countryside, even with the misery of colonisation, the traditional tribal fraction, the *firqa*, continued to operate and mobilise – particularly in the mountain regions – regardless of the administrative division of tribes into *douars-communes*. The real council, below the official colonial structure, continued to function and provide the social and political organisation of peasant life, regulating village life and providing a united front against the outside world. McDougall describes how widespread anti-conscription revolts in World War I and social banditry in the mountains were all signs of 'this vital, sustained rural social solidarity'.[18]

In small towns and cities, following the 1901 French Law on Associations, civil society organisations and spaces emerged, as did new French- and Arabic-language press outlets, although these were controlled by the colonial administration. By the 1930s professional associations, trade unions, cultural clubs, the Scouts, secular charities, intellectual circles known as *nadis*, cafés and religious organisations all flourished. Liverani writes that the *nadis*, in particular, by the end of the 1930s, had become 'the centre of socialisation for the Algerian intelligentsia and radically transformed the political opportunities of upper-middle class Muslims'.[19] The cafes represented a space of socialisation for the working classes and for men in particular. With increasing urbanisation, it was in cafes that 'the newly urbanised exchanged news from home regions, and rumours about events in the capital and the country in general'.[20] It was, then, within the formal structures of the colonial associative experience, such as the unions or sports clubs, that these two populations, urban and rural, were able to meet and, despite control by the colonial administration, to socialise, politicise and mobilise. The lack of political space under colonialism pushed many Algerians to less-obviously-political forms of activity, such as football or boxing clubs, theatre groups or popular music like *chaabi*, in order to actively try to create an Algerian public sphere. Within the restricted spaces of French Algeria, McDougall describes how, similar to the coming together of the multi-ethnic *Français d'Algérie*, 'Algerians from the Mzab to Kabylia, from Tebessa to Tlemcen, recognised their own shared condition and found ways to contest it' in a process of political community formation.[21]

Many of these associative structures played an important role in the nationalist independence struggle in more subtle ways, ranging from everyday resistance to more active mobilisation after World War I. This is illustrated by episodes such as the mobilisation around the Popular Front in 1936.

The 1920s saw the beginning of new, organised political opposition to the French colonial state. In 1926 a combination of migrant workers and Communist Party activists in Paris created the Association *Etoile Nord Africaine* (ENA). Messali Hadj was elected as its charismatic Secretary General and spoke in Brussels the following year, laying the grounds of the independence movement and politicising the Algerian population both in France and in Algeria. By 1933, the *Etoile Nord Africaine* had a clear political programme for independence through non-violent means. Active both in Algeria and in Europe, it effectively became the first Algerian political party. When the ENA was dissolved by the French authorities in 1937, Messali Hadj went on to create the radical nationalist *Parti du Peuple Algérien* (PPA), the Algerian People's Party, which was also suppressed. It was transformed once again in 1945 into the *Mouvement pour le Triomphe des Libertés Démocratiques* (MTLD). With the PPA and MTLD parties dominating Algerian nationalism up until 1954, its splinters would go on to form the basis of *the Front de Libération Nationale* (FLN) and its armed wing, the *Armée de Libération Nationale* (ALN).

In a competing version of Algerian nationalism, the *Association des ulama musulmans algériens* (AUMA) was founded in 1931 by Islamic scholars, including Abdelhamid Ben Badis in Constantine. Publishing a weekly and monthly review since the 1920s, Ben Badis' Ulama aimed for social improvement, political freedom, Arabic education and the renewal of Islam in Algeria. As a religious organisation, they managed to unite different strands of the resistance forces to articulate a united nationalist agenda. Horne notes that many considered that 'it was the religious doctrine which, more than anything, had kept alight the fires of nationalism in Algeria' and that 'their philosophic influence was of primary and inestimable significance'. He goes on to write that 'the Ulema did more than any other body to rekindle a sense of religious and national consciousness among Algerians, but, tied up in their own theological coils, they failed to find pragmatic applications of their doctrines'.[22] It was the energy of revolutionaries such as Messali Hadj that would fill this gap.

Whilst in 1933 Messali Hadj was already speaking of revolution, universal suffrage and total independence for all the Maghreb nations, and the AUMA reformists were becoming increasingly politicised, many forces within Algeria still supported the reformist, assimiliationist vision of politicians such as Mohammed-Salah Bendjelloul, who took leadership of the *Fédération des élus* in 1932. Alongside Ferhat Abbas – who had been leader of an association whilst at university in Algiers – as a third strand of Algerian nationalism, they envisioned the emancipation of Algerians through access to French education, the vote and reform of the system. The wide membership of the *Fédération* included urban professionals but also many associated circles (*nadis*) reaching into the rural population. In 1936, Abbas and Ben Badis became engaged in contestation over the very meaning and existence of the Algerian nation. Ben Badis argued that the nation, whose existence Abbas denied, 'has its history, filled with great deeds, it has its religious and linguistic unity, its particular culture, its customs, its moral character'.[23] These contestations over the meanings of the Algerian nationalist struggle were not truly divisive, however, and many Algerians saw no contradiction in supporting both the Ulama and the *Fédération*.

New legislation drafted under the Blum government of the Popular Front in the 1930s proposed that 21,000 Muslims in Algeria would have the same vote as the European settlers and that the size of colonists' properties would be limited. After massive protests by the European *pied noirs*, the government finally dropped the Blum-Violette plan in 1938. As Rebai Maamri points out, this served to entrench the divisions between Muslim and French communities and aggravated existing tensions, whilst also 'sounding the death knell for the assimilation movement'.[24] The disillusionment of the liberal moderate wing of Algerian nationalism under Ferhat Abbas, who had consistently fought for greater equality for Algerians within an assimilation narrative, brought him closer to the position of the other Algerian nationalists.

Abbas' disappointment and betrayal by the French colonial government, seemingly at the hands of the European *pied noirs* settlers, further fed into the revolutionary sentiment.

Political activism and associational life in the 1930s were significant for their mobilising capacity and the legacy they created for the nationalist movement after World War II. By 1936, the ENA had 20 local sections in Algeria and the same in France. By 1939 there were 2,500 members in Algeria and 1,500 in France. In 1937, 25,000 Algerians marched in a separate cortege on Bastille Day behind a green flag and slogans of 'Freedom for all' and 'Respect for Islam', and the PPA virtually occupied the entirety of the main square in Algiers.[25] The repression of the movement had led to increasing demands for the complete emancipation of Algeria and all sides began to move towards demands for a 'multi-confessional, sovereign and democratic Algeria with equal rights for all, under a reformed French aegis'.[26] The imprisonment and exile of Messali Hadj during World War II simply reinforced his status as a charismatic popular leader and his martyrdom enhanced the prestige of the nationalist movement. As a radical grassroots movement, the PPA had a significant effect on political life and mobilisation. However, in such a difficult context, the factions within Algerian communitarian politics persisted, and divisions between the different organisations through the 1940s and 1950s ultimately led to the disintegration of the MTLD as a political party, together with the PPA's paramilitary wing the *Organisation spéciale* (OS), which had sought to prepare the armed struggle for independence.

The end of World War II and the liberation of Europe were critical moments in this process of mobilisation, for Algerian civil society and for the battle for equality. During the war, European freedom had been fought for by many tens of thousands of Algerians, and other North Africans, who had battled on the front line in Italy, France and Germany. Yet, upon liberation Algerians returned to their lives as colonial subjects. The values and liberties they had shed their blood to defend were denied on a daily basis at home. In a segregated state, Algerian Muslim children were still refused education and democracy was absent. Poverty, low wages and unemployment were the reality for most Algerian Muslims, compared to the relative luxury of their European neighbours. With the liberation of Europe, the nationalist movements for democracy, self-determination and civil liberties gained strength.

Many more Algerians began to demand freedom from their liberated colonisers. On 8 May 1945, in Setif, the colonial government brutally suppressed one of these uprisings, leading to the deaths of at least 15,000 Algerians. Around 100 Europeans lost their lives. May 1945 was a turning point for Algerian civil society and for the demand for civil rights and justice.

Extreme repression by the state and the further split in the nationalist movement contributed to the creation, in March 1954, of the *Comité Révolutionnaire d'unité et d'action* (CRUA), the secret revolutionary avant garde group that would subsequently form the *Front de Libération Nationale* (FLN) and launch the independence struggle on 1 November 1954. The FLN clearly sought to bring about mass participation in the War of Independence, and not only in the major cities. The process of mass mobilisation of the nationalist struggle involved a defining role for intermediary towns, which had perhaps preserved their links to traditional or rural life, as well as their spaces of socialisation, more successfully.[27] Within these spheres, the FLN succeeded in uniting the rural and the urban, the masses and the intelligentsia, through cafes and *nadis* across the country, where increasingly politicised Algerians had joined together over the previous decades. The work of transnational, underground associations in France and Algeria facilitated the financing of and provided moral support for the liberation struggle. During the War of Independence, from 1954 to 1962, both formal and underground associations played an important part in this mobilisation. Similar to the processes Asef Bayat describes across the Middle East, it was the important local community activism as 'a significant locus of struggle for (urban) citizenship and transformation' from the 1930s onwards, as well as the different mobilising forces of the ENA and the AUMA, which revolutionised the Algerian people and made change seem possible. Ultimately, it was 'through their quiet and unassuming daily struggles'[28] and the refiguring of new communities in different urban and rural realities that, as Bayat writes, 'In a major social and political upheaval, the Algerians overthrew French colonial rule in 1962 and established a republic.'[29]

Civil Society in an Independent Algeria

After eight years of bloody war, as a newly independent state in 1962, Algeria faced serious challenges. From artificial borders with the outside world to weak institutions within its territory, Algeria was left with little infrastructure and insufficient means with which to govern the country. Few Algerians had benefitted from a university education, which had been reserved for French citizens. With continued French terrorist actions at the end of the independence struggle, which saw the Secret Army Organisation (OAS) – a right-wing French paramilitary organisation – destroying any infrastructure they could lay their hands on (including burning down the national library), Algeria had to rebuild a nation. The difficulty of constructing a united identity meant there was little room for pluralism. One of the constraints of the FLN narrative was that it had been constructed in response to a colonial one. FLN narratives had emphasised the dichotomy of good versus bad, coloniser versus colonised, enemy or traitor versus insider. The enemy had now gone, however, and there was a need to create a new strong, heroic narrative and a single conception of what the Algerian identity and nation should be. The re-adaptation of historical texts and the creation of a national education system in the Arabic language played an important part in this process. The official version of the liberation struggle 'expunged the fraught internal history of the PPA-MTLD from its memory'. Messalists were labelled traitors, Abbas was framed as a bourgeois assimiliationalist and Ben Badis became the figurehead of the nationalist movement, which was reimagined and taught to the next generation as a cultural and religious quest for 'restoration' of 'a purified community'.[30]

Following Algerian independence, support from other Arab states also led Algeria to draw on closer links with the Middle East and pan-Arabism, thus seeking to strengthen a unified Algerian identity founded on Arabic and Islam as a common cultural heritage. Algeria's new leaders drew on messages from pre-independence activists, particularly the *Association des ulama musulmans algériens*, and Ben Badis' famous quote: 'Islam is my religion, Arabic is my language, Algeria is my country.' Yet, despite similarities and strong cultural links, the historical contexts, colonial legacies, socio-economic development, languages and structures of society varied hugely across the Arab world. The diversity of cultural identities within Algeria also meant that the idea of a unified Arab identity was laden with tensions and challenges.

One of the difficult challenges facing the newly independent Algerian nation was that of language. French had been the sole language of education, legislation and the political sphere for over a century, along with the repression of Arabic culture under colonialism. Upon independence, the introduction of modern standard Arabic was viewed as a unifying force, although this differed significantly from the Algerian Arabic spoken in most homes across the country. Arabisation was generally viewed by most Algerians as an important 'matter of cultural decolonization and social equity'.[31] However, the fact that most Algerians had received their education in French meant that Arabic education required the recruitment of teachers from abroad. It also meant that the educated class would now struggle to find a means of expression in the public sphere. Equally, Berber languages, spoken by a third of the population, were sidelined, strengthening rifts created by the divide-and-rule tactics of the colonial state, which had prioritised Berbers over Arabs. Whilst huge improvements were made in literacy and education, language policies presented a new barrier for much of the population and for civil society.

Given these tensions in the post-colonial period, under the first President, Ben Bella, associations were originally tolerated rather than openly embraced. However, the fear of independent, mobilising and divisive forces that might stem from Islamic associations, foreign organisations or other powerful actors increasingly led subsequent President Boumediene's regime to channel all popular civic participation through the mass organisations steered by the FLN itself. From the sole trade union, the *Union Général des Travailleurs Algériens*, to the student body, the *Union Nationale de la Jeunesse Algérienne*, the FLN dominated. In a Soviet-style model of culture throughout the 1960s, 1970s and early 1980s, the post-independence state claimed its hegemony over Algerian cultural life and social order. From 1962 to 1989 a nationalistic model was followed, through which the promotion of Arab-Muslim cultural identity and the anti-colonial struggle as a unifying force were at the forefront. Some critical organisations existed as political parties without legal recognition; for example, the left-wing *Parti de l'Avant-Garde Socialiste* (PAGS) was born out of the Algerian Communist Party and it infiltrated many of the major unions. However, in general, the state controlled almost all social and economic activity in society through nationalised industries, collective farms and mass associations. Professional unions and corporations were created by the FLN with the sole objective of giving unconditional support to the single party and the Algerian revolution. The legal apparatus reinforced this deep level of control.

There was no longer any space for associations. The fragility of national unity and the importance of consolidating the revolution were the implicit reasons given by the FLN for their domination over the social, economic, cultural and political life of the nation. Whilst this strengthened the state and embedded the revolution in everyday life, it also resulted in 'an impoverished and anaemic associative life, void of any real anchorage in society'.[32] In Algeria, and beyond its borders, associations again became a question of inherent importance to the legitimacy of the Algerian state. Threats to the stability of the new nation meant that the regime sought to incorporate any form of opposition or non-oppositional grouping within the single-party FLN structures. The populist project, Addi writes:

> did not want Algeria to be a civil society with its conflicts and diverging individual or group interests, wishing rather that Algeria be a national family, unified by the memory of the ancestors and the martyrs.[33]

In terms of legislation and control, a rather ambivalent situation existed in the early years of independence, with the retaining of the French 1901 legislation. In practice, a more restrictive approach was put in place, blocking any social organisation outside the state.[34] Omar Derras quotes the ministerial circular of 1964, which requested the regional prefects

> to prevent the constitution of associations which, under the cover of a social, cultural or artistic activity, try to pursue political activities which would bring prejudice to the internal or external security of the state.[35]

Although the French Law of 1901 still guaranteed the freedom of association, the reality of repression was made clear in the circular of 1964, in the political statements of the regime and in the actual application of the laws in the new state. This ambiguity was lifted in 1971. The law was changed and President Boumediene reinforced a deep level of control over independent organisations. The ordinance passed in 1971 instituted an obligatory double ministerial authorisation for an association to gain legal status. Model statutes were imposed and the state gained strong powers to dissolve any association. This effectively prevented the development of any real autonomous organisations outside official state-controlled channels. Under Boumediene, only FLN-affiliated associations were truly able to function. With the new legislation in 1971, restrictive practices were legalised into a text which rendered extremely difficult the creation and running of any independent organisation. This repression of associational life for Algerians was also mirrored in France – the ban on Messali Hadj's association of the 1930s was never reversed with independence. Algerian associations in France were also highly controlled. The *Amicale*, formed from the *Fédération de France* of the FLN, had a monopoly over the Algerian community in France. This was the case until 1981, as Collyer writes in his article on the 'Transnational political participation of Algerians in France', when foreign nationals were finally allowed to form organisations without the consent of the French Minister of Interior.[36] Similarly, whilst the legislative framework in Algeria was tightened, new 'state associations' were set up by the FLN structures. Derras describes how,

> In parallel to the process of cleaning up the spaces of socialization [...] the state begins progressively the creation and diffusion, across the country and institutional levels, of an ensemble of state partisan associations which would have for their role the creation of unconditional support structures, and also an effective means to frame, control and manage society.[37]

Liverani describes how the state began 'co-opting the discourse of the most vocal and combative groups'. He shows how the huge state-led associations were the 'first tool to this end'.[38] By the 1980s, the failures of this approach, and increasing political tensions, fed into discourses of inclusion and exclusion – of us versus them.

Malika Rebai Maamri describes how the exclusionary nationalist tendencies of the Algerian state fuelled the rise of identity challenges in the early 1980s. She describes how 'three types of identity contestation manifested themselves almost simultaneously on the Algerian political scene'.[39] Berber, women's and Islamist voices, through active organisations and movements, lived in constant tension with each other and with the state, providing a real – although divided – opposition.

The FLN structures under the presidency of Chadli Benjedid initially tolerated these new voices, and increasingly manipulated them, playing the different actors off against each other and increasing the divisions in Algerian society. The rise of the Berber movement following the Berber Spring riots in 1980 began the initial challenge to the unicity of Algerian state-imposed identity. The Berber Cultural Movement, a loose clandestine network, demanded the recognition of the Berber language, culture and identity. It also initiated the ideological material and actors of the future Berber political parties – actors who were increasingly frustrated by imposed narratives of the purely Arabic identity of post-colonial governments.

Similarly, Algerian women were often disappointed by the Algerian state's positions after independence. Women had played an active role in the liberation war, which had been widely recognised and celebrated. The women's movement grew after independence, but increasingly faced chauvinism and repression from the state after 1962. Contradictory speeches rejecting Western feminism and embracing Islamic socialist values, but insisting women would be emancipated, frustrated the increasingly well-educated young population. A circular, issued in 1980 and preventing women from travelling, sparked protests and a questioning of the meaning of Algerian nationality and citizenship. In 1984, what was considered to be a highly regressive family code provoked massive mobilisation. The new code, inspired by elements of sharia law and conservative forces in Algeria, relegated women to the status of minors. It legalised polygamy and allowed men, in the case of divorce, to retain the family home with no obligation to support their families. It went against the 1976 Algerian Constitution which guaranteed equal rights of all citizens and proscribed prejudice on the grounds of gender, race or profession. The feminist movement and protests proved incapable of overturning it, in part because the Chadli government had played strongly into the hands of the Islamist movement which had increasingly taken over the public space. The strongest area of associational activism throughout the 1980s was, by far, that of the Islamic charities, of which there were over 11,000 by 1987. In an appeasement to religious factions within the FLN and as a tool with which to play off the different modes of opposition – the feminist and Berber movements – the FLN had facilitated the rise of these organisations. This was a move which would soon backfire upon them.

On both sides of the Mediterranean, the repression of Algerian society proved unsustainable. The real nature of the artificially created associations soon became apparent. As claims for rights and for a meaningful place in the public sphere for Berbers, women and Islamists were all equally frustrated, the gap between state and society in Algeria grew wider. In 1987, the oil crisis and economic instability led to mounting tensions across all echelons of society and all across the country. As well as social instability, Algeria's economic situation worsened throughout the 1980s, and economic upheavals and austerity culminated in uprisings in 1988. State–society relations had broken down and were increasingly defined in antagonistic terms such as 'hogra', the contempt or disregard for the masses, by those in power, known as *le pouvoir*. This climate of mistrust, symbolised by the penchant for conspiracy theories, fed into the breakdown in relations and into an explosion of contestation. In 1988, intense nationwide riots were witnessed across Algeria. Rising prices, unemployment and poor governance fed into the frustrations of the young Algerian population and hundreds were killed as symbols of the state were targeted by rioting protesters.

Democratic Opening and the Black Decade

In response to the riots, and, indeed, prior to the collapse of the Soviet Union, Algeria launched its democratisation project in the late 1980s. President Chadli Benjedid revised the constitution and brought in legislative reforms to open up the political scene to voluntary associations and political parties.[40] In 1987, already, President Chadli had introduced a new Law on Associations which was passed despite reticence from the more conservative branches of the FLN. Under the new, more liberal law the need for 'prior authorization' of an association was removed and replaced with automatic approval after a 60-day period. This reform programme very quickly allowed for a degree of political pluralism, for freedom of the press and for a considerable degree of freedom of association. In this reform process, the state and civil society, which participated in drafting the new legislation, sought to redefine the limits of public space through the new constitution and legislation. In 1987, 1989 and 1990 state–society relations were reformed in terms of freedoms of associations, of the press and of political parties. The 1990 Law on Associations removed even more of the restrictions. As well as removing the need for prior authorisation, thereby enshrining the declaratory regime, an association could now either register at the district level or with the Ministry of Interior if it had national ambitions. The administration had to deliver a receipt of registration, again within 60 days. Should the association be considered contrary to the dispositions of the law, the administration had to launch a legal enquiry within 52 days following the deposit of registration, otherwise the association was automatically considered to be officially constituted. Many commentators felt that the 1990 law was a founding moment for the associative movement in Algeria, freeing it up from political and administrative constraints and interference from a heavy administrative machine.[41] The opening-up in 1987 had already inspired a strong associative dynamic, and many felt it was the context, more than the text, which had enabled civil society. The period 1988–92 had truly favoured a liberal opening-up of society. Following the 1990 Law on Associations, the number of registered associations soared as national and local groupings formed and registered their status officially.

The new legal reforms also opened up the political scene to different political parties. On the back of Islamist mobilisation through charitable associations in the 1980s, the new Islamist opposition party, the *Front Islamique du Salut* (FIS), made significant gains in the communal elections across Algeria in 1990. Subsequently, during the first free national elections held in 1991 and after having dominated post-colonial Algerian politics for 30 years, the FLN suffered a massive defeat. The FIS fought and won on a theologically inspired programme – promising to bring sharia law to Algeria – and on what was seen, particularly by the secular opposition, as an anti-democratic programme. Following this defeat in the first round of the elections, a military *coup d'état* was orchestrated. With significant support from many sections of Algerian society, including those targeted by the Islamist programme such as the left, feminists and intellectuals, the coup halted the electoral process, removing President Chadli and preventing the FIS from taking power. The succeeding bloody and prolonged conflict between Islamist insurgents and the military regime resulted in the reversal of the democratic opening which Chadli had launched, and in another deep trauma for Algerian society. Islamist insurgency under the armed wing of the FIS, the *Armée Islamiste du Salut* (AIS), took aim at the Algerian state, which had deprived it of its place in political power. More radical splits within the *Groupe Islamique Armée* intensified the violence and caused factions such as the *Groupe Salafiste pour la Prêche et le Combat*. These armed groups increasingly targeted Algerian civil society, intellectuals, journalists, writers, artists, educational establishments and any person deemed an enemy, for contradicting the Islamist ideology or for somehow supporting the Algerian state. The decade of conflict caused the deaths of an estimated 200,000 Algerians; whole villages were wiped out in mass atrocities and many more fled the country to live in exile. The coup, the conflict and the resulting state of emergency imposed upon society all contributed to reversing the democratisation process launched by the Algerian state in 1989. Algeria returned to a seemingly unavoidable state of authoritarian control.

Conclusion

Algerian history still deeply influences the space and conditions for civil society organisations across the country. The traditional roots of Algerian civil society, in the consensual approaches of the village communities and the religious structures from the ulama to the Sufi brotherhoods, still underpin social organisation and civic life, as well as influencing more recent styles of government. The growth of civil society under what was a repressive colonial regime indeed framed the liberation movement as one of rights, democracy and justice. The coming together of different sections in society in the formal colonial structures of associations, clubs and unions reinforced this movement. The legacy of the French legislation on associations also promoted, but then subsequently hindered, the development of associational life, particularly from the 1970s on, as the political context changed. The difficulties in rebuilding a nation divided by bitter conflict following the War of Independence are still as evident today, despite significant economic and infrastructural advances in the country. Accepting plural opposition was problematic for post-independence leaders fearing division, betrayal, fragmentation and violence, linked to the collective memories of struggle and conflict. Perceptions that contestation threatened the unity of the nation prevented the vibrant civil society, which had emerged from the 1920s and 1930s, from playing a meaningful role in the state-building process during post-independence. The memory of colonial violence and the repression of Algerian cultural identity still complicate the processes by which Algerians seek to redefine and reassert the rich cultural heritage they hold in terms of art, literature, religion and language.

The challenges caused by tensions between civil society and the central state, from the Ottoman Regency through to the violent colonial conquest and liberation war, have led the Algerian state to be characterised simultaneously as nepotistic, authoritarian and weak. Yet, from the late 1980s, political decisions did allow for openings and for one of the most progressive democratisation processes in the region. The opening up of the associative sphere led to a vibrant civic life and to a more collaborative form of co-existence. Despite the violent context of the 1990s, the progressive texts meant that, notwithstanding the hard realities of conflict, many associations were created to fight for liberty, freedom and democratic rights, to seek justice for victims of the conflict and to resiliently continue the debate about the nature of Algerian heritage, identity and culture, ongoing throughout the twentieth century.

CHAPTER 4

CIVIL SOCIETY AND THE STATE

The relationship between civil society and the state in Algeria is complex, close and often conflicting. James McDougall writes of the 'ferocious strength' and the 'simultaneous fragility and limitations' of the Algerian state over time.[1] There have been multiple legal, political and linguistic challenges to constructing a unified Algerian nation and identity, both prerequisites for consolidating the state and allowing plural opposition. In the last century, citizenship and belonging in Algeria were based upon the creation of a *communauté de résistance* against colonial domination.[2] This *communauté*, the *Front de Libération National*, and ultimately the future state, were in many ways the product of associational life and mobilisation from the 1920s onwards. For the same actors, once in power in the post-colonial period, the position was uncomfortable. To avoid contestation of the new state's legitimacy, the symbiotic nature of state–society relations was further strengthened under the single-party system. The boundary between the state and civil society has remained blurred ever since the main actors of the contemporary Algerian state emerged from the liberation struggle in the 1960s.

The state's legitimacy in the twenty-first century still rests on its historical role in the War of Independence and on the civil society, revolutionary movement which was part of it. The specificities of the institutional setting and complex state–society relations also make it difficult for external actors to engage with both the Algerian state and civil society. Chapter 2 showed the limitations faced by donors such as the EU, which has a significantly lower budget in Algeria than in any other country of the region. To engage with civil society in Algeria, foreign actors are obliged to grapple with the complexity of state–society relations and to understand the law and practices which regulate both these relations and their own presence. Whereas most commentators point to the authoritarian nature of the Algerian state as the main barrier to foreign actors and to an effective civil society, others claim that it is a 'weak' state that still lies at the heart of the problems of civil society in Algeria today.[3]

The interface between what constitutes the state and what constitutes society is difficult to define in any context. Elusive state–society boundaries, as Mitchell argues, are erected internally through complex power relations.[4] The power to regulate is not simply a capacity stored within the state; there are often conflicts between the state and organisations – just as there are between different government agencies within the state – which shape that power. The state is not a coherent object clearly separate from society. In Gramscian terms, civil society is a sphere of hegemony; it is part of the state and, as such, is responsible for creating consent in those subordinated to it. Relations with civil society require mutual recognition, and whilst civil society needs the state's recognition for its own existence and legitimacy, under certain conditions civil society can be a potential realm of contention and can act as a counter-hegemonic force to state authoritarianism.

In the Algerian context, as discussed in the previous chapter, post-independence civil society did not represent a counter-hegemonic force, due to the governing FLN party's 'refusal to accept politics and conflict' and the general 'denial of plurality'.[5] This denial of plurality, and the blurring of state–society boundaries, is what made the beginnings of civic life so difficult in the post-colonial era. For Addi, this non-recognition of opposition politics meant that opposition had to be expressed outside legitimate state channels. Such lack of legitimate channels often led to opposition being expressed in a violent way against whatever was the prevailing nature of the state at the time. Chapter 4 examines these interactions between the Algerian state and civil society organisations, exploring contemporary relations since the 'black decade' and the failure of dialogue. It will interrogate how this relationship has been affected by the Arab revolutions in 2011 and new legislative reforms, drawing on a number of case studies of specific organisations and networks of associations in different areas of the country.

State–Society Relations and the Failure of Dialogue

The period of political change between 1987 and 1991, which effectively opened up the political system, did allow for new forms of opposition to the state. McDougall describes how,

> The opening of public space to associational life – for everything from clubs for former students of particular schools to proselytising Islamic associations like shaykh Mahfoud Nahnah's *jami'yat al-irshad wa'l-Islah* (the Guidance and Reform Society) – a proliferating and remarkably free media, and a massive social mobilisation, especially through near continuous strike action across all sectors of the economy and the professions, certainly liberated and encouraged an immense outpouring of social energy and enthusiasm as well as anger and dissent, especially among younger Algerians.[6]

Despite this 'wind of freedom', McDougall argues that events up until 1991 had not constituted a promising transition to democracy suddenly overridden by the army; rather, it had been 'a case of manipulative crisis management gone awry'.[7] The conditions for the transition of this energy into a tolerating and democratic polity were absent. The only organisation readily mobilised was the radical Islamist *Front Islamique du Salut*. Presenting itself as the *fils*, the legitimate son of the wartime FLN, an 'incorruptible, religiously based opposition to oppression', the FIS claimed to be the true inheritor of the revolution that 'corrupt apostates had stolen from the people' and it directly and virulently attacked the failures of the post-independence Algerian state.[8] Taking on the generals and the established system, the FIS also faced strong anti-Islamism from left-wing human rights activists, such as those in the *Parti de l'avant-garde socialiste* (PAGS). The PAGS, which took over from the Algerian Communist Party after independence, had been a strong critical voice, particularly of the single-party system under Chadli. Their opposition to what they saw as a fascist form of Islamism now overrode their dislike of the regime. Playing on Algerians' profound attachment to religion, capturing the energy of young people and offering a radical vision for the previously disenfranchised, the FIS gained its massive protest vote. However, for many of the Algerians who had voted, this was a protest at the Algerian state rather than a vote for an Islamic theocratic state, with many arguing 'we voted for them, but we didn't want them to win!' The cancellation of the elections and the state of emergency imposed in 1992 further entrenched the state dynamics of control. Despite progressive laws, the increasingly violent conflict meant that the 1990s saw a return to more rigidity and greater powers for the regime and the military generals, the *janviéristes*, who had overseen the deposition of Chadli in January 1992 and who went on to ruthlessly crush the Islamist insurgents. In such a context, the reforms of the 1990s, which introduced freedom of association, could not bring more constructive relations. The climate of mistrust between the state and newly created organisations intensified. Whatever the focus of the new associations, even if they did not directly challenge the regime, their existence reinforced 'the mutual defiance that exists between civil society and the state apparatus'.[9]

For many of the civil society activists interviewed, the advances of the 1990 law, such as the simple declaration method to set up an association, only ever existed on paper. Due to ordinary people's lack of knowledge of the legal regime, or through diverse local interpretations by officials, the administration still managed to block associations from registering, from modifying their statutes, or from carrying out their activities and accessing funds. Whilst such interpretations of the legal system varied across the country, this ambiguity nevertheless highlights the fragility of Algerian state structures and the importance of individual actors, such as regional *walis* or governors, mayors and ministers, rather than of institutions. The Algerian state, like all states, suffers from its own internal incoherencies. Brahim Salhi recalls the frustration of associative members at the fact that 'there is not one State in Algeria, but States. Each *wilaya*, each *daira*, each *commune* interprets the law to its will'.[10] Despite the new law, the possibility of this kind of obstructionism continued. Associations were inherently in contention with the state. Associative networks were grounded in a 'repressed counter-culture', and, whatever gains they could make, 'their discourses invariably contribute to the popular resentment against the ruling elite'.[11]

Yet, despite the violence, the retracted democratisation process and the clampdown on political parties, the late 1990s witnessed a steady and continued increase in formally registered civil society associations. By 2007, the number of associations registered at local and national levels grew to 78,000, making Algeria the most active country in the Middle East and North Africa in terms of civic life. Many associations emerged in the social, charitable and medical sectors, but also in promoting human rights and protecting the victims of violence. Increasing numbers of associations fostering religious and cultural education, preserving Algeria's heritage and safeguarding the environment also confirmed a sustained interest and engagement within formal civil society organisations in the debate about rights, citizenship and identity. The originality of the new organisations was in their areas of work and in the populations who were mobilised, often for the first time, to work on issues such as human rights, women's rights or cultural heritage. Omar Derras writes that this was linked to a 'very strong demand for social emancipation' engendered by the 'frustrations of specific social categories'[12] who finally found a voice.

The black decade saw the fragility of the political order – which had fallen apart so quickly – replaced by a 'ruthless brutality with which it was reconstituted' for the benefit of a small elite and to the exclusion of most Algerians. The state was indeed resilient, in its 'core of coercive force', and its 'increasingly predatory relationship to the population'.[13] At the same time, the unsustainable nature of the all-encompassing state was increasingly felt and is reflected in the term 'hogra', which is still used today in Algeria to describe the idea of government contempt towards society. The term defines the rupture between the state and the people; the ongoing mistrust heightened by a lack of communication between the rulers and ruled. For their part, most Algerians viewed the state with 'irony and disgust',[14] condemning the self-serving incompetence of the elite *apparatchiks*. In *Islam and Democracy, the Failure of Dialogue in Algeria*, Volpi concludes that, given its specific history, only a new generation of political activists, such as the vibrant Berber associations he praises, could advance the participation of the *demos* in the Algerian political system.[15] A decade on, it is from these associations that new actors are currently emerging to stand in local elections across Algeria and to challenge the structures which had impeded their development.[16] However grave the situation in the 1990s, relations between state and society were capable of being rebuilt. In addition to formal institutions and new-found voices, Algeria 'put itself back together', writes McDougall, 'through long-established practices of informal politics and even older institutions – *jama'a, ashira and zawiya*'.[17] In the new millennium, Algerians 'tentatively rebuilt their social space on the basis of a broad consensus of values, within which social and political divisions could be played out without recourse to arms'.[18] Since 2011, in the wake of the Arab revolutions, the Algerian state and civil society have once again been locked into a new negotiation process in order to redefine the limits of each other's competences, rights and obligations.

The Arab Spring, Associative Action and State Responses

Between December 2010 and March 2011, Algeria experienced significant social unrest and demonstrations related to unemployment, housing, food prices, inflation, lack of political dialogue and corruption. These protests happened in parallel and were fuelled, at least to a certain extent, by the successful movements for change in Tunisia and in Egypt. Distinct from the social protests a decade earlier, these protests were of a global nature. They were neither Islamist, nor organised on ethnic lines. Yet they did appear to be the expression of frustration at the same issues that lay at the heart of the Islamist and the Berber demonstrations of the past: the role of the security apparatus, the arbitrary character of many state policies and the lack of accountability of state institutions.[19] Social exclusion and unemployment clearly triggered fragments of unrest but, similar to regional discontent, one of the main problems was that Algeria still presented 'a population frustrated by an unresponsive state administration' and the lack of 'a meaningful political debate'.[20] Whilst socio-economic problems underpinned much of the frustration, the main argument was political.

On 21 January 2011, at a meeting of a number of associations and political parties, the National Coordination for Change and Democracy (CNCD) was created. This new movement was intended to act as a platform which sought systemic political change and aimed to pilot mobilisation and demonstrations. However, the movement did not appear to have a united overall plan or a loyal enough, broad-based following and this fairly weak coalition of left-leaning opposition groups seemed to fall apart rather quickly. In February 2011, one of the main Kabyle parties, the *Front des Forces Socialistes* (FFS), thanked the CNCD and praised the joint analysis of the political problems in Algeria but stated that it currently did not prioritise participation in a march, though it supported the right of other actors to do so.[21] The joining together of radically different opposition organisations, from the fierce secularists to the former Islamist FIS leader Ali Benhaj, chanting very different slogans, undermined the credibility of the CNCD.[22] Marches were heavily repressed by a police force which was significantly larger than that of the demonstrators. The limited traction with the Algerian public and the very different conditions in Algeria compared to those in Tunisia or Egypt, countries where the presidency had become a position for life, meant that the CNCD had a short lifespan. The reticence of the Algerian population to engage in protest appeared mainly to be due to the desire of the vast majority for peace and stability over violent upheaval. The desire for change could not come at the cost of more human life. Bozzo points out that the Algerian demonstrations two decades earlier had been the very first of all the demonstrations in the Arab world, even though now, 'atomised, divided, traumatised, Algerian society has shown itself apparently to be in retreat compared to the wave (of protest)'.[23]

At the same time as the Arab Spring, the bombing of neighbouring Libya by a former colonial power also had an important impact on Algeria. Hugh Roberts points out that this was the first NATO intervention in North Africa since the FLN defeated the French in 1962.[24] Perceived threats to the stability and security of the Algerian state increasingly became the subject of popular debate. Fear and outrage at the possibility of invasion by Western nations, or by the former colonial power, helped distract a still-antagonistic population and channel discontent away from the internal structures of the state and towards foreign actors. This distrust of foreign actors grew across the region during the Arab Spring, with the Egyptian regime in 2012 taking a number of American NGOs to court and imposing heavy fines and prison sentences for interfering in national politics. The Algerian regime had always been clear on the limited space it allowed for foreign organisations. Yet many associations also shared the same fears about foreign interference, pointing out that external funds could come from extremist Salafist groups which would risk destabilising Algerian society. Both secular and Islamist associations were suspicious of meddling by European and Americans in particular, and these suspicions were reinforced by nationalist discourses and by contempt for European discrimination against Algerians, particularly in visa regulations.

As such, the place of foreign NGOs in Algeria was again put on the table after 2011.

As a first reaction to the protest movements, in February 2011 President Bouteflika lifted the 19-year State of Emergency laws. These had been a source of much frustration for those demanding the right to protest. With continuing fragmented unrest across the country, the region in turmoil and legislative elections due the following year, in April the president announced a series of further reforms. These reforms would revise the constitution to re-establish presidential limits and revise the laws on political parties, the media and associations. Seeking all opportunities to defuse the frustration of the population, at the same time the state also put in place further price subsidies, accelerated public works programmes, attributed grants and increased loan schemes. Whilst this practice of *arrosage* defused or reduced certain tensions, it did little to fully tackle the underlying causes of discontent: social exclusion, unemployment and the desire for a more meaningful political debate.

In the slightly calmer political environment in spring 2011, the state began a process of political dialogue. In April 2011, a wide consultation process was launched at national and local levels to discuss reform. This was piloted by the *Conseil National Economique et Sociale* (CNES) and was described by one of the EU officials in Algiers as 'by far one of the more progressive responses to the wave of discontent in the region'.[25] In June 2011, the *Assises de la Société Civile* regrouped a considerable number of actors in Algiers. At the national level too, in October, the Ministry of National Solidarity, together with its Social Development Agency, organised a large conference on local development and the future of social policy in Algeria. A significant number of active associations were invited to participate in a national debate – some of these had had considerable difficulties with the authorities in the past.[26] One association which presented its work to the conference described it as 'the opportunity to air our grievances, show what we have achieved and ask for support to prevent interference from the regional level in our functioning'.[27]

At a more local level, the consultation processes were carried out across the country and were received with varying degrees of enthusiasm by the respondents. In Oran, some associations indicated that they had been consulted by the local authorities through written questionnaires which asked for recommendations for the new law. However, these consultation processes were received with certain scepticism. Some associations considered them to be rather pointless and held that their opinions were unlikely to be considered if they were thought to be contravening the will of the state. Consequently, a number of associations chose not to respond. Public consultation meetings with organisations were limited to the rather weaker associations. A member of one association described the state, in this consultation process, as 'unable to communicate and therefore dialoguing only with itself'.[28] In contrast, at the same time, in Laghouat, 400 actors from eight different regional *wilayas* were invited by the CNES to participate in a large consultation process on local development.[29] The associations themselves, and the local authorities who participated, gave reports which were rather more positive: 'it was quite emotional to find all the associational actors who had worked together over the last years, come together to discuss with the authorities for two days local development plans for the region.'[30]

These consultations were followed by a massive communication campaign. Ministers were increasingly seen to 'be visible' in public settings, with constantly organised inaugurations. Public grants and loans were hastily signed with little control of the quality of the dossiers presented. The message from the state appeared to be, 'we have understood the problem and are acting'. This, in some ways, further exacerbated the problems of disconnection between state and people and the general feeling of cynicism and contempt at the lack of real opportunities for the increasingly qualified young population. Huge mobilisations were required for flash 'ministerial appearances' and these were highly disapproved of by many. People were taken away from their jobs and then made to wait pointlessly in order to assist once the dignitary appeared. One interviewee complained,

> we were requested to travel 4 hours to participate in the inauguration, which lasted five minutes, for the cameras. We had to show all the work which had been done by us, and there was no interest in exchanging or even speaking with us.[31]

The state's reaction, therefore, did not always succeed in improving its strained relationship with civil society associations. Nor did it remedy the 'listening deficit', as one EU official framed the problem. However, in addition to the consultation process, the state promised concrete, legal reforms, together with a new dialogue process, and the new Associative Law of 2012 was drawn up.

Civil Society and the 2012 Law on Associations

Continued repression of civil society organisations, despite the liberalisation in 1990, emanated from the state's fears of both internal and external forces of change. Yet this urge to control was not truly in response to any real risk or threat from associations, often described by Algerian and external actors as weak, fragmented or co-opted by the regime and in most cases incapable of accessing external funding or support. From my interviews with associations, it seemed that repressive state responses were perceived by them as coming more from feelings of competition, a certain jealousy of active associations and even a fear of indigenous organisations doing better than state structures. Some associations working on cultural, heritage, social and youth projects in collaboration with local authorities reported that instead of encouraging them, institutional actors often wanted to take over, appropriate or restrict their initiatives. All associations, whether or not they focused on sensitive topics, such as the role of the security services in the black decade, had to tread a diplomatic fine line to maintain their existence and avoid a number of potential problems. Poor relations with the regional administration could result in statutes being withheld, accusations of mismanagement or the association being forced to shut down. In this context, and with the Arab Spring uprisings, the new Law on Associations in 2012 was initially sold as a means of transforming this situation and recognising the importance of associations in the country. Opposition parties were quick to state that this was an inadequate and insufficient response and argued that the genuine application of the current laws was what was really needed, rather than any tinkering with new ones.[32] There were many fears that the new law would simply legitimise the repression which had progressively entered into the application of the law by the administration.

The following findings from one national networking initiative and from two active local associations in different regions of Algeria show some of the recent developments and challenges in relations between the state and associations. The first networking initiative concerns the new law introduced in January 2012. The second case concerns an association active in the health sector and the last one is about an association active in environmental and heritage protection. Their interactions with local state structures highlight the diverse state responses and uneven application of the legal framework by different actors.

The associative lobby against the law on Associations 2012[33]

In September 2011 the Algerian state drew up its new draft law on associations and launched a restricted consultation process. A number of significant associations received the draft text, notably those from which the state feared a strong reaction, such as the eloquent and highly critical Fédération Algérienne des Personnes Handicapées. These associations in turn disseminated the text as widely as possible so as not to appear to have dominated the debate and outcome, whatever that might be. A number of network events and large meetings were used to discuss the proposed reforms. Through these meetings, the draft law was analysed in detail and assessed in comparison to the current Law on Associations of 1990.[34] In the draft text, the associations felt that there appeared to be a significant level of self-awareness on the part of the legislators, who openly acknowledged the failures of the 1990 law's application. The preamble to the new draft law itself stated,

> In truth, the current legislation has finished, and this is an acknowledged fact, by being perceived, rightly or wrongly, as the expression of a wish to hamper any initiative and to close down the spaces of the associative movement.[35]

The stated objectives in the preamble of the draft outlined the wish to facilitate, simplify and reduce the administrative burden on associations. The new law would

> 1. Lighten the conditions to constitute an association taking into account the territorial and diverse nature of associations; 2. Enlarge the field open to associative action and access to justice to protect their rights and interests; 3. Simplify the organisation and the transparency needed for the functioning of any association; reduce the excessive and inoperative controls and complex and

constraining procedures, which come from an unacceptable mistrust of associations [...].³⁶

It proposed to facilitate the creation of associations, giving powers at the local level of town halls to register associations and reducing the number of founding members required. The articles that followed, however, also significantly increased the administrative burden and control by the executive. The draft law strengthened control over foreign NGOs and donors, strengthened the powers of the executive and reinforced the reporting obligations of associations. According to many associations, if embodied in statute the state could then maintain a legitimised form of repression through the legal framework, rather than having to rely on the more vague interpretations of the 1990 law.

In response to these proposals, a group of associations in Oran took legal advice and launched an in-depth reflection process to assess the likely impact of the law. After consultation, they judged the law to be far more restrictive than the current situation. They felt it represented a step backwards from the regime that had opened up the associational movement in 1990. In the minutes of the final sitting of the inter-associative meeting concerning the new law, they noted,

> In this new draft law, there is a fundamental flaw which appears from the first articles, notably article 9. In effect, it is the administration (wilaya) which accords itself the right to decide whether or not an association can or cannot exist. However, the administration is an executive power at the service of the citizen, it is for the judicial system to take such a decision. In a democratic state, it is not the executive which judges or which decides the non-existence of an association. The normal procedure would be to inform the administration, which can then consult with the judiciary in a case of non-conformity.³⁷

Identifying a series of anomalies, they launched a petition for the withdrawal of the new law on the grounds that it reinstated an authorisation rather than a declarative regime.³⁸ A common communiqué was drawn up, pointing out that the law was anti-constitutional and would also be contrary to Algeria's international commitments on the freedom of association. They called for a national fund, a tax system to favour volunteering and a rapprochement between civil society and the state. They demanded the right to be consulted in any new legal framework discussions.

Similar lobbying campaigns and ad hoc networks came together across the country. Communications were issued by these networks, or by their lead associations, such as that transmitted by Amusnaw in Tizi Ouzou, arguing that the new law would represent 'a programmed death of civil society'. The Algerian League of Human rights, within the Euro-Mediterranean Network of Human Rights, issued a memorandum stating its fear that the new law would not guarantee freedom of association, as enshrined in the constitution and in international conventions which Algeria had signed. Following these lobbying campaigns and the diffusion of the communiqué to a significant number of deputies, particularly in Oran, the law was then debated in parliament on Sunday 27 November 2011. The deputies strongly criticised the law, arguing that it was not constitutional and that it went against the spirit of partnership with civil society organisations.[39] They also used the opportunity to frame a number of grievances, regarding, amongst others, prejudicial treatment of religious associations, mainly from the religiously oriented MSP (the ex-Hamas party), and the plotting of foreign actors against Algeria's national interests.[40] It seemed that the draft law was to be blocked and that the Parliament had somehow asserted its role in the democratic and legislative processes of government. It had, moreover, responded to the lobbying efforts of the associations and networks.

Yet less than a month later, on 14 December 2011, the law was passed by the Popular Assembly, as it stood, and it was subsequently adopted by the Council of the Nation. It was published in the official law journal on 15 January 2012, as Law 12–06. This is perhaps a striking comment on the limited role of the Parliament. Amel Boubekeur has previously pointed to the significant pay rises, including a 300-per cent wage increase for deputies in 2008, as having contributed to this co-opting of the Parliament. She writes:

> It is rare that a law proposed by the government is rejected. Lack of independence from the government inhibits members from fulfilling their basic responsibilities as lawmakers and acting in their role as mediator between institutions and citizens.[41]

Whilst the outcome seemed a regression, there had been significant progress in the consultation process. Algerian associations had initiated a political dialogue and a lobbying campaign which resulted in the questioning of the law in parliament. This campaign continued. On 7 January 2012, the network of associations from Oran published a communiqué criticising the unconstitutional nature of the law and proposing solutions to achieve the stated objectives of the presidency.[42] Pointing out the contradiction to Algeria's international commitments on civil and political rights, the petition noted that the law 'puts into question the declarative system in place in all democratic countries and creates multiple obstacles to voluntary associative action'.[43] Whilst the new legislation appeared to have done little to reverse the negative effects or ambiguities of the previous law, it had nevertheless launched a debate. It had at the same time officially recorded many of the reasons to be optimistic about the associative movement. The preamble to the draft law stated the achievements of associations, noting that 'despite all the difficulties met with in the management of their activities, they have nonetheless managed to give meaning to associative life, a level and dimension of which the reality is undeniable'. Outlining the goals for the associative movement, the preamble continued:

> Recognised in its work, re-established in its mission and role, supported in its goals and objectives to support the common good, the associative movement will contribute by its vitality and vigour to participative democracy, of which it is an essential part, more meaning and reality.[44]

Consulted in early 2012, a number of associations that had participated in this networking initiative stated that, whilst deeply disappointed, they had experienced more positive interactions with state actors when trying to understand the obligations of the new law. For them, it remained to be seen how the law would be implemented in practice and how the different political levels of the town halls, regions and ministry, now responsible for associations, would interact with them. A few years on, the results vary significantly according to region. When interviewed in 2016, a number of associations still felt that the 2012 law had 'codified the previous transgressions of the state'.[45]

A socio-medical support association in Medea

The city of Medea suffered more than most in terms of grievances, trauma and suspicion during the conflict of the 1990s. This was not only in terms of specific grievances and violence suffered by the population, but also the insecurity that contributed to a weakening of the provision of services to the population. Across Algeria, many of those involved in religious charitable organisations encountered difficulties in their work during the tense political situation of the decade. Some associations continued, and some actors used their previous experience to set up new, single-issue or sector- oriented associations to deal with social questions, issues of public health or problems related to personal grievances.

In Sidi Fredj, in 2003, two men from Medea met in a health centre. They both suffered from spinal problems. They had had to travel for hours (whilst in severe pain) by road to reach the centre and thus began to question the lack of services and information in their home town. On their return, they spoke with other friends and contacts, particularly parents of disabled children suffering from similar problems. The following year, drawing on practical experience of charitable work in religious organisations, they set up an association named Echifaa, meaning 'healing' in Arabic. The goals of the association were:

> To create a space to meet and think about the ways and means to accompany patients who suffer from different pathologies of the spine, in their search for health care, and above all to intervene to prevent such illnesses which can be avoided through certain changes in lifestyle and daily practices and behaviour, changes which could be easily available for everyone.[46]

Following its creation, the group organised information and awareness campaigns, and an annual conference. They organised the distribution of wheelchairs, crutches and medicines to those in need of support. With the help of an EU-financed project, co-sponsored by the authorities and Sonatrach, the national petrol company, a medical centre was set up in 2008. Through the centre, those suffering could be treated locally for a symbolic membership fee. In 2006, there were already almost 500 members of the association. By 2011, there were almost 5000 members. The centre was quickly operational and all the basic service activities continued or were scaled up. A website and Facebook page now communicate the activities of the association to members and other interested parties, and they are supported across Algeria and by a number of international friends of the association, in Europe and Canada.

The association provides a service to the population via a functional centre which opens for six days each week: three days for female patients and three for male patients. It has a staff of over 20, supported by social development authorities, whose wages support approximately 30 families. Procuring much of the services and supplies as locally as possible and recruiting regionally, the association in its own way also contributes to the local economy. In its more international outlook, the association made a request to recruit a Palestinian doctor who, resident in Medea, had asked to help.

In terms of any political role, or ties to the Algerian state, the association was asked to and did support the presidential electoral campaign in 2009 in its logistics. It was also involved in distributing posters and transmitting information about communal events. In 2010, the governor of Medea promised the association a disused swimming pool which could be renovated for the treatment of patients. On a number of occasions, the association has been able to present its work and activities at national level. Speaking in the autumn 2011, the president of the association indicated that,

> In the national seminar in October 2011 in Tipaza, under the patronage of the Minister of National Solidarity, under the theme Social development, experiences, risks and challenges, we were invited to participate to explain how our project has been able to self-finance and be sustainable. This is thanks to the participation of the members who multiply day by day, today they are 4942. As such, this summer we were able to extend the centre.[47]

Through a combination of local initiatives and modest outside help, it was, on many fronts, a clear success story which served genuine local needs.

However, at the time of being interviewed, the association was uncertain of its future. There had been a change of regional governor, and suddenly it began to receive letters and convocations from the authorities. The association was summoned to present its case to the regional authorities, which had accused it of making a profit, charging patients and acting outside the *wilaya* of Medea by treating patients from Algiers. This, it implied, affected its regional status. A police enquiry was sent to the association. The statutes, which had been updated due to the rotation of the president and presented to the authorities, were withheld at the *wilaya*.[48] It was made clear that there was a problem and that they would perhaps not be 'approved'.

Members of the association team were seriously affected by the interference and accusations to which they were subjected, but they continued to operate the centre and seek solutions to the problems resulting from conflict with or misunderstanding by the regional authorities. Speaking in December 2011, they complained:

> We are disappointed that our false problems are still not resolved, we received last Thursday a visit from an inspector sent by the Minister of Health, but he was unable to do anything due to the matter being in the hands of the justice system. He even spoke with the *Wali*, but it is the same story. As a result, the health directorate has broken its convention which allowed the detachment of two doctors to our organisation. We are trying to recruit now a doctor specialised in re-education who could be the medical director of the centre and paid by the association. We have already contacted two doctors and await the response. Hopefully we can recruit one as soon as possible.[49]

The association's key members felt they had to invest all their energy in responding to negative and intrusive requests from the authorities to present their accounts and activities, whilst at the same time having been recognised by the state as a success story. After two years of investigations, audits and questions, and the reduction of their activities to a minimum, the association was finally acquitted of all accusations by tribunal in Medea in October 2012. Their experience provides a not uncommon example of a soured relationship between the associative sector and the state authorities. With a complete turnaround from the authorities, the association's fortunes changed for the better. Their previous torment, however, and their continued anxiety, demonstrates the fragility of associations; they are vulnerable to accusations, jealousy and the complexity of apparently arbitrary relations between state structures internally, and with civil society actors.

Environmental and heritage protection association in Ghardaia
About 500 km south of Medea, in the Ghardaia region of Algeria, the Association for the Protection of the Environment of Beni Isguen (APEB) was created in 1989 to respond to the needs of local populations and to restore oases. It currently groups together a number of teachers, biologists, agronomists and citizens of Beni Isguen. The association set out to mobilise funds for projects to protect palm groves, local traditions and agriculture. It targeted, notably, the ancient water systems which protect Beni Isguen from the flooding of the desert riverbed, the *oued*. Serious flooding in 2008, some of the worst in over a century, killed over 30 people and displaced many, bringing home yet again the importance of preserving traditional flood protections. One of the larger projects carried out by the association was to rebuild the walls which channel the waters in the event of floods. When the rains arrive, these water channels protect the town, irrigate the different terrains within the oasis and fill the wells. This sustains the agricultural activities and livelihoods of many citizens. It also saves lives and infrastructures, diffusing the pressure of intensive flood waters and gradually channelling them to safe reservoirs. Such systems have worked for thousands of years in the oasis towns of the Sahara and for six centuries since the creation of Beni Isguen. They have historically been managed and maintained communally by the local population.

However, in contemporary Algeria, with a population continuously migrating towards the capital, many of the oases face ruin. The association is trying to salvage and recreate the maintenance of the irrigation systems as a communal project. It has worked largely with a Spanish association and once with the EU. One of the association's recent projects was the construction of a training centre for agriculturalists from oasis towns across Algeria and the Maghreb region. A programme was drawn up taking into account the specificities of the target students, and the training programmes were launched. The association is a key player in the RADDO network, which links up associations working on development issues related to oases and which represents associations in the south of Europe, Morocco, Tunisia, Mauritania and Algeria.[50] Eleven Algerian associations are members, and APEB is trying to work to strengthen the national Algerian network of these organisations. The national network, according to the association's members, was much more challenging.

There is a particular density to associative life in Ghardaia. The Mozabite population in Algeria is known for its solidarity and its structured organisation at the local level. For APEB, the town hall has offered a building in which activities can be managed, in addition to the training centre built by APEB in the palmary. APEB's president reports that the *wilaya* is now far more open towards the association. The last renewal of statutes went smoothly. Today, the Minister for the Environment recognises the work of APEB and has suggested drawing up a convention with the association in clear and positive recognition of the work it has achieved.

In Ghardaia, many associations were registered in the late 1980s at the beginning of the opening up of civil society in Algeria and with the more relaxed laws on association in 1987 and 1990. Associations thus have had a longer lifespan than elsewhere in the country. The region also suffered less during the conflict of the 1990s, when Ghardaia was isolated from the more violent incidents which affected the north. However, in 2013 violence between the different ethnic groups in Ghardaia and Berriane highlights the continued potential for instability, particularly with regard to the regional turmoil not far away at the Libyan border. The association is keen to work hard at the local level to preserve the local heritage and ecology, and to encourage young people to stay, invest in and develop the region. Activities in Ghardaia have inspired trends elsewhere in the country and APEB now works with other associations across Algeria. APEB's successful management of its relationship with the state is in marked contrast to the misfortunes of the health association in Medea and illustrates the varied experience that associations encounter as they interact with the state in different parts of the country.

Conclusion

Despite persistent difficulties in state–society relations, and the general mistrust of the state, there are nevertheless, as well as repression, numerous examples of negotiation and compromise; these are highlighted across the different case studies. Demonstrations during the Arab Spring revolutions in 2011 were heavily repressed, yet they had been fragmented before they even began. With the backdrop of a decade of violence in the 1990s, Algerians had no desire for further upheaval or bloodshed. The CNCD marches did not provide the solution, although the bringing together of radically opposed factions of Algerian society was symbolic of the capacity for reconciliation and the ongoing struggle to shape the future polity, with shared values around social justice. The relationship between state and society in Algeria was influenced by the Arab revolutions and the profound changes in the region, but there were arguably more subtle changes in Algeria that were less visible than the anger demonstrated on the streets of Algiers in early 2011. Though fearing an open dialogue on Algeria's problems, the regime did attempt certain reforms. New legislative proposals were introduced but the new legal texts redefined relations between civil society, the state and external actors in a context of mistrust not only of foreign interventions, but also of local associations and civil society, and they generally represented a less enabling environment. What was initially more interesting, however, was the coming together of associations at local, regional and national level to challenge the state, using the legal and parliamentary process. The negotiations amongst associations, individuals and politicians to influence the legislative process ultimately failed when the state stepped in to restrain the parliamentarians. However, dialogue and discussion between very different actors about the Algerian state's methods of obstruction were an important part of renegotiating access to the public sphere. So, while the outcome may be contested, the impact of the consultation process is significant.

The wide public consultation that followed the 2011 uprisings led to certain optimism amongst some actors as to the potential for change. Yet fear and distrust appear to have limited this opening, as shown in the case above of the network of associations which challenged the new law. The experiences of the two associations in Medea and Ghardaia illustrate the arbitrary nature of the authorities' interactions with associations. Although there are examples of improved cooperation, emerging transnational networks and recognition of an association's achievements by the state, the mechanisms of disruption – as in institutional slowness through withholding of statutes – the invention of complex and shifting rules, or the co-opting of organisations into ministerial visits, still exist.

Yet associations are far from passive receivers of state tactics to maintain control and hegemony over associational life. They have their own strategies of response, through lobbying or through building networks. Ultimately they are already engaged in the heart of the Algerian predicament, namely the need for political dialogue and the involvement of a far wider public in the political debate. They are actively renegotiating the place of associative actors within the political system and challenging the terminology of violence and rupture to describe the Algerian predicament. To further understand these processes from the perspective of associations, the next chapter takes a more in-depth look at the make-up of Algerian civil society.

CHAPTER 5

ASSOCIATIONS IN ALGERIA

The nature of Algerian associations, their focus and their geography, can be illustrated through developing a new typology, building on current categorisations of associations by contemporary researchers,[1] but also drawing on discussions with many associations over the last ten years about their own perceptions of their organisations and the role they play in Algerian society. Such a typology should determine which types of association exist, whether – as they have previously been categorised – they are self-serving and co-opted or, on the contrary, whether they provide services to the population. Do associations contribute to political change, either in terms of social, cultural or environmental policies, for example, or through promoting rights and tackling injustice? Recently published figures from the Ministry of Interior show a certain degree of transparency in terms of access to information about associations registered in the country. Ministry figures, which are available online, indicate a predominance of local associations, religious charities and social associations. Associations dealing with culture, heritage and youth are also predominant. Using the Ministry's figures, in combination with recent research on active associations, this chapter sets out to identify where associations are most active in Algeria and on which sectors they are most likely to focus. It builds also on Brahim Salhi's detailed study in 2011 and on Omar Derras' research in 2007, into the profiles of associational actors. To explore associations and their work in Algeria, the chapter presents, first, a general overview, including a typology of different associations. This draws on official sources and previous research to identify the overall breakdown of these organisations. It questions whether previous typologies have been overly pessimistic in their categorisation of Algerian civil society, failing to consider that there may be more positive reasons for Algerians joining associations and more constructive outcomes of their work. The geography of associations across the Algerian territory is investigated, and a sectoral breakdown considers their main areas of interest and focus.

A New Typology of Associations

As discussed in the first chapter, in *Some Propositions about Civil Society and the Consolidation of Democracy* Phillipe Schmitter argues that at a general level, civil society can have a positive role in consolidating democracy. This is the case when it regroups information; it inculcates civic behaviour; it provides closer channels for expression; it governs towards collective commitments; and finally it provides a source of resistance to tyranny. However, similar to Jamal, who argues that civil society cannot function well in authoritarian systems, Schmitter argues that civil society can also present risks for democracy. Depending on the specific organisations and the governing system, this occurs if it makes majority formation difficult, biases influence, compromises political life or is potentially ethnically or culturally divisive.[2] A positive role for democracy therefore depends on the nature of the organisations, particularly whether they are broadly encompassing enough, balanced in their capabilities and able to be well governed. If such conditions are met, then there is a chance for genuine social dialogue. Otherwise, Schmitter suggests, the promotion of civil society may simply reproduce conflicts and organisations incapable of agreeing on a common cause. According to Schmitter's framework, it is important to study the nature of associations at grassroots level to understand how representative they are and whether, through shared experiences and learning, they create social capital, or, on the contrary, tend to be divisive and self-interested. Hardig takes issue with the previous dichotomy of describing civil society in the MENA region as either 'strong and antidemocratic or weak and irrelevant'. He argues that the Arab revolts of 2011 presented the clearest challenge to such a dichotomy as 'CSAs proved to be both interested in democratization and capable of mobilizing for that end'.[3] Hardig suggests the need to understand the potential for MENA civil society to broaden the political space and improve governance, as well as the need for coalitions, not only across civil society, but across the whole political sphere.

Previous studies have attempted to regroup into a typology the different kinds of associations in Algeria. To different degrees, these previous typologies have generally classed Algerian associations rather negatively. The typologies have sought to measure their usefulness in terms of altruism and independence from the state, but generally concluded that Algerian associations were neither altruistic nor independent. Ammar Belhimer, for example, identifies three categories of associations: first, those which are created purely by the state; second, those which are created by independent actors but are then co-opted by the state; and finally, those that appear to be mainly opportunist in a situation of scarce resources and which seek financial or personal gain.[4] At the opposite end of the scale, other research adds a more positive category of associations: those which are politically active and motivated by the real needs of the population, through militant activism or socially inspired actions.[5] Derras categorises these as associations of contestation. For Cavatorta, many associations fit into this category. However, for him, these associations, whilst not co-opted by it, are limited by difficult relations with the state and with each other and this prevents independent and effective action.

Using Schmitter's framework, it is possible to first question whether there is a divisive element in Algerian associations. Cavatorta's research into associations that question the Reconciliation Charter suggests that there is a difficult relationship between those organisations which come from an Islamist perspective, blaming the Algerian state for their losses, and those from a secular background which might hold the Islamist insurgency as primarily responsible for Algeria's painful conflict of the 1990s. Yet Cavatorta points to many cases of cooperation between divergent organisations. In interviews with *Djazairouna*, one of the key organisations in this area, the president of the association confirmed the more nuanced understanding of most Algerians about the conflict, the general desire for peace, and, for *Djazairouna*, that 'we work with all tendencies to fight for justice, we exclude nobody'.[6] The regional make up of civil society is also important in this regard, particularly to determine whether there is a class or group bias, or a divisive element along, say, ethnic or cultural grounds. For example, in Algeria the strong presence of associations in the Berber regions of Kabylia or the M'zab could imply such divisive forces. Yet, the case discussed in the previous chapter of the environmental NGO in the M'Zab would seem to refute this. The federating methods of the organisation seemed to imply a more inclusive nature. Equally, Frédéric Volpi's research on Kabyle associations would seem to confirm the more consensual, bridge-building approaches of associative life in Kabylia. Whilst there is a small independence movement in Kabylia, the main aim of the Berber associations is far more about cultural and linguistic identity and justice within Algeria. Volpi describes their ability to build the 'organic connection between rulers and ruled' and more structured approaches, valuing Kabyle culture and heritage rather than any divisive or purely regionalist perspective.[7]

The risk of biased self-interest is usually seen through the lens of being 'co-opted by the regime' in Algeria. Such ties are demonstrated when associations mobilise presence for political rallies and ministerial visits as the obligatory return for freedom of action and small grants. Associations under the single party were indeed attributed such a role, namely to mobilise the population and support for the regime. Despite the changes in the political configuration in Algeria since 1987, this practice of involving associations in political life continues. As seen in Chapter 4, associations are called upon to invite participants when state actors are visiting or to mobilise support for electoral campaigns. What was clear in the interviews, however, was the clear disdain for this approach from many associations and the feeling of being used. When interviewed, most were quite critical of the lack of support received from the state. They felt that when they did receive support, such as placement staff from the Social Development Agency, it could often quite arbitrarily be taken away, not necessarily for failure to support the state, but for random motives about which they had little understanding – such as personality conflicts or unfounded accusations, as described in the case study in the previous chapter. The state did try to co-opt associations and grants had been 'given out willy-nilly' in the past, but this was very negatively viewed by most of the associations interviewed.

In order to determine whether associations are able to inculcate democratic behaviour and to channel expression, as Schmitter suggests is important, the following chapters will present case studies of associations to examine the motivations, goals and profiles of the founding members as well as exploring how they and their main activists participate and enter into dialogue with local politics at the communal and regional levels. These case studies will explore whether they provide sources of resistance or opposition politics – as suggested by Cavatorta – arguing that the associational sphere is indeed now where politics happens.[8] First, it is useful to set out a range of categories in which associations can be placed. This can be done based on previous research and recent interviews with associations. Recognising the more critical vision of these organisations, as well as the ideal type, the following criteria and typology are proposed. Associations can be divided into three different categories:

- partisan associations which seek personal gain, or which are sleeping 'briefcase associations' with no real permanent activity or anchoring in society, such as those described by Belhimer. This category would include both the 'assisted associations' and the 'collaborating associations' also described by Derras;
- associations created for more personal reasons – for personal grievance, loss, injustice, maybe recognition either of a cause, a person or trauma, and which may become a life project. This would include the associations Cavatorta describes, which work for families of the disappeared and the many foundations set up since the 1990s;
- associations which are created from altruism, political will or militant goals, to improve social, cultural or environmental wellbeing, possibly along ideological or religious lines, including Derras' *'associations de contestation'*.

This typology can be visualised in Figure 5.1.

Such criteria are not static and an organisation, and its members, could move between categories or belong to more than one over different time periods. This volume argues that previous typologies and analyses have focused too much on the first box. It argues that the predominance of opportunist or partisan associations has been overstated in the language of academia, policy makers, the media and donors for a number of reasons. One of these is that researchers have perhaps insufficiently engaged with associations on the ground to understand the difficulties of their environments. Omar Derras' typology, drawn up in 2007, is detailed and insightful. It clearly describes a whole range of different

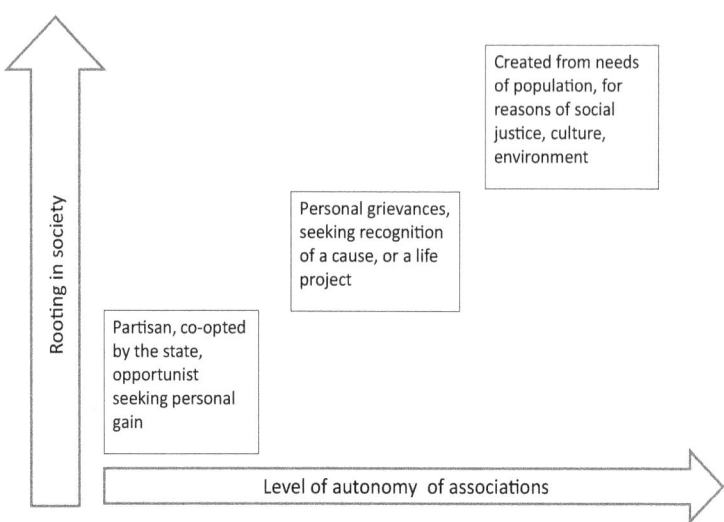

Figure 5.1 Typology of associations, reasons for creation and levels of autonomy.

types of associative actors, from social, humanitarian, politicised and self-interested, to youth-oriented organisations. Derras acknowledges a real role and independence, however, only for associations of contestation. These in turn, for Derras, 'are marginalised and controlled by the state'. The following chapters will assess Derras' findings about the roles of these different structures more closely, through specific case studies. The next sections will, first, assess the ministry figures and previous research, hoping to shed light on the regional and then the sectoral breakdown of associations in Algeria by exploring where associations are most active.

The Regional Focus of Algerian Associations

In early 2012, the Ministry of Interior published online a detailed typology of all registered associations in Algeria, by section and region.[9] Whilst it is not clear whether all the associations are active, the figures are nonetheless instructive. They indicate, at the very least, the will of the population, across different regions, to act in the public sphere in a particular sector and in the form of an association. As a minimum, this involves uniting 12 founding members, as specified by the law,[10] defining objectives and agreeing on statutes, managing a bank account and presenting the association's dossier to the regional authorities. From interviews with donor agencies and Ministry officials in Algiers, most presumed that the south of the country was relatively less represented in terms of associative life; or, at least, that the south is deprived of the national or international support mechanisms for associations. Analysis of recent figures from the Ministry of Interior shows that on the contrary, per capita, the south is far more densely populated with associations than the north.

The regions with the most associations registered per capita are almost all in the southern Sahara. Those with the least associations are the more urban, populated regions of the north – Relizane, Annaba Oran, Sétif and Djelfa. Oran, due to the visibility of its associations, is often seen as the strongest region in terms of associative activism. Yet the figures indicate that Oran is one of the lowest in terms of numbers of registered associations per population across the *wilaya*. Overall, the population of Oran has created far fewer associations than in other regions. It is perhaps the environment in Oran – better connections, its status as an economic capital, the prevalence of the French language, all contributing to better access to external funding opportunities – that has meant that newly created associations could flourish and be more visible than those in other contexts. Overall, however, fewer associations have been created in Oran. Equally, although the capital Algiers has the

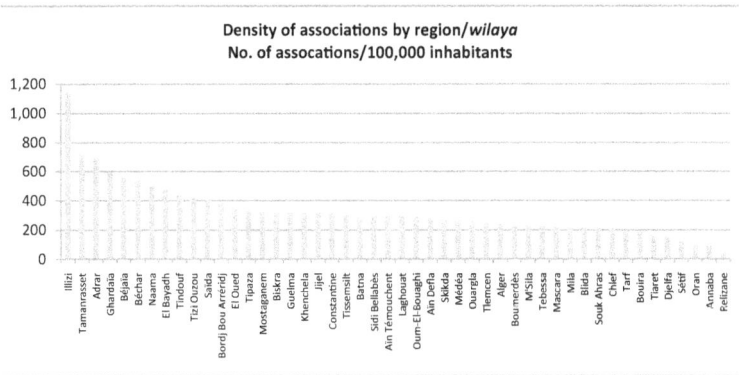

Figure 5.2 Density of associations by *wilaya*.

highest number overall, with over 7,000 associations registered, the huge population, particularly with the migrations during the violence of the 1990s, means that the ratio is comparatively low compared to many of the more isolated regions of the country.

Reasons for the density of the south could be many. In the south, many associations work on cultural issues and are thus perhaps easier to set up and are less conflictual. The needs are perhaps greater than some of the northern regions and distances are greater, indicating a need for localised organisations. There is also the long history of associative or community action in the south, as well as the fact that traditional networks and religious structures were less affected by the colonial project and its destructive aims than in the north. As one member of an association in Ghardaia, the Mozabite region at the gates of the Sahara, described it: 'here we have links of solidarity which have existed for centuries. We have lived in harmony in the same composition for so long. People understand us and support the association'.[11] Figure 5.3 reflects this density of associations by region, in terms of the populations of the different *wilayas*.

In contrast, Figure 5.4 highlights areas in which associations successfully competed for grants under the EU's support programme for associations from 2006 to 2010.

The two maps, of associative density and of donor-funded associations, appear to be directly opposed. Whereas the densest area of associations per inhabitant is in the south, the majority of funding is in the north. Whilst a large proportion of the population resides in the north, there are nonetheless a large number of associations in the south. Conclusions drawn from these figures about the regional distribution and stronger associative activism in the south, far from the sources of funding, could be multiple, including: that there is no link between the presence of donors and the existence of associations; that donors primarily target associations in proximity to the capital due to logistical difficulties related to the geography and size of the country; that, for language reasons, one part of the country's associations has been more successful in obtaining grants; or that there is a greater reluctance to work with foreign actors in certain regions than in others. The reality probably lies somewhere in between. Derras' study shows how the 'lack of means' is one of the main factors for abandoning or becoming disillusioned with associative life.[12] Yet, in a parallel with Algeria's position in the MENA region as the smallest consumer of foreign 'civil society support', it appears again that lower

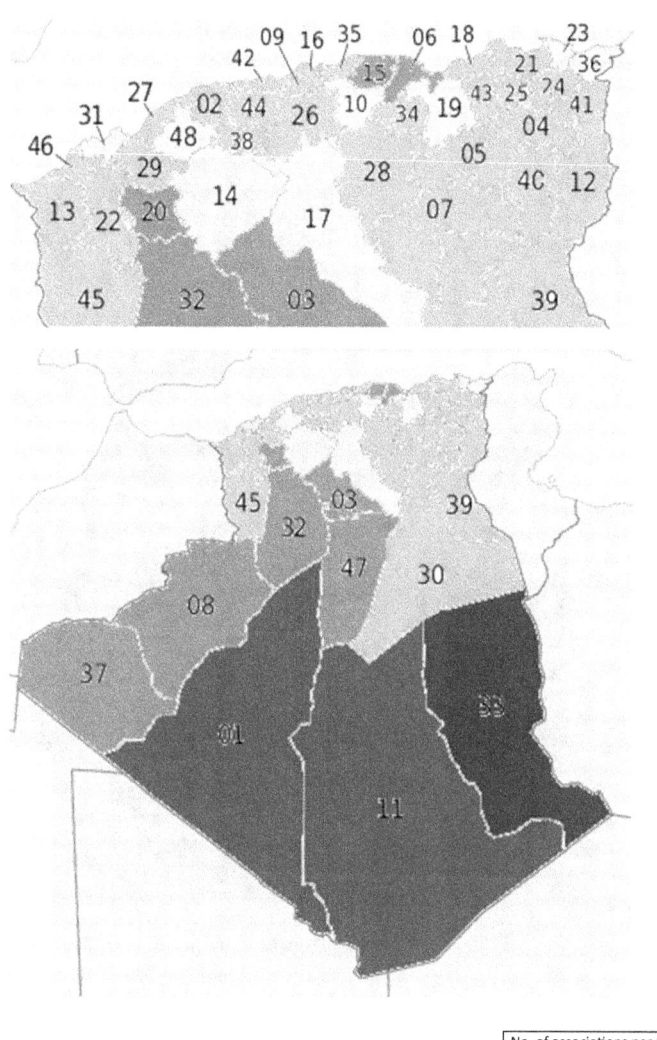

Figure 5.3 Association density map of Algeria by *wilaya* and population.

Repartition of associative projects financed by three EU calls between 2007 and 2009
Data from the EU funded ONG2 Project, 2009

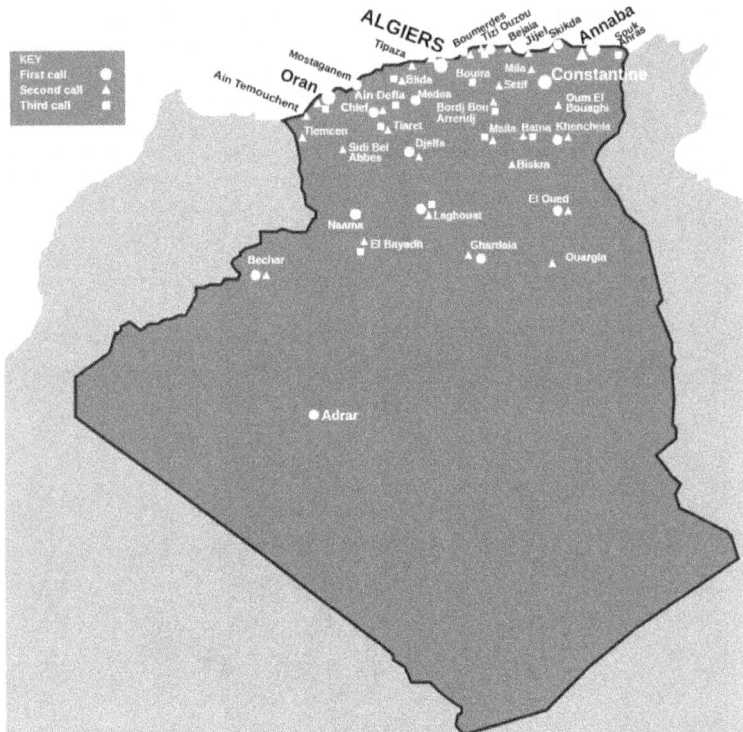

Figure 5.4 Map of EU-financed NGO projects in Algeria.

funding and greater isolation do not necessarily mean that civil society is less present. The strong presence of associations in the Algerian south, despite limited support, implies that any discussion of civil society in Algeria needs to include the activism, ideas and areas of interest of organisations in the Sahara.

The Sector Focus of Algerian Associations

Several studies have analysed the sectoral bias and distribution of the associational phenomenon across Algeria.[13] According to Salhi, 46,000 organisations were created between 1990 and 1997. The vast majority of these were, in order of their representative weight and importance, parent-teacher associations, followed by mosques and religious associations, then sporting, cultural, humanitarian, local, youth, rural, disabled and women's associations. In 2007, Omar Derras carried out an extensive, nationwide research project on the associative phenomenon in Algeria, which was financed by the German foundation Frederich Ebert Stiftung. Derras' research selected 'active' associations according to a set of criteria. These included the existence of a permanent office, space or address from which the organisation's activities were run, a programme of previous and ongoing activities and the presence and relative stability of the members of the board.[14] In his study of 446 'active' associations in 2007, Omar Derras notes 43 per cent in the social sector, followed by 28 per cent in the cultural sector. Youth organisations represented 14 per cent, health organisations 5 per cent and religious, women's and rural associations represented only a small fraction of active organisations.[15]

The 2012, sectoral and regional Ministry of Interior figures indicate a slightly different breakdown. For the sectors of activity of the 92,627 'local' associations registered at regional level, 22 per cent were local *comités de quartiers*, whereas religious, sports and parent-teacher associations each made up 16 per cent of local associations. The next significant group was cultural associations, which represented 10 per cent of officially registered associations. The remaining associations represented, in much smaller proportions, a number of sectors including the professions, environment, youth, old age, health, disability, solidarity, women, tourism and humanitarian aid (Figure 5.5).

At the same date, 1,027 'national' associations were registered with the Ministry of Interior in Algiers. They are deemed, by their registration at this central level, to be competent to work right across the national territory. The areas and priorities of the national associations differ slightly from those of the local associations. The main areas of activity are the representation of the professions – through the professional national trade unions, which make up 21 per cent of national registered associations – followed by health associations and cultural associations. Of these 143 cultural associations, most deal with art, culture and education, and a small percentage tackle national heritage (Figure 5.6).

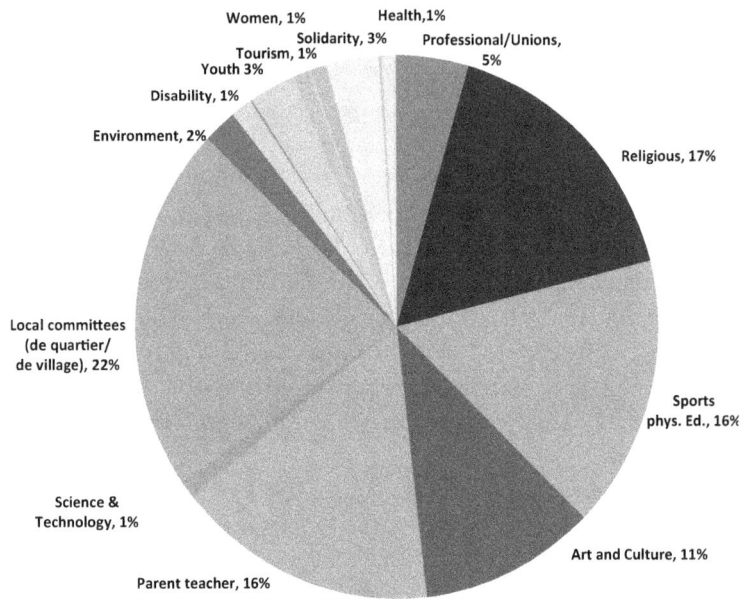

Figure 5.5 Local associations in Algeria and their sector focus. Source: figures from the Algerian Ministry of Interior, 2012.

The high number of registered associations in Algeria reflects a wide variety of actors across many sectors. From the figures above, it is clear that many have a specific and well-defined role, such as the management of a school or the charitable actions of a mosque. The case studies in the following chapters seek to explore those associations which go beyond these well-defined roles and act more widely within the community. Associations working in the heritage sector may protect a specific monument or area, yet may simultaneously engage in the national debate about Algerian history, train other associations or lead a national network of similar organisations. Social sector associations may provide services that the state struggles to deliver, such as caring for people with disability, perhaps motivated by the personal experience of one of their members. However, they are often also in dialogue with the state about needs on the ground, training state officials or sharing information and

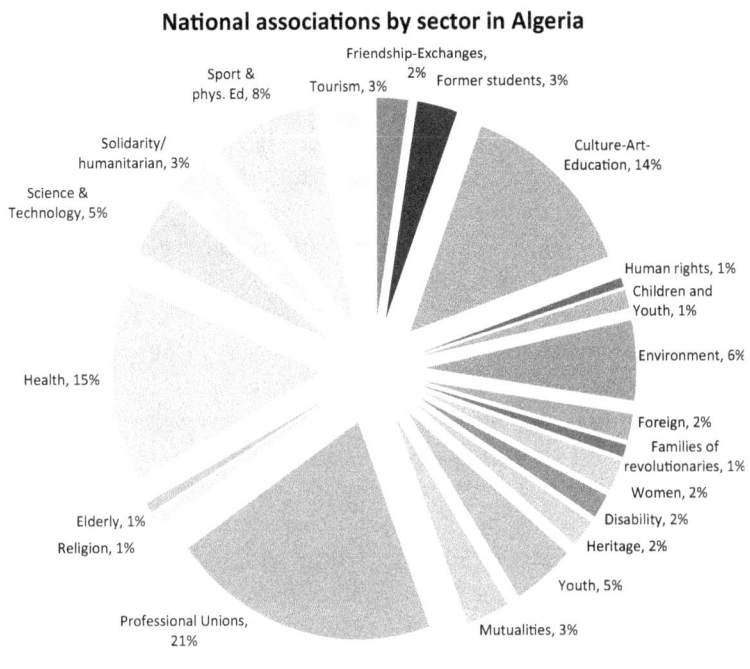

Figure 5.6 National associations in Algeria and their sector focus. Source: figures from the Algerian Ministry of Interior, 2012.

expertise through regional and international networks. Whilst perhaps less overtly political than human rights organisations or the feminist movement, the social and heritage sectors are those most targeted by the 'active' associations studied by Omar Derras in his 2007 project and as such merit more exploration in the following chapters.

Many of the associations interviewed in these sectors were also engaging in public debate at some level. This was not always easy to manage, particularly when it touched on questions of national identity, say, in the heritage sector, or on state capacity in the social sectors. If comments were seen as too critical, state actors would '*mettent des bâtons dans les roues*' or 'throw a spanner in the works' of the association. Yet, the fact that such public debate takes place indicates that such organisations are not simply co-opted actors, nor are they regrouped family structures seeking personal gain. The actors involved in the associations are often qualified, retired, public sector officials, such as teachers or managers. With reasonable pension schemes and early retirement, they have the energy and the means to dedicate themselves to associational life. They have also felt perhaps more strongly the frustrations of half-a-century of independence and the huge expectations of Algeria in the 1960s, which remained unfulfilled in the following decades. For such reasons, older members of associations indicated the importance of 'creating projects which directly target young people, offering them new skills and opportunities to learn about Algerian heritage and contribute to the development of the country'.[16] Secular association members felt that through the organisation, they could stand up to obscurantism of the Islamist threat, particularly to Algerian heritage and identity. In more Islamic charities, members also spoke about job creation, education and building bridges through dialogue with different actors and, as well as moral salvation, that they could provide new opportunities for the predominantly young population and contribute to a more positive vision for the future of Algeria. There were many such cases of intergenerational dialogue within many of the associations interviewed. This points increasingly towards a perception of associations and their networks as a space rather than just a membership. As Hardig suggests, in Gramscian terms, civil society then becomes 'a realm of contention, where strategies are devised, alliances are built, and activity is inherently political'.[17]

Conclusion

From an overview of associational life and by breaking it down into a new typology, the potential for a more positive categorisation of associations and their place in the political and social life of contemporary Algeria can be deduced. The geographic and sectoral distribution of associations across the country also perhaps contradicts previous perceptions. The findings from these figures suggest that, as Omar Carlier described for the processes of mobilisation in the nationalist struggles of the 1950s, it is not necessarily the big cities where profound and unexpected changes can take place, and where a defining role in structuring the mobilisation happens.[18] 'Intermediary' towns, which may have managed better to preserve their links to traditional or to rural life, as well as their spaces of socialisation, should not be overlooked. Although there may be more dramatic experiences of the associations in Oran – exemplified by mobilisation around heritage questions which will be explored in the next chapter – the figures show that there is a far greater concentration of smaller organisations in the south of Algeria and Kabylia, and generally far from the urban centres.

When the maps of association density and donor programmes are compared, it also appears that there is no clear relation, in Algeria, between financial opportunities and the creation of associations as has been so clearly documented in other contexts.[19] People create associations to respond to their own individual or communal preoccupations, which have in many cases been prompted or exacerbated over a decade of insecurity and violence. Whilst donor interventions may give short-term project support or grants to associations in some of the sectors, their absence from most of the Algerian territory, particularly the south, is notable. It is the relationship with the state, with members and any beneficiaries, that matters more to the associations interviewed and which either breaks or consolidates their work.

Many associations emerged in the heritage sector, despite serious practical difficulties. They worked to protect tangible artefacts or monuments at the time of the violence of the 1990s. It was an equally difficult sector in political or strategic terms, given the huge rifts which emerged over the nature of Algerian identity, heritage and culture. Similarly, many of the local associations set up in the 1990s were established to support schools as parent-teacher associations. This was at a time in Algeria when simply sending a child to school was a risk due to insecurity, with targeted attacks on teachers and the school arson campaign of the radical Islamist *Groupe Islamique Armé* (GIA). During the 1990s Algerians engaged in a wide variety of associations, often with considerable risk to their own safety. With little or no financial incentive, either from the state or from international donors, they continued to demonstrate a desire to contribute to the reconstruction or even the 'salvation' of Algeria in a time of conflict.

Although critical, many members wanted to build bridges with the state. Almost all interviewees felt strongly about protecting the Algerian nation and its population following the traumas of the last century. These factors constrained the yearning for radical protest against the state. The vast majority of associations focusing on the social sectors, as identified by Derras' study, could be taken as a comment by civil society on the failure of the state to care for its population. Yet, this was not the only discourse emerging. The work of the associations can also be seen, conversely, as reflecting the will of the population to participate in social care, in volunteering, in charitable work. The state does clearly accord the opportunity for associations to take an active role in the social sector, and through the national insurance scheme of the *CNAS* it supports this work financially. This appears to demonstrate a relationship which, whilst clearly contentious, maintains several channels for mutual recognition, cooperation and dialogue for improvement in the future. Drawing on these initial findings from the general make up of associations in Algeria, the following chapters will explore in more detail these significant sectors of heritage and social welfare to see how these organisations contribute and how they engage with each other, and with the state, in the public sphere.

CHAPTER 6

ALGERIAN ASSOCIATIONS PROTECTING THE PAST

State–society relations in the realm of cultural heritage have always been sensitive and complicated domains for Algerian associations. After the painful anti-colonial struggle, establishing a new cultural identity was a major challenge in the post-colonial era. This construction of an Algerian cultural identity was both a psychological and a physical task, given the suppression of Arab-Muslim culture under colonialism and the destruction of cultural institutions during the War of Independence. The re-writing of history in line with a new nationalist perspective was an important tool with which to tackle the previous injustices, the marginalisation of Arab-Muslim and Berber culture, and the divisive myths of colonialism. It was in this context that Arabisation became a 'matter of cultural decolonization' and a question of social equality.[1] The promotion of the Arabic language would open up education and culture, and allow full access to basic social services for the predominantly Arabic-speaking population which had, under colonisation, been denied such rights.

In the 1980s, resentment over the denial of ethnic differences, in particular for Algeria's significant Berber population, fuelled the desire to promote wider, more inclusive cultural heritage, identity and language policies. Increasing numbers of cultural organisations were created and by 2012, 10,000 were registered in the ministry of interior's figures as cultural heritage associations. With violent conflict throughout the 1990s, and a relative abandoning of the cultural sector by the state, these associations saw their purpose as being to protect a wide range of Algerian cultural heritage which was at risk. They carried out their mission under the daily threat of violence from the extremist insurgency. In response to their demands during the 1990s, the Algerian state did facilitate their role through legislative reform. The law for the protection of cultural heritage of 1998 identified as national heritage all artefacts, buildings, monuments and traditions, upon and in the Algerian soil, from pre-history to the current day. Article 4 of this law allowed that such heritage be managed by associations, regulated under the terms of the Law on Associations.

With the end of the conflict and a new Minister of Culture in the late 1990s, a national cultural policy was re-launched. During this phase the state set out to monopolise many aspects of cultural life, with the result that national institutions and large-scale, state-organised festivals consumed most of the significant state budget. Algerian cultural policy was seen as being mainly limited to grandiose events such as the Pan African Music Festival, or launching huge infrastructure projects such as the new Chinese-funded Algiers Opera House. Very little funding was given to civil society. Cultural organisations and the independent sector received only 0.2 per cent of the culture budget. Against this backdrop of renewed state hegemony in the cultural sector, cultural heritage associations have been contributing to reflections about Algerian national and cultural identity in recent years. In an examination of how they protect historic buildings, preserve archeological sites and promote different forms of religious identity, specific case studies will highlight how they cooperate, challenge and come into conflict with the Algerian state in the task of preserving the country's cultural heritage.

Heritage Associations in Algeria

Since the 1990 Law on Associations, and the subsequent 1998 Law for the Protection of Cultural Heritage, thousands of Algerian associations have been created across the country to protect Algeria's heritage. Statistics published in 2012 by the Ministry of Interior, on the numbers and sectors of registered associations, show that cultural associations represent over 10 per cent of regional and 16 per cent of national orgainsations. According to Omar Derras' 2008 study of active associations the figure is higher, with almost a third working in the cultural heritage sector. The regions of the country where cultural associations appear most prominent are in the south. According to the ministry's figures, Illizi and Adrar in the Sahara have the highest number for their populations. The northern Berber *wilayas* of Tizi Ouzou and Bejaia in Kabylia also have high numbers. Table 6.1 illustrates the figures for cultural associations by *wilaya* in Algeria.

These figures can also be visualised in Figure 6.1.

The *wilayas* with the lowest densities of cultural associations are the northern ones of Chlef, Oran, Annaba, Tarf and Relizane, although vibrant organisations exist in the main cities of these *wilayas*. Derras' study also confirms that the southern *wilayas* (Tamanrasset and Adrar) are the densest in terms of cultural associations. While these, he suggests, are mainly artistic with limited ambitions, such as organising traditional music for local festivities, they represent 'local community associations which deal with everyday problems, social solidarity and preserving communitarian and social links'.[2] Regional, rather than national, associations make up the vast majority, and these mainly focus on their immediate environment, or one particular form of cultural

Table 6.1 Association density – cultural associations per 100,000 inhabitants (ten densest regions).

	Wilaya	Number of culture and heritage associations	Population in thousands	Associations per 100,000 inhabitants
1	Illizi	96	52	183
2	Adrar	498	399	125
3	Tamanrasset	206	177	117
4	Bechar	311	270	115
5	Ghardaia	401	364	110
6	El Bayadh	191	229	84
7	Tindouf	39	49	79
8	Tizi Ouzou	801	1 128	71
9	Bejaïa	513	913	56
10	Naama	89	193	46

Note: Figures taken from the Ministry of Interior, 31 December 2011. For most recent figures see www.interieur.gov.dz/images/pdf/Thematiquedesassociations.pdf (accessed 18 March 2018).

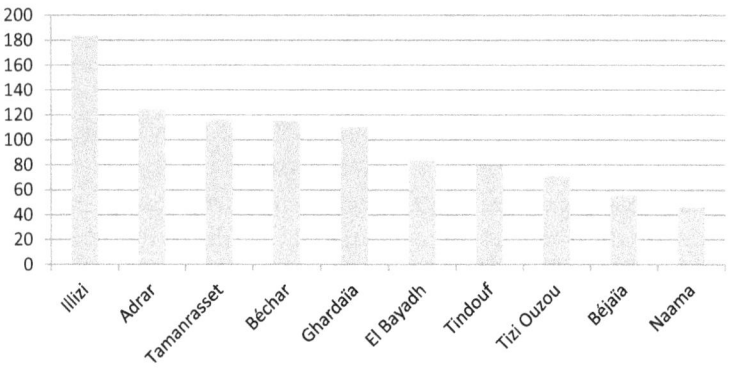

Figure 6.1 Regions with most cultural associations per capita.

expression. However, networks also enable organisations to interact at the national level. Thirty per cent of associations interviewed in Derras' study maintain relations and networks with other associations.[3]

Whereas many cultural associations' actions are focused on the local level, say providing music for weddings, Benramdane describes the increasing which take on more ambitious projects. He writes that 'many CSOs mobilize for heritage protection, such as "Bariq 21" which works with the association "friends of Skikda" on the renovation of the old Neapolitan quarter and stands up to the developers'.[4] The preservation the European colonial buildings in Skikda against the priorities of the Algerian state and its promotion of Arab-Muslim architectural heritage, whilst also standing up to corporate interests, in an area where housing shortages are critical, is a challenging area to work in.

On people's reasons for joining a cultural association, Derras reports that this comes from the desire to find a framework within which to defend certain values, to contribute to the construction of the country, to protect religion or national heritage or to defend a certain identity.[5] Layish writes of how across the Muslim world traditional religious authorities had seen an incremental loss of their independence over a long period. As it became increasingly incorporated into the state establishment, through colonial rule or nationalist projects, 'contemporary Muslim society has lost a vital element of civil society'.[6] Yet it is also true that religious associations during the 1980s grew in importance, particularly in the social sectors, providing grassroots support to communities which were neglected by the Algerian state through most of that decade. They also took on the protection of Algeria's cultural heritage, such as preserving religious texts as exemplified in the work of the *Association Abou Ishak Ibrahim Tefayech pour le Service du Patrimoine* discussed later in this chapter. As a religiously inspired organisation, set up to commemorate the works and manuscripts of the Ibadite Sheikh Tefayech, the association's goal was to preserve the heritage of the M'zab region and to educate people about the importance of these religious manuscripts. Since the end of the violence of the 1990s, during which the *zawiyas* of the Sufi brotherhoods were often directly targeted, many religious associations have been created or revived with the support of the Algerian state, and President Bouteflika in particular, to preserve this religious heritage. In Mostaghanem, in the Alawiyya Sufi order, the success of Sheikh Khaled Bentounes in setting up associations in Algeria and France is one clear example of their reach. Capable of mobilising tens of thousands within Algeria, Bentounes is clearly influencing policy making in Algeria and in France. Also working with UN institutions, Bentounes' associations seem to have greater international ambitions too.[7]

The role that a number of cultural associations played within the short-lived *Coordination nationale pour le changement et la démocratie* (CNCD), the platform set up in 2011 in the context of the Arab revolutions, highlights their interlinking desire to impact upon the whole of Algerian society; to preserve its culture but to also improve its political life and governance.[8] In a sector where expertise and public action remain weak,[9] these new Algerian associations have increasingly contributed to public debate in the cultural sector, covering identity, national heritage, history and religion at the local level. The following examples will explore these developments, their impact upon the associations themselves and also upon the state. The information comes from interviews and discussions with heritage associations from different towns across Algeria between 2007 and 2016. These orgainisations come from a variety of regions including Oran, Chlef, Tiaret, Kabylia, Adrar and Ghardaia and the experiences they share mirror those of similar cultural heritage organisations from across the country.

Associations and Urban History

In involving themselves in the protection and promotion of Algeria's historical monuments and the architecture of its cities, associations face a number of difficulties in terms of organisation, regional state actors and public response. Most suffer from poor infrastructure as well as limited resources and capacity. One of the most successful in overcoming such constraints, and developing its activities and reach, is the association 'Bel Horizon', based in Oran. This association was created in 2001 in the context of the celebrations commemorating 1,100 years since the foundation of the city by Andalusian merchants in AD 901–2. Through tours, advocacy and restoration work, Bel Horizon seeks to promote a shared heritage and real appropriation of the city of Oran by its inhabitants. Historian Diana Wylie describes how Bel Horizon focuses on the city's architectural heritage, embracing all the cultures which make up Oran, in particular the city's Mediterranean outlook. She writes of the passionate and committed approach of the members of the association, and their desire 'to make people feel at home in their beautiful, but beleaguered, city'.[10]

One of the association's first projects was to restore the sixteenth-century Spanish Santa Cruz Fort in Oran. This project was significant, first, in that renovating a Spanish vestige clearly diverged from the state's priorities in terms of primarily preserving Algeria's Arab-Muslim heritage and therefore conflicted with the state's vision of which parts of history should be primarily 'remembered'. Second, the restoration involved securitising a whole area of the city. The mountain route up to Santa Cruz Fort had been off limits during the 1990s when Islamist insurgent groups occupied it. Returning this space to the population was highly symbolic. The Bel Horizon association, through its negotiations with local people, the authorities and the police, as well as its engagement with the historical truths of colonialism and the more recent history of violence, managed at the same time to both challenge and cooperate with the state.

Bel Horizon organises regular cultural activities, music festivals and an annual heritage walk. This walk takes the population, in its thousands, through the different historical areas of the city and up to the Spanish Fort, thus publically reclaiming this space for Oran's citizens. In 2011, this attracted over 20,000 people, highlighting the popular interest in cultural heritage, but also the capacity of the association to inspire both its members and the public.[11] Despite this success, or perhaps because of it, relations with the authorities have never been straightforward. Defining heritage has national implications, but can also call into question local urbanisation policies as well as the authorities' capacity to manage development and protect historical buildings. A number of conflicts have emerged, particularly concerning the status of colonial and Jewish buildings and over how best to preserve Oran's heritage. In interviews, the president of the association reaffirmed its priority to promote *all* Algeria's heritage, including the Arab, Muslim, Berber, Roman, Jewish, Ottoman and European cultural heritage of the country, and he criticised the authorities' lack of interest in doing the same.[12]

In an interview with *El Watan* newspaper, the president of Bel Horizon explained that the association's motivations for publishing books – such as *Oran, Une Ville de Fortifications* in 2012, *Oran, la mémoire*, in 2004 and *Oran, études de géographie et d'histoire urbaines* in 2003 – were based on the desire to both document and celebrate the diversity of the city's local heritage. He argued that whereas in Europe many books had been published about Oran, only two had been published in Algeria and that this demonstrated both the lack of interest on the part of state institutions and the distance between the inhabitants and their elected leaders in the city.[13] The president also gave his views on what he saw as the state's ideological reasons for its denial of local cultural narratives across Algeria, particularly in Oran, and how the city's distinct cultural identity, its local elites and its narrative history have suffered due to the homogeneous identity imposed since independence:

> In the minds of a conservative authority within the cultural domain Oran was a bad example. At times accused of being Spanish, at other times colonial, wasn't it the most European Algerian city? As a result it represented unsettling values. A policy of blame has been put in place which claims that Oran's participation in the war of liberation was only lukewarm, that its moral values were permissive. As a result, local elites and leading figures became more circumspect and have largely been neutralized.[14]

Such claims are echoed by cultural associations across Algeria. Many associations challenge the state's refusal to accept certain narratives of local or regional identity, along with the linguistic issues that these raise, and seek to overcome this rejection through actively preserving the past.[15] They also sometimes go further by standing for local government in order to have a direct impact on the decisions relating to the city and its heritage. Members of Bel Horizon and the Santé Sidi el Houari, another active cultural association in Oran, have seen their leaders go on to be elected members of local government at the Communal Council (APC) level. Through this transition from civic to political activism, associative actors have been able to gain experience of local politics as well as access to information and a better understanding of local government.

As a predominantly francophone organisation, language is another challenge for Bel Horizon. French remains the working language of most of its meetings as well as that of its formal documents and publications. This goes against the policy preferences of the state and even the Law on Associations itself which, until revised in 2012, required all associations to produce their main publication in Arabic.[16] This was largely ignored. During a planning meeting in Oran, one of the younger activists passionately asserted – in reaction to negative responses from the authorities and the accusation that they were protecting colonial vestiges – that Oran was 'our city' and was formed by different external influences. He pointed out the contradiction that the authorities, like much of the population of Oran, spoke the language of colonisation, while simultaneously rejecting it. Why should they not value all the different cultures, he asked, which make up the richness of the city? As a francophone organisation, moreover, the association has enjoyed easier access to international funding from the EU and other donors such as the French Embassy and the Cervantes Institute, who issue their funding calls predominantly in French and who have been increasingly targeting the heritage sector. This is much less the case for mainly Arabic-speaking associations further south, such as the Association Rostomid Artisanat or the Association Salaam el Akbar, both in Tiaret,[17] and which, given the challenges of writing or translating all documents into French for an international donor, felt it unrealistic to even try, looking rather for small grants from regional state institutions. Bel Horizon networks with other heritage associations around the Mediterranean, including exchanges with organisations from Spain and France, such as members of the French funded *Programme Concerté Pluri-Acteurs* (PCPA) network. Funding from EU programmes has enabled the association to purchase technical equipment and material and to widen its funding sources.

Formal and informal networks exist, bringing associations working in the heritage sector together, primarily from neighbouring *wilayas*. Bel Horizon is a lead actor in these networks, encouraging other heritage associations to take ownership of historical narratives which help to define Algeria. Benramdane writes that Bel Horizon and the similar association Santé Sidi El Houari work closely with the authorities, providing expertise as well as volunteers and professionalising the sector. He describes how Santé Sidi El Houari even set up a training school for restoration work, which the Ministry of Culture subsequently proposed as a national pilot.[18] The organisations and their members challenge state narratives, participate in local government and encourage young people to engage in a more constructive political debate. Wylie writes of Bel Horizon:

> What it rejects is an authoritarian vision of the world, one that refuses to accept cultural sharing as normal. Bel Horizon, in short, is acknowledging that architecture, like music, has enormous power to express, and to shape, who people think they are and what they believe in.[19]

Promoting more inclusive, open identities, Bel Horizon seeks recognition of the country's cultural diversity through promoting a much wider conception of the country's past. McDougall describes the need, in twenty-first century Algeria, for a space 'creating new, and freer, histories'.[20] Through their daily activities, heritage associations such as Bel Horizon, as well as Castellum and APPAT described below, aim to create such a space for reflection on history and the state's and society's role in preserving it and incorporating it into enabling narratives of identity. Bel Horizon, through its significant public support and legitimacy, appears to have secured this space, at least in the short term and within the city of Oran.

Preserving Roman History in Algeria

The association 'Castellum Tingitanum' was named after the Roman town previously standing on the site of current day Chlef, in the west of Algeria. The decision to take a Roman name was symbolic at different levels. The French colonial conquest in the nineteenth century had specifically drawn on the Roman history in Africa to organise and then justify its invasion of Algeria. The colonial project sought to perpetuate a Western tradition of Roman civilisation in French Algeria; the meshing together of Rome and France was presented as 'different stages of the same oeuvre'.[21] Using a manufactured memory of the grandeur of the Roman Empire in North Africa, and France's colonial conquest as its logical continuation, Lorcin writes that the French could then be framed as the 'true masters' of an area destined for colonisation.[22] The marginalisation of the Arabs and Berbers, their presence and culture, was achieved through the idea of 'a modern "Latin Africa" as a continuation of an ancient Roman Africa' and this, she writes, 'fed into the Eurocentric imperial narratives of the *mission civlisatrice*'.[23] In the decolonisation period, the works of Taoufik El Madani were important in directly countering this narrative, particularly his re-framing of history, presenting Carthage as the enlightened North African power and Rome as the barbarian invader.[24] This narrative was strongly taken up by the FLN, and whilst the Roman ruins of Tipaza, Djamila and Timgad were state-run, there was no great interest in their preservation.

Yet increasingly over time, local associations began to question the manipulations of Roman history and the state's subsequent neglect of the significant Roman and other heritage sites in different locations across Algeria. The organisation Castellum was one of these. Set up by the current president (a journalist and businessman committed to working for the protection of the region's heritage) in April 2001 during Algerian heritage month, it had the goal of identifying, codifying and then restoring all the cultural and historic heritage sites of the region of Chlef. It was as a journalist himself, in the early 2000s, that the founder had felt a certain responsibility to protect the heritage of the region and had been upset by the lack of interest or care in maintaining sites which he considered important to the Algerian collective memory.

In cooperation with the museum of Chlef, the association began to collect ancient texts, documents, geographical maps, postcards, etc., in order to set up and develop a database of local heritage sites. The goal of this work is to include the sites in international classifications such as that of UNESCO and to then gain recognition at local, national and international levels, so as to carry out restoration work. The association carried out an exhaustive census and audit of all historical vestiges, sites, objects and ruins across the region. These include artefacts from the prehistoric, Phoenician, Roman, Islamo-mauresque and colonial periods. The members have also implemented communication strategies and awareness campaigns aimed at local authorities and the general population concerning the degradation of the sites and have organised visits and debates with professionals, to launch restoration programmes. The association also carries out education initiatives for young people to raise awareness about the importance of the historical sites around them. Excursions and creative activities such as photography competitions are organised for school children of all ages. Its website now details all sites of historical interest and concern across the region and identifies the progress made in ensuring their protection.[25]

The association received limited financial support from local sources and functioned mainly through the personal commitment of the team until an EU grant allowed it to develop the work significantly in 2008. To receive European funds to preserve Roman heritage in Algeria might have created some antagonism from the state, but this was conveniently followed soon after by support from Sonatrach, the national energy company, whose partnership was necessary in order to co-finance the EU-funded activity. The president himself admitted to a degree of real surprise at the success he encountered in 2008, when the association's work truly took off. For him, this was due to the dynamism of a number of the younger members, experienced in the communications sector, who enjoyed designing and implementing the visibility materials and generating publicity for events. Others were more interested in the restoration work, and, as a team, the overall impact was much greater due to this successful cooperation and communication. The practical work is cyclical and has slowed down to some extent, but the database is protected within the association and publically available via the website. The work of protection and restoration is, however, still ongoing and the need for this work remains significant. The association has carried out the first important steps: those of identification and recording, and continues to work with different actors on issues of protection.

Relations with the authorities appear to be relatively smooth and cooperative. In many ways this would seem to be due to the respect for the person and position of the president as a successful entrepreneur in the community. Decisions are taken mainly at his level, but younger members propose new ideas which are often implemented. The levels of self-confidence of the younger volunteers therefore appear to have risen. Equally, all members' knowledge about public affairs, the role of the state, local authorities and associations in the protection of national heritage has increased. This is due to the practical role of the association in the public sphere and also to networking activities and participation in training initiatives, alongside other associations in neighbouring regions, such as those launched by APPAT in Tiaret.

Algeria's Archaeological Past

The wealth of Algeria's archeological past, from pre-history to the preserved Roman sites and cities such as Tipaza and Djemila, has been widely acknowledged to be unique in the region and in terms of world heritage. The steppe region of Tiaret is known for its numerous heritage sites, including a necropole dating back six millennia. The ancient tombs of the 13 impressive 'Djeddar' monuments date back two millennia to the rule of the Berber Kings of North Africa. Near to the city of Tiaret, the neighbouring town of Frenda is the location of the cave used by the philosopher Ibn Khaldun to write one of social science's most important historic works, *The Muqaddimah, An Introduction to History*, in the fourteenth century. The region also hosts the site of Tihert, from which the Rostomid dynasty ruled from AD 761. Tihert became the capital of the most important kingdom in the Maghreb. The site of Tagdempt, another state capital, under the Emir Abd el-Kader in the nineteenth century, was the military, political, economic and cultural capital of Algeria for seven years from 1835 to 1841.[26] As one of the most important protagonists of the resistance struggle against colonial invasion, the Emir has particular symbolic importance for Algerian nationalist history. The ruins of the Emir's house are still visible, as are the sites where gunpowder was made and the first coins of the Algerian state were minted. More recent is the *Jumenterie*, the largest stud farm in North Africa, dating from the mid-nineteenth century (the colonial period) and still an important site for horse breeding today.

The 1990s were difficult for citizens of the region of Tiaret. This was particularly so in rural areas, which were the targets of extreme violence by Islamist insurgents, resulting in a mass exodus towards the main city. Kidnappings, bomb explosions, false police barricades, executions and requisitioning of farms and produce were regular occurrences. Far from the capital, with imposed curfews and weakened state security structures, the citizens of the region suffered intensely. To leave one's house was seen as an act of bravery; to venture into the surrounding countryside to explore abandoned ruins in an effort to protect the Algerian heritage and culture, which many felt was under direct threat from the obscurantist extremist ideology, was both a political and personal act of genuine courage.

Working to protect and value all the sites described above, a local heritage association, the Association for the Protection of the Archaeological Heritage of Tiaret (APPAT), was created in 1992, thanks to the will and dynamism of a retired teacher who became its president. The APPAT organisation registered as a regional association with the *wilaya* of Tiaret. Over the last 20 years, APPAT sought to identify and list all the archaeological sites of the region. Four hundred and fifty-two monuments were listed, of which five were subsequently classified by the Algerian state as national heritage sites.[27] The members of APPAT were passionate about the heritage of their region, but felt that knowledge about the importance of these sites was insufficient amongst the local population and amongst Algerians generally. This was also the case for the state, it seemed, as even sites of symbolic importance to the Algerian state were left unpreserved. Weaknesses in state structures, the years of violence and limited awareness at all levels of society had led to many of the sites being neglected. The association carried out civic education amongst the population, for visitors to the region and in schools, it and trained local guides to ensure that these sites gained the necessary protection and were accorded a place within Algeria's national heritage.[28]

With a small grant from the European Union in 2008, APPAT launched a regional network of heritage actors to coordinate approaches and to develop joint training programmes with other associations on legislation relating to, and methods of identifying and preserving, historic sites. They initiated a new training programme for university students seeking to work in the tourism, heritage and archaeological sectors. Trained as heritage guides, and in methods of conservation, the trainees were sent to different sites across the region to learn about their history and about guiding techniques. With help from a former director from the Ministry of Culture, the association worked with other heritage organisations in the west of Algeria to complete a common database of sites around the region, from prehistory to the present day. In collaboration with the Chamber of Commerce, discussions were launched with a view to developing a comprehensive distance learning diploma for young people.

Concerning relations with regional government authorities, when interviewed in 2011 the president of the association felt these to be positive, although this perception was later to change. The authorities maintained regular contact with the association and if any ruins or archaeological sites were discovered, they were the first organisation to be consulted. Relations with local authorities were generally good, thanks above all to personal support from the director of the Chamber of Commerce, who had given much of his personal time and commitment to helping this association and others. Clearly, personal relations matter but funding, he noted, was still an issue.

The association had been lobbying local government authorities for a museum to promote the history and archaeological wealth of the region. This request had been turned down. They were then surprised to learn that the region was planning to inaugurate a museum commemorating the Moudjahid and the history of the Algerian War of Independence funded by the Ministry dedicated to that cause. As in Oran, there is a sensitive debate between the state and associations concerning the representation of history and national heritage. That said, state narratives of national identity are not necessarily always even in conflict with those of individuals and associations who seek to promote their histories, monuments and traditions. In Tiaret, the state's previous neglect encompasses *all* heritage sites, including those which would seem to be of key importance to its own perception of Algeria's national identity. For example, the association was keen to protect sites of importance to the nationalist struggle, including the site from which the Emir Abd el-Kader launched the rebellion against the colonial invasion in the nineteenth century. The state's antagonistic responses to its requests for help with this might well have been a result of its recognition that it had failed to recognise the importance of protecting a site marking a significant moment in the history of anti-colonial resistance, or its inability to do so in a context of violence and insecurity, or that it resented a small association willing and brave enough to take up that challenge. Indeed, state heritage services, at regional level, had themselves been frustrated by a lack of training, a lack of security, a lack of direction from the Ministry of Culture and rigid, hierarchical decision-making structures. These factors had been compounded by the traumas of the 1990s. Associations such as APPAT had been filling the gaps, providing new solutions to promote Algeria's heritage and insisting on broader historical narratives to include all the periods which had played a part in the *wilaya's* history. This included the nationalist struggle and Islamic heritage but also pre-history and colonial history, recognition of which, they felt, could enrich the life of the city of Tiaret and its citizens.

APPAT had managed to achieve the first steps towards recognition of this broader, more inclusive history by taking a constructive approach rather than an oppositional one. With limited means, the organisation received popular support and was recognised by state institutions for its work on the region's heritage. However, in 2014 the association suffered a complete breakdown in relations with regional authorities. Banned from holding a high-level conference on Berber history at the Ibn Khaldun University in Tiaret in 2013 with guest speaker Jean Pierre Laporte – an expert on North African history – the association was targeted by the authorities and prevented from working by accusations and administrative obstacles, for no apparent or communicated reason.[29] Not dissimilar to the experiences of other previously successful associations across the country, the debate about history, access to the public sphere, and the capacity to speak about and represent Algerians and their history remain highly contested domains and often difficult ones for associations. Since 2014, severely demoralised, the association's future has been unclear, as the detailed work of restoration and classification of the region's archeological heritage slowed down. The future of associational autonomy and the limits within which the state will allow associations to function and act as ambassadors for Algerian heritage remains a fine line to be negotiated by the different organisations and state actors.

Religious Heritage and Traditions

Another important area of Algerian cultural and religious heritage is found in its ancient manuscripts, which are conserved in places such as the National Library in Algiers, and in private and family collections across the country.[30] What is now Algeria has traditionally been a crossroads for intellectual life, ideas and learning in North Africa. This explains the abundance of these important religious manuscripts held in Algeria today by state institutions and private families, although the existence of the manuscripts held in private homes is little known both inside and outside of Algeria. Across the Muslim world in the seventeenth and eighteenth centuries, the growing Sufi brotherhoods, the *zawiyas*, had sought to communicate with remote, rural, often illiterate communities. The vernacular, *darija*, was used to take Islam and its spirituality to the countryside, mainly through mystical poems written in a language the people there could understand. Levtzion explains that:

> The need to write down oral mystical poetry in folk idioms arose also with the growth in scale of the brotherhoods, whose leaders sought to communicate with affiliates living in remote communities. Poems in the vernaculars, which had earlier been transmitted and recited orally, were committed to writing in the Arabic script, and copies of the written texts were sent out to the literate representatives of the *shaykh* in different localities who then recited these texts to an illiterate audience.[31]

In her detailed ethnographic research carried out in two regions of Algeria, Scheele describes the complex processes involved in the current desire to conserve and to promote the value of these manuscripts across Algeria, together with the resulting tensions between different groups, associations, families and the state. She explores the work of two heritage associations in Kabylia (*Groupe d'études sur l'histoire des mathématiques à Béjaïa* – GEHIMAB) and Adrar (*Association des recherches et études historiques de la région d'Adrar*), both concerned with protecting religious manuscripts. She describes how the protection of this particular religious heritage stirs up conflict over political and social legitimacy, and notes,

> The sudden revival of interest in manuscript collections that occurred from the mid-1990s onwards was thus not an isolated occurrence, but part of a larger 'rediscovery' of Algeria's long-neglected intellectual and religious heritage, and of ongoing conflicts over social and political legitimacy between central government and local actors.[32]

Scheele feels that the challenges around the conservation of these manuscripts relate not to technical capacity, nor to the colonial destruction of Algerian culture, but more to the 'problematic relationship that many contemporary Algerians maintain with their history and with local traditions of knowledge and scholarship.'[33] Written in the vernacular Arabic, rather than classical Arabic, it is the language of these texts that raised problems for both organisations that Scheele explores, given the strong focus primarily on Berber identity and language in Kabylia and the devalued place of Algerian Arabic in much of the country. In the Kabyle case, the GEHIMAB association was able to use external support from the Canadian Embassy to gain local legitimacy and it avoided conflict by maintaining the manuscripts in the local vicinity. In southern Algeria, the case of the historical research association of Adrar was more complex. Their ambitious project to create a centre for the conservation of manuscripts, involving state funding and an institutional structure, thus added to local conflicts, and to mistrust and insecurity over the value and rightful place of that heritage. The history of the Sufi brotherhoods in Algeria, and the double attack on them – first by colonialism and later by reformist orthodox Islam of the nationalist movement – meant that the legitimacy of many of the families who were descendants of the sheikhs and scholars who wrote the manuscripts had been damaged. Local Islam as represented by the *zawiyas* came to be seen as 'morally tainted' and inferior to the orthodox Islam of the Middle East, although the strength of such discourses still varies across regions of Algeria. Direct physical and verbal attacks on the *zawiyas* during the violence of the 1990s presented a further barrier to the valuing of the heritage they reclaimed and actively preserved.

Yet, increasingly, certain associations have managed to overcome these multiple obstacles to conserving manuscripts. With the place of the *zawiyas* increasingly recognised in the political sphere, and the current president's known affinity with them, practical solutions have been drawn up by associations, perhaps more successfully than those of state institutions. Ignoring divisions and problems of language or identity, some associations have sought simply to conserve the manuscripts and explain their importance in the public sphere. One such association in the M'Zab, Ibadite region of Algeria, is the *Association Abou Ishak Ibrahim Tefayech pour le Service du Patrimoine*. Since 2007, this local association has been involved in a technical project working with three local libraries to digitalise and conserve over 1000 manuscripts as part of a larger project to protect all religious manuscripts in the M'Zab region of the country. Funded initially by a small grant from the European Union and local contributions, their project honours primarily the memory of the Ibadite Sheikh M'Hammed Ben Youcef Ben Aïssa Tefayech, who was born in Ghardaia in 1821 and died in 1914 in Beni Isguen.[34] Self-taught, he acquired and transcribed many religious manuscripts, purchased whole libraries and dedicated much of his life to the education of others, receiving students from across the region and writing more than 300 manuscripts himself. In addition, the partner libraries also hold manuscripts from religious scholars coming from different sects and ethnic groups, including Ibadite and non-Ibadite sheikhs. At present, the association has managed to successfully conserve all these manuscripts in an inclusive manner, compiling them in digital format. It has trained young people from the region in conservation techniques, as well as launching a discussion on the intrinsic value of the documents themselves. As such, the association has managed to avoid conflict, both within the community and with state structures, by presenting a predominantly technical project that is also inclusive, aimed at preserving one part of a common, traditional, religious heritage of Algeria.

Conclusion

In their work with tangible historical monuments and objects, and also with the intangible heritage enshrined in living cultural expressions and traditions, heritage associations have dealt with questions of identity, language, moral convictions. They have also mediated state–society relations, whilst conserving Algeria's national history. This is a history which spans the Berber, Roman, Jewish, Arab, Muslim, Ottoman and European cultural heritage of the country. Conflicts in this sector seem to emanate, however, less from a contested idea of the Algerian nation and more from competition between state actors and civil society organisations over who has the right and the skills to represent, conserve and provide a voice for Algerians in their collective memory. Lloyd writes that the concept of civil society itself needs to be wide enough to encompass such conflicts, not only with the state but also with regard to religion, gender and ideological power structures.[35]

She laments that too much focus on violence and conflict has 'obscured the courageous resistances involved in Algerian civil society'.[36] McDougall also challenges the endless clichés of 'fury' and 'revenge', arguing for 'a critical exploration of the relationship between forms of historical self-perception, Islamic culture and the nationalist struggle in colonial Algeria'.[37]

Through associative networks, such as those maintained by Bel Horizon in Algeria and across the Mediterranean, social actors can resist oppression 'and formulate new social visions'.[38] In the Algerian case, specifically, with exile after the War of Independence and more recent migration during the 1990s, the boundaries of the nation state have become increasingly blurred. With the changing profile of migrants in recent decades, Algerian associations are increasingly able to operate beyond the borders of the country and Algerian associations in France are able to contribute to the debate within Algeria.[39] Due to the immense disparities in the means available to conserve, revive and restore Algerian culture and heritage, civil society actors have had to negotiate with external actors like the EU to gain technical and financial support, and they are increasingly Mediterranean and transnational in their outlook. They are also more strongly connected with local populations, who are keen to support hard working associations if they see results. This contrasts starkly with the immense means of the state, gained from the windfall oil wealth, and its limited capacity to manage such budgets and to connect with the Algerian population.

Heritage associations continue to play an important if sensitive role in Algeria, as intermediaries between the state, international actors and the population for the protection of Algeria's past. Negotiating with state actors about how to preserve history, they are at the same time developing their technical, diplomatic and political expertise. Some associations expressly include state actors in their training and education campaigns, restoring trust between the state and civil society. Overcoming conflicts such as those experienced by Bel Horizon, and more severely by APPAT, is part of a drawn-out process in the revival of Algerian civil society which challenges and negotiates with state actors for a voice within the public sphere.

CHAPTER 7

ALGERIAN ASSOCIATIONS AND SOCIAL WELFARE

Upon independence, Algeria's health and welfare system was almost inexistent and there were only 300 doctors across the whole country.[1] Health was a major priority for post-independence governments and huge progress was made. By 1990 there were 23,000 and by 2010, 41,000 doctors, according to WHO figures. Life expectancy in Algeria now stands at 75 years. Health care spending has increased as a percentage of GDP, the government having invested significantly in the health and social sectors. Ensuring the quality of the services, however, as well the improving the infrastructure, is an ongoing challenge. Human resources, equipment and medical supplies are still often insufficient. Algeria is working with the EU and the WHO to modernise the health sector; however, there is criticism about poor-quality services, notably in hospitals, which leads well-off Algerians to use private health clinics or to travel abroad. In 2014, the Algerian human rights NGO LADDH criticised the fact that about 24 per cent of the population lived below the poverty line. In 2015, they estimated this to have risen to 35 per cent. With the crash in energy prices, the weakened economy and the resulting austerity measures impacted heavily on the population. The 2017 Finance Bill was again heavily criticised for its austerity measures, although social sectors were supposed to be protected from cuts.

In Algeria, as elsewhere, associations often emerge to fill the gaps that the state's social services are unable to fill, caring for vulnerable sections of the population. Their importance is high for the families and communities which depend upon them. However, there is also much potential for conflict or competition with a state which sees its role from an all-encompassing perspective and brooks little criticism in certain areas such as the role of the security services in the violence of the 1990s. Such criticism is punishable by law. Associations working on social welfare, in contrast to the heritage associations, are often created to deal with personal grievances affecting a family or a community, for which the existing solutions are either inadequate or non-existent. Many members of the social associations interviewed, although not all, had a family member suffering from a particular illness or disability which was supported by the association. Associations were also at the front line in supporting victims of trauma and injustice from the 1990s conflict. Organisations such as *Djazairouna*, for the families of the disappeared, offered very practical support to those who had lost their loved ones. The Boucebci Foundation, which commemorated Professor Boucebci, assassinated by insurgents in 1993, counselled over 1000 children a year and offered workshops and family therapy to all victims of violence who came to its centre in Algiers.

Social sector associations make up a huge proportion of associational life in Algeria. They provide services to the population and also work with the state, critically engaging with the authorities about the quality of social care and support to vulnerable populations. They play a role in bringing people together around questions of rights and social justice. In providing services, they are often negotiating the parameters of their responsibilities with those of the authorities. The following pages provide an overview of social associations across Algeria, and then specific cases illustrate the work they carry out on the ground.

Social Sector Associations in Algeria

According to the Ministry of Interior's figures, associations involved in social work are classed under the following criteria: children, youth, disability, retired persons and the elderly, health, social solidarity and humanitarian organisations. At the local level, it seems relevant also to include religious associations, which represent 16 per cent of the total and which often carry out important charitable health and education work. Combining these figures, it can be seen that roughly a quarter of the total registered associations in Algeria, at both national and local levels, deal with some aspect of social policy or work. At the local level, there are 20,178 associations that have been created to work in fields related to the social sector (if we include all religious associations). This represents 22 per cent of the total number of associations in the country, as represented in Table 7.1.

At the national level, there are 269 associations that have been created in order to work in fields related to the social sector. This represents 27 per cent of the total number of national associations in the country, as represented in Table 7.2.

The above figures are demonstrated in Figure 7.1.

Such figures are not always easy to interpret. For those 'active' associations from Omar Derras' study, which were directly asked to define their sector, an even higher figure of 47 per cent saw themselves as working in the social sector. The Law on Associations does allow associations to work in the social sector, to receive public grants for works of public interest and to acquire goods and property in order to implement their goals. Furthermore, many of the associations working with disabled children received the *prix journalier*, a daily payment from the CNAS, the national insurance scheme. This is a state contribution of 300 dinars, or around three dollars, per child who receives full daycare from an association. Such support is in recognition of the work of the association and the fact that the national education system does not then

Table 7.1 Local social sector associations.

Sectors of local social associations	Number	% of total local associations
Religious	15,304	16.0
Childhood and youth	2,677	3.0
Disability	1,234	1.0
Retired and elderly	152	0.2
Health	644	1.0
Humanitarian	167	0.2
Total	20,178	21.4

Source: Figures taken from the Ministry of Interior website dated 31/12/2011 (consulted on 29/10/2015). For most recent figures see www.interieur.gov.dz/images/pdf/Thematiquedesassociations.pdf.

Table 7.2 National social sector associations.

Sectors of national social associations	Number	Percentage of total national associations
Childhood and adolescence	14	1.0
Youth	50	5.0
Disability	18	2.0
Retired and elderly	8	1.0
Health	151	15.0
Solidarity – humanitarian	28	3.0
Total	269	27.0

Source: Figures taken from the Ministry of Interior website dated 31/12/2011 (consulted on 29/10/2015). For most recent figures see www.interieur.gov.dz/images/pdf/Thematiquedesassociations.pdf.

provide for that child. This appears to represent, in a way, national recognition of the organisation as a professional, qualified service provider. Not all associations working in the disability sector received this, which was a source of contention; some claiming that the selection criteria are not systematically applied across the country.[2]

In terms of the regional distribution of social sector associations, as for the cultural ones, the south once again figured most prominently in the number of those registered. Yet the more northern urbanised regions

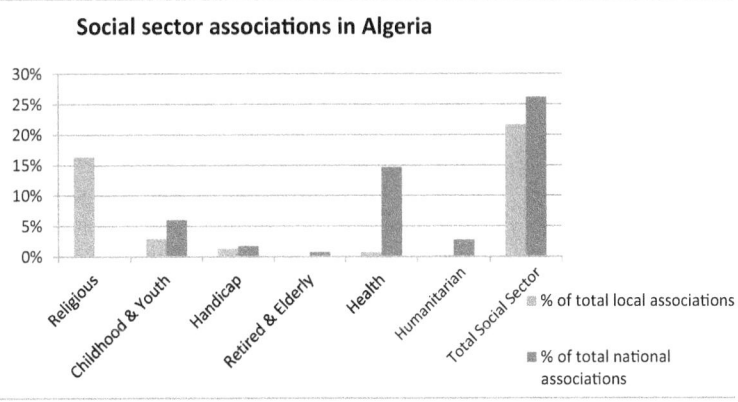

Figure 7.1 Social associations in Algeria.

of Saida and Bordj Bou Arreridj also figured amongst the densest regions in terms of social sector associations. The ten regions with the most per population, according to the Ministry's figures, are shown in Table 7.3. This can also be seen in Figure 7.2.

The regions with the lowest densities of social associations were Tiaret, Blida, Annaba and Oran and the lowest, once again, was Relizane. However, the following case studies show that these figures do not necessarily reflect the quality of the work carried out by social associations in these regions, with Oran having particularly active organisations.

The importance of social associations to the populations they serve often depends on whether the latter look to such organisations for support for vulnerable members of a family. Personal experiences often guided individual judgments as to the utility and relevance of such associations to people's lives. There were also very varied perceptions from state officials about these associations, often depending upon specific experiences of cooperation. Social associations were significant not only in the services they provided, but also in that they represented

Table 7.3 Association density – social associations per 100,000 inhabitants (ten densest regions).

Wilaya	Social associations	Population	Number of social associations per 100,000 inhabitants (ten regions with highest density)
Illizi	128	52,333	245
Adrar	710	399,714	178
Tamanrasset	297	176,637	168
Naama	262	192,891	136
Saida	429	330,641	130
Bordj Bou Arreridj	732	628,475	116
El Oued	739	647,548	114
Ghardaïa	411	363,598	113
Tizi Ouzou	1169	1,127,607	104
Bejaia	922	912,577	101

ALGERIAN ASSOCIATIONS AND SOCIAL WELFARE 143

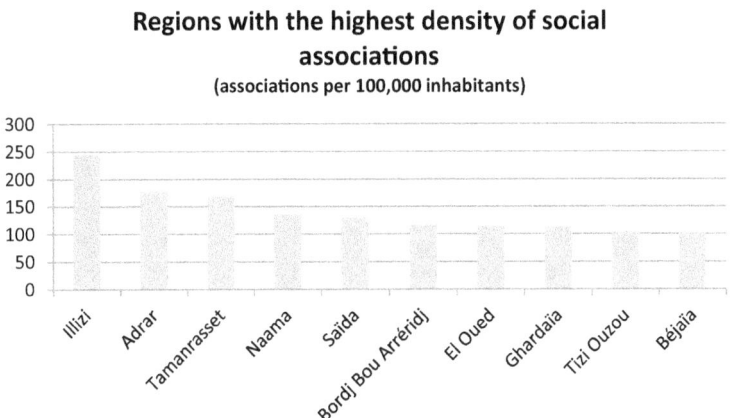

Figure 7.2 Regions with most social associations per capita.

channels for the exchange of information between the state and the population. Whilst this relationship remains strained and sometimes competitive, a complex process of recognition by the state was seen to be ongoing. The Social Development Agency, for example, was slowly developing tools to integrate associations into the work of its regional branches and to cooperate in the provision of social services. The fact that the national insurance scheme finances the running costs of certain associations taking care of disabled children was also a step in formalising a more cooperative relationship. The following case studies describe the work of a number of social sector associations working in different regions across Algeria – in Oran, Tizi Ouzou, El Oued and Algiers. The associations' leaders, staff and members were interviewed on several occasions between 2009 and 2016. During visits to the associations to observe their work, and in follow-up communication, discussions included aspects about their relationships with the population, with other associations and with the state.

Social Work, Disability and New Voices in Oran

The association *Nour*, for children with cerebral palsy, was set up in Oran in the year 2000. It is managed by the parents of a child suffering from this condition. Well-educated, francophone and similar to many

Algerians, these parents had significant connections in France. During their travels they had witnessed the achievements of different associations in France that helped children with cerebral palsy. From this experience, they decided there was no reason why this could not be replicated in their home city of Oran. Commencing with two children in 2000, by 2012 they were caring for 80 children daily in two centres. Association *Nour* was made up of the children, their parents, the board and the professional staff. The children participated in different workshops, including painting, pottery, craftwork and music, developing different skills with the help of staff members. Outlining the regular activities of the association, and its progression over the last decade, the president described her usual daily programme:

> We now manage two programmes in Oran with 39 children and 46 adolescents in daily workshops. Each centre has a head of the centre, a psychologist and facilitators. We begin work at 7.30 in the morning, opening the first centre, then we move on to the second. We are volunteers and we manage all the administrative side. The other members of the team here are professionals and so are paid a salary. There is now a waiting list of 50 children. We look after them for free. The parents have very little means.[3]

The association functioned with the financial support of the Algerian social insurance scheme, which paid the daily grant per child of 300 dinars. This ensured reasonable salaries for the staff. The president was keen that all staff be well treated in order to retain them within the association over the long term. In discussions, the association's members felt it was highly justified that the state should contribute to covering the basic running costs – through the daily grant – as the association took on this particularly difficult task. *Nour's* children attending the centres, they felt, were the responsibility of the Algerian state and education system, to which they were denied access by their disability. The board applied for project finance from various donors to renew the equipment and to implement training programmes both for the staff and for the parents in how to care for the children.

At the time of the interviews, *Nour* was the only structure in Oran caring for children with cerebral palsy. For the association's leaders, it was unthinkable that they should stop their activities. It was also highly important that the state supported them and that they in turn worked cooperatively with the state. The president pointed out:

> Cerebral palsy is often related to problems in the medical follow up during pregnancy. It is therefore linked to the health care system. It is an issue which therefore falls within the responsibility of the state. These children are the responsibility of the state, the state must do its best to take care of them and support us in this task.[4]

Concerning their interactions with state institutions, the association's leaders were of the opinion that, despite seeking to work for the general interest of the Algerian population, associations in the past were continuously blocked. For them, the changes brought in by the 1990 law significantly improved the situation. Associations in the social sector had hoped that changes in the legislation in 2012 would lead to yet greater recognition of the status of a 'public interest' organisation, with greater support from the state. This sadly did not materialise. Relations with the authorities were not always smooth, especially regarding the association's choosing to work with the EU in the early 2000s. However, the fact that the EU chose to implement its next programme in collaboration with the Algerian authorities very much facilitated the work for *Nour*. According to the president, there was less distrust the second time around.

The implementation of a number of projects since the association was set up in 2000 has helped to structure it in terms of financial management, communication and professional support for the children, their parents and teachers. Furthermore, common training programmes have helped to reinforce exchanges and networks between different actors in the region, and in the sector:

> the training programmes have put us into local and national networks of organisations working on the same sector. Today there are links which exist. It is also possible to have a debate about the new legislation proposals, because we now know the other associations.[5]

For *Nour*, its relationship with the state improved due to efforts on both sides. On the part of *Nour*, this effort consisted of lobbying, awareness raising and networking carried out to advance its cause within state structures. Increasingly, the association reached out to the administration. Civil servants were invited to their training programmes, which were now well respected by state and civil society organisations and seen as innovative. There was, on the state's side, an opening up towards the association, despite certain competitive tendencies persisting. According to *Nour*, associations need to 'manage relations' with the state but also 'to strive to be a source of new ideas, initiatives and proposals', as the president argued.[6]

According to the association's leaders, a less critical and more structured, coordinated approach would better serve the interests of vulnerable populations and lead to a more effective civil society. This was difficult, they felt, as certain subjects remained difficult for Algerian society. There were a number of opportunities for associations to work together in networks, such as the French-supported PCPA, the women's network WASSILA or the NADA network for children and youth organisations. The president felt that, whilst useful, these networks were not functioning as well as they might. Associations with heavy workloads on the ground often did not have the time to participate. Despite being very busy, *Nour* was present in a number of networks. Handicap International provided them specific support and the PCPA provided a national framework in which social associations could come together. NADA, the network of associations working with children, was also an opportunity to exchange information, even if members did not agree on all aspects. The president of *Nour* had been voted onto the board of the French cooperation's PCPA network of Algerian associations. This was a position of prestige and involved her travelling to Algiers to represent the other associations of the region in board meetings, alongside delegates from across Algeria. This had enabled the association to have an insight into the national vision of the role and potential of the associative movement. From this perspective, she felt that associations were 'not even aware of the importance they have'. Whilst it is easy to get absorbed in the daily activity of the association, the president acknowledged that at the same time 'we now realize that we have all actually gained financial support, knowledge, training, and ideas. Now, for networks to develop there needs to be a real desire to work together'.[7] Overall, the association felt that a constructive approach was necessary. The political situation in Algeria was still fragile and *Nour*, as an association, had no desire to destabilise or create controversy. The main goal was to be able to continue the work with vulnerable populations in Oran. Apart from that, there was always the hope that the political and legal framework within which social associations worked would develop in a way that could encourage greater cooperation in the future.

Contesting State Provision in Kabylia

The association for the parents of disabled children in Tizi Ouzou was created in 2007 to provide a space, education and support for children and young people with mental and physical health disabilities. It was situated on the outskirts of the capital, in a relatively poor *quartier* of the *wilaya*. The founding members had little experience of associational life prior to this. They were parents of disabled children who suffered from the absence of structures to effectively care for their children in the region. The organisation was set up mainly through the inspiration, hard work and dynamism of the president, a carpenter and also a parent of a disabled child. After slowly building up the capacity of the association over a number of years with limited means, by 2012 the association was taking care of 72 children and young people from Tizi Ouzou with different degrees of disability. The education authorities had given the association an old school on the outskirts of Tizi Ouzou in which it had set up a carpentry workshop as well as formal education classes. The conditions were basic but the work was clearly carried out with great commitment and kindness towards the children in their care.

Describing the functioning and financing of the association and the relationship with regional authorities, the president explained the difficulties they faced and his anger at the lack of support:

> It is difficult to function with the means we have. We are not recognized as a centre, just as an association. We receive the daily grant from the state of 300 dinars per child, but this does not cover our running costs as we need a number of specialized staff to care for the children. We visited the Social Development Agency but promises of support do not seem to become reality. Not one member of the regional office of the agency, nor anyone from the wilaya, has been to visit us to see the work we carry out.[8]

Building on their experience of allowing young adults to participate in income-generating activities, the association set up a workshop in 2008 with a small grant from the EU. The workshop continued to function four years on, at the time of interviews, and the president and his team had different ideas as to how to further develop the work and care of the beneficiaries. Despite serious financial difficulties, the work still continues. The association's activities appeared to function well and were appreciated by the children and their parents. All energies were invested into the daily functioning of the centre, which was split between two localities: the carpentry workshop and, a few hundred metres away, the formal classes in part of the old school.

Despite their experience, the association's leaders felt they did not have time, between their own working lives and voluntary commitment to the association, to participate in wider debates or networks related to issues of disability. They preferred to invest time within the centre, trying to engage with the authorities to ensure its sustainability and quality of care of the children. The president was critical of state run centres. He indicated that:

> Our work functions as well as, if not better than the state run centres, with fewer means. This is because we are a family for these children. I am here because of my personal commitment as a parent of a disabled child. I am not specialized in a social sector but I want to learn.[9]

From the state, they sought not only financial support, but professional advice, training and support which they did not feel to be forthcoming. The association's members argued that they would like to see a more collaborative approach, from both the state and donors who only rarely visited associations which received grants in Tizi Ouzou. They questioned whether either state or donor ever really carried out any follow-up or evaluation of the support given to associations.

The association's members felt that, despite limitations, there had been achievements since its creation in 2007. A number of other associations in the region also now worked in the disability sector. However, they worried that children's needs were far greater than the services offered by both the state and associations. Many children could not be taken care of due to the lack of space and facilities. A greater capacity to respond to these needs was essential. For them, this was both 'a moral obligation and clearly feasible!' given the means available in Algeria. Better care for these children, specialised staff, training and greater cooperation between the state and associations was urgently needed across the country.

Associations, Faith and Health Care in El Oued

Health association *Tej pour la santé* was created in 2005 by a group of health care professionals, doctors and paramedics. They wanted to deal with the lack of health services for poorer sections of the community, particularly for nomadic populations and for those suffering from a disability. The association was based in the town of Guemar, in El Oued province in the east of Algeria and near the Tunisian border. Guemar is a Saharan oasis town. The population targeted by the association included many nomadic communities who travelled across the province of El Oued, and who were often unable to access health facilities.

The reasons behind the creation of *Tej* were in line with the religious, Islamic convictions of the founders. Much of the support came from donations through the religious obligation of all Muslims to give alms, *zakat*, and these were often from anonymous benefactors. The goals of the association were to help those in need who were sick, to offer medical training and to organise awareness campaigns about health issues, particularly for those with limited access to health care and information. *Tej* means 'crown' in Arabic, and the motto of the association was established from the popular saying that 'health is a crown upon the heads of the healthy, only visible to those who are sick'. The orgainisation was managed by volunteer doctors and paramedical staff, who were the key members. There were also a small number of professional staff, paid by the association to manage the centres and a number of permanent activities and services provided by *Tej*. Non-qualified volunteers received training so as to effectively contribute to the work of the association.

In terms of its activities, since its creation, the association had organised blood donation campaigns and mobile campaigns for small operations (hernias, cataracts) in the desert; it had delivered psychological support to patients, run medical caravans for communicating about health issues and held a number of training and information days for doctors and paramedical staff in El Oued. It cooperated with other Algerian local and national associations and with Franco-Algerian associations such as SoliMed. Despite key members being mainly Arabic-speaking, the association cooperated with donors such as the EU, the French development cooperation and the Belgian Embassy, which all required documents to be translated into French. It ran a centre for children with hearing difficulties, a pharmacy, a system of support to patients needing medical advice and loans of medical equipment such as wheelchairs. On religious holidays, it orgainised hospital visits and gifts for patients, mainly sick children, in the region of El Oued.

In 2008, *Tej* was proud to be selected amongst the top 25 per cent of associations competing for support from the EU's support programme.[10] It was attributed a contract with a grant of just over 30,000 euros. *Tej* had proposed a project to put in place a centre for deaf children in El Oued, where the children would receive very specific professional care. The centre also included support mechanisms for the integration of deaf children into the education system, information about rights for families, support and training for parents and help to individuals seeking to create associations for the deaf. In this way, they would be able to support the creation of further initiatives and to share *Tej's* experiences.

Speaking at the end of 2011, the president of *Tej* indicated that the association now had good structures in place, with 'a rotating presidency, decided on the basis of elections and decisions are taken in regular meetings of the administrative council. The association now has over a hundred members'. The president described relations with their partners as 'very constructive'. In turn, the Paris-based, Franco-Algerian NGO, SoliMed, described the association as a 'very dynamic, reliable partner and a pleasure to work with'.[11] The regional adviser of the EU-financed support programme described the work and management of the association 'as extremely professional, committed and transparent'.[12] The association pointed out that successful evaluations of its work with deaf children between 2008 and 2009, and the creation of an educational centre for them, led to a positive response from the Belgian co-operation, which then agreed to finance mobile operations to carry out 77 cataract operations across the *wilaya* of El Oued. This was an action of which they were particularly proud. One member explained that, 'it is our proximity campaigns, for which we now have the material and logistical equipment necessary, which really make a difference and are needed by the populations'.[13]

The Association *Tej* had positive and cooperative relations with both secular authorities and religious structures in the region. They indicated that the town hall and regional direction of the Social Development Agency were all supportive of the organisation. The Ministry of Solidarity had promised financial support. According to the association's members, there were gaps in the provision of care for vulnerable populations, particularly the disabled, poor families and nomadic communities. The association believed it had found new, innovative ways to respond to these gaps and provide a more personal response to the problems in the health sector at the regional level, supported by the religious structures of the region. Whilst identifying such gaps in the public sector provision of care, the association did not appear to take a confrontational position against the authorities. The members were less critical than the Association for the Parents of Disabled Children of Tizi Ouzou, discussed above, for example.

Compared to previous social associations, *Tej* differed in that it appeared to be the religious or moral convictions, rather than personal motivations, that drove key actors to create and continue to manage the association. Equally, *Tej* appeared to have both a wider range of activities and a wider support network, receiving financial and material help from both religious and secular sources, foreign and national ones, and making the association less dependent on the state or on any one donor. Its wide support base also avoided any possible suspicions by the authorities of Islamist funding that other associations were sometimes accused of. It was more the proven track record that evoked the interest of the authorities, who promised further funding for the future which was later confirmed and provided. Its members contributed to dialogue with other associations, and with the authorities, to identify opportunities and to cooperate to improve health care in the region.

Dealing with Trauma

Many social associations were born out of the conflict of the 1990s. The intense suffering of the population, the loss of state legitimacy and the common experience of injustice were behind many of the decisions to create associations. National organisations were created, both Islamic and secular, with the aim of caring for and seeking justice for families of the disappeared.[14] Foundations were created to commemorate the politicians, intellectuals and activists who were assassinated. Charitable associations were set up for the psychological care of orphans and families of the victims. Such associations are important in their very existence in that they commemorate and shape the narrative history of Algeria. They equally play a practical role in reconciliation, in a context where the state struggles to do so. The 2005 Reconciliation Charter ruled out many possibilities for truth as part of the reconciliation process in Algeria, and rendered it an offence to criticise the role of the army during the conflict. This opting for compensation rather than truth has been heavily challenged by many Algerian associations.[15]

One such social association set up in the 1990s is the Boucebci Foundation in Algiers. The Foundation commemorates the life and work of internationally renowned psychiatrist Professor Mahfoud Boucebci, who was assassinated by Islamist insurgents in 1993. During his lifetime, Boucebci fought for the rights of those excluded from Algerian society: single mothers, drug addicts, abandoned children and detainees. As a founding member of the Algerian League of Human Rights in 1985, he fought for the respect of basic rights for all in society and for a secular democracy for Algeria. He was highly critical of the intolerant direction of Algerian society and with the rise of Islamism and the rejection of vulnerable groups, but was also critical of the repressive nature of the Algerian regime. He was instrumental in the creation of a number of associations, working for family planning, caring for disabled children and those supporting adoptive families. His assassination was thus a direct attack on Algerian civil society, progressive thinking and freedom of association.

The Boucebci Foundation was set up by his family, his wife and children, in 1993. They waited a year to receive notice of its legal registration and, despite other obstructive measures, have managed to operate over two decades to continue his work and philosophy. At the time of interviews, it had one permanent, paid member of staff, Social Development Agency staff on secondment and 12 psychologists who regularly volunteered. Its aim was to be a multidisciplinary social project; its primary purpose to support child victims of violence.[16] Initially set up to house the library of Professor Boucebci, the family soon realised the gravity of the situation in Algeria, along with the importance of sending out a message of a 'non-violent' Algeria and an alternative to state representations of Islamist violence.[17] Annette Boucebci, Professor Boucebci's widow, was reported in the Algerian press in 2005 as saying, 'when my husband was assassinated, I thought they had succeeded in silencing him. But I soon realised I was wrong, never has a dead man spoken so much through the voice of others'.[18]

The Foundation, its members and the families and friends who created it were horrified by the statement made by Anwar Haddam, the FIS parliamentarian who obtained asylum and who styled himself as the FIS delegation in the US, that the assassination was 'not a crime but a sentence carried out by the mujahidin', a statement he repeated in 2012.[19] They were equally critical of the regime – which they believed may well have been happy to have had Boucebci silenced. At the very least, the state had been negligent in protecting those Algerian intellectuals who were at serious risk. It had also failed in its investigation of the crimes. European and American politicians had equally failed Algeria by harbouring those who continued to promote the violent ideology of the FIS and its armed wing, the GIA (Groupe Islamique Armée).

In the first years of its existence the Foundation commemorated the life of Mahfoud Boucebci. It ran cultural events and annual conferences on societal challenges such as drug addiction or mental health, which led to publications. Finally, in 2001, it managed to obtain offices in Mohammadia, Algiers, with support from UNICEF and the Canadian Embassy. As well as housing Professor Boucebci's library, the organisation began to provide practical training for the Foundation's psychologists, who went on to support over 1000 children annually. In partnership with the local authorities, with the aid of a small grant, the association launched a research initiative to tackle violence in schools. Through this project it worked with local authorities to improve teacher training and to contribute to the debate about how to reduce violence in the education system. It also provided support services, with its own staff being made available for teachers from the selected schools.[20] The association had hundreds of members, in Algeria and abroad, and was funded through membership fees, local donor funding and private sector donations.

Interviews with voluntary and paid staff indicated the importance to them of the practical role of the association, for its legitimacy and success. Young staff members, working as psychologists with child victims of violence, highlighted this role and their feelings about their work: 'I feel free working in an association; here people give us their trust.'[21] On personal reasons for working in such an organisation, another staff member also pointed out how it assisted her own research into family therapy, but also gave meaning to her work.[22] The Boucebci Foundation, like many associations, provided a new sphere for people to defend their values, and to contribute to social projects, indirectly or directly targeting the trauma Algerians had suffered. Volunteers worked with local structures of Algerian society – town halls, education and health authorities – and appeared to be trusted by the population. Internally, like most of the associations interviewed, the foundation organised an annual general meeting, elected its leaders and reported back to its donors about funding and activities.

Members of the association were critical of the urban policies and education system, particularly in the area of the capital city where they worked, which saw thousands of families rehoused in high-rise flats during the insecurity of the 1990s. However, they were not only critical. To deal with this, the Foundation engaged with local authorities to improve approaches to tackling violence and conflict in classrooms and homes.[23] The success of the Foundation on different fronts made them sometimes victim to jealousies from other associations, but also from commentators, who assumed they were funded, and therefore co-opted, by the state – something which, on consulting the finances they openly shared, I could see was clearly untrue. The Foundation did receive staff from the Social Development Agency and funding from European and North American donors, but this did not prevent them critiquing the policies of either. Similar social organisations, supporting vulnerable families across Algeria, in particular those campaigning for those with disabilities, are also particularly vocal in their criticism of the state. Organisations such as the *Fédération algérienne des personnes handicapées* have become necessary consultees for all political reforms in the social sector, but also for legislation concerning associations generally.[24] Social associations have thus become part of the policy making process, and, whatever their limitations, they have had an input.

Conclusion

From the official figures and from the examples shown in the cases above, it seems that the 1990 Law did enable a number of active social associations to emerge. These associations have been providing services to vulnerable populations, in some ways filling the gaps left by the state, since the 1990s. They also play a role which could not be provided by the state in any context given the personal commitment of the associations' leaders. Social organisations are perhaps less engaged in public debate than heritage ones, as their position is weaker, often labour-intensive and therefore necessarily dependent on the state for support. Yet, even principally 'service providing' associations such as *Nour* have become active in the public sphere. Associations supporting victims of trauma and violence, such as the Boucebci Foundation, are inherently involved in the public debate about the future of Algeria and how to deal with the past. Most associations sought constructive dialogue with the authorities and recognition by state institutions. They lamented the ongoing obstructionism but, ultimately, primarily sought for themselves an improved capacity to care for the population.

The legitimacy of the actors seemed to come from individual convictions and proven success in managing activities rather than just from the personality or position of the presidents of the associations. From interviews with the associations, a main motivation for their leaders appeared to be that of being involved in a project of importance to Algerian society. As well as more altruistic goals, of course, presiding over an association was also a position of responsibility and respect – one which facilitated contacts beyond the constraints of the family or immediate social circles, potentially linking with international actors and likeminded thinkers in a period when social relations in Algeria were fraught with tension and mistrust. It also gave meaning, a way to fight back and a new life project to those who had lost everything when their loved ones were assassinated, or to those whose lives were so affected by the absence of any support to their disabled family members. The personnel on the ground, who were perhaps less personally entwined with the aims of the organisations, nevertheless indicated their wish to bring positive changes for the future of Algeria rather than focusing on the conflict or the past. In interviews at the Boucebci Foundation, and in similar discussions with the SARP association and *Djazairouna*, members referred to the importance of rebuilding Algeria, responding to the needs of the victims and dealing with the trauma which had been passed on to children in particular due to the experiences of their parents. Whilst still facing numerous challenges, such organisations provide new spheres of activism in which qualified personnel are also involved. They create autonomous spaces in which people can exchange, contest and propose critical reflection and analysis. In organisations such as the Boucebci Foundation or *Djazairouna*, such discussions also covered an area in which the state has attempted to rule out open debate through the restrictions of the Reconciliation Charter. Through their practical work with victims of violence, many associations are able to challenge certain discourses of the authorities. They represent the population and provide forums for discussion,[25] channelling information and contributing to political debate about social policy, welfare and reconciliation in a challenging political context.

Civil society associations can be classified on a scale ranging between dependence and autonomy, as presented in the typology of associations in Chapter 5. It would seem that these social associations are not purely dependent on the state, but neither do they feel they have full autonomy. They appear to have been created mainly from needs arising in the population, for the protection of vulnerable populations, often from personal reasons, such as supporting a family member. Whilst the original motivation may have been personal, they act at the community level, supporting a significant number of children and their families. They often become the life projects of the leaders of the associations, yet they are still far more about shared grievances than personal ones. These associations openly challenge the state, despite needing its support. They recognize the state's weaknesses and question public policy choices in the social sector. Social associations cooperate with state structures, despite persistent obstructions, and seek dialogue both to fulfil their aims and to pursue their ambitions for a different vision of how Algerian social welfare provision could function.

PART III

DONORS, DEMOCRACY AND THE LANGUAGE OF OTHERS

CHAPTER 8

EUROPE, CIVIL SOCIETY AND DEMOCRACY IN ALGERIA

Algerian cooperation with the EU, particularly in more sensitive programmes targeting civil society, is conditioned by difficult historical relations with Europe, notably in tensions between Algeria and France, the former colonial power. For Algerians, Europe had shown an equivocal commitment to human rights during the War of Independence and, more recently, had given little support during the conflict of the 1990s. Many Algerians felt that Europe had actually worsened the conflict by giving asylum to 'terrorists' in its capitals. This, coupled with the closure of the EU delegation in Algiers in the 1990s, further complicated the potential for a cooperative relationship. Civil society programmes depend on a tangible diplomatic presence and in Algiers this presence had been weakened. Algeria was now a significant energy supplier for Europe and an increasingly important military power in Africa. It had also recently renewed its foreign policy ambitions.[1] These different factors all contributed to a re-balancing of power, and the partnership with Algeria became one in which the EU was relatively weak and the Algerian state relatively strong in negotiations. Despite the historical challenges and technical difficulties, the EU has nevertheless been the most important foreign donor for the Algerian government, particularly in terms of support to non-state actors. The EU was the first donor to launch country-wide programmes to support civil society. Personal and cultural ties, linked to the significant Algerian diaspora in France, also encouraged diplomatic cooperation with Europe, as did the absence of other options. Strong links with the Chinese, whilst financially significant, focused primarily on the state and the construction industry. There was also wariness of accepting funding from the Gulf due to previous Salafist influences from the Middle East and also to Saudi Arabia's support of the Armed Islamic Group in the 1990s and problematic representations of Algeria by Al Jazeera.

In such conditions, and with its renewed foreign policy, Algeria had to engage with the EU. The Algerian Government had to negotiate around the EU's general approach in the region, categorised by others as a rather one-sided 'hub-and-spoke' model through which Europeans imposed their agendas.[2] For Algeria, however, the mechanisms through which the EU normally supports civil society needed to be different.[3] The normative, value-laden and euro-centric language of EU institutions, as well as the rigidity of procedures, meant that programmes and often not-so-independent European NGOs would not work in Algeria. Moreover, as Aliboni describes, in other countries in the region,

> Arab governments have limited the participation of nationally-based NGOs in EU programmes as much as possible and most of all have prevented their NGOs from receiving funds from the EU. Many sectors of society [...] rejected the offer of co-operation which they regarded as gross political interference.[4]

Interviews with associations confirmed the perception, on the Algerian side, of an imperialist approach and a neo-colonial agenda on the part of the EU that prevented them seeking EU support. Yet, many of these same actors acknowledged that their perceptions had changed. Since 2004, the Algerian Government itself has also softened its position towards the EU and has accepted funding for a significant number of national organisations. In its first 'associations support programme', from 2000, the EU financed 76 associations. Under the second programme, from 2006, a further 127 associations were supported through small projects. Training opportunities were also widened to include not only associations but also a number of other institutional actors as well. The change in approach, to include rather than sideline the state, was noted by associations on the ground like Association *Nour*, discussed in the previous chapter, and this facilitated their working with the EU.

Initially, the Algerian Government had refused to accept any NGO funding programmes linked to the implementation of democracy or human rights. This, it was felt, was on the grounds that Algeria would not accept such a moralising approach from the EU. Algerian associations confirmed this, arguing that they had 'nothing to learn from the EU about human rights' protection, given that Europe had condoned torture and given amnesty to its perpetrators'.[5] Yet, during the same discussions, it was clear that the Algerians did seek technical and capacity support for both institutions and associations. They sought the opening up of Algeria to greater contacts in the neighbouring region and wished for increased exchanges of information and expertise. Still, this had to be on their terms, with respect to national legislation, traditions and customs, and in concordance with the capacities of Algerian associations.[6] As such, it seemed that the nature of cooperation became intertwined with questions of mutual respect, the need for recognition of historical truths, and appreciation of Algerian culture and national sovereignty.

European Diplomacy in Algeria

The European Union's relations with Algeria date from even before the country's independence from France in 1962. Whilst Tunisia and Morocco were already independent in 1957, Algeria, though fighting a bitter anti-colonial war, remained a French territory at the time of the signing of the Treaty of Rome. Algeria left the EEC on acceding to independence and signed up to separate trade agreements to ensure continuity for trade in certain goods. This, coupled with piecemeal decisions from the EEC, member states and the Algerian Republic, meant that adaptation was possible but it also created 'discrepancies which, in the long term, led to an anarchical, juridical situation'.[7] With these complex beginnings, the EU also faced many further difficulties in establishing a functioning cooperation with Algeria, stemming from ongoing historical tensions. Algeria's colonial experience had been so brutally destructive that, as Entelis writes, it 'naturally engendered hostility to France and the West'.[8]

Despite this hostility, the French authorities, according to Daguzan, sought to create 'a new form of post-colonial co-operation,' and one which would be 'exemplary in the eyes of the world'.[9] After losing its colonies, 'the driving force of France's policy in the developing world was the desire of its leaders for the country to be a global power'.[10] France would use European integration to further this objective. Relations with Africa were the means by which France could retain global power and maintain its sphere of influence, particularly after the traumas of its recent history in Algeria. After independence, France continued to dominate relations with Algeria and up until the end of the 1990s, France was reluctant to allow any form of European cooperation with its former colony. Daguzan writes,

> The exemplarity which France made of its interactions with Algeria transformed this into an exclusive relationship. This led, as a result, to the French Authorities keeping the European Union well away from any political interventions concerning the country.[11]

The Algerians, on their side, struggled to deal with their European partners in the aftermath of the bitter War of Liberation. Human rights, such as the protection of prisoners, enshrined in international law, had been violated by the French authorities. The systematic, state-sponsored use of torture was evident. If Algerians, individually, had not witnessed atrocities first-hand, there were enough reminders made public by many of the victims – for example Henri Alleg's book *The Question* (1958) – and even on the French side, there were admissions from perpetrators such as General Massu in 1972 and General Aussaresses in 2000. French denial, censorship and amnesty concerning the atrocities and war crimes continued to feed the animosity and the 'environment of fear, suspicion, and distrust', that Entelis describes. Heartfield writes of the 'contradiction between humanism and imperialism', whereby the colonial power actually 'denied Algeria its freedom in the name of the Rights of Man'.[12] Despite winning the War of Independence, it remained difficult for Algerian leaders and their diplomats to manage relations with France and Europe. The injustice of the war crimes was exacerbated by the limited form of debate in France and the censorship of books and films which dealt with the war.[13]

The Algerian Government also questioned the sincerity of European interests in Algeria, doubting that these were motivated primarily by economic interests, particularly in the energy sector. Despite the legal, historical and diplomatic complexity of these initial relations in the 1970s, the Europeans did manage to establish a more formalised cooperation with Algeria within the framework of the Global Mediterranean Policy. Van Reisen points out, however, that this also coincided with the oil embargo following the 1973 Arab–Israeli war and the ensuing increase in oil prices. She writes that in the 1970s, 'One of the few options the EC had to secure energy imports was to urgently intensify its relations with the southern Mediterranean and Arab countries, with Algeria and Libya.'[14]

Within this context, Algeria continued to negotiate with the European Communities, but with reservations as to their underlying motives. Longstanding suspicions blighted the European Mediterranean Policy (EMP) generally, and reinforced the reluctance of southern Mediterranean countries to fully cooperate with the EU. Del Sarto writes that:

> The EU's tendency of giving a far greater importance to its own economic and security interest than to the liberal principles of the EMP inevitably nurtured the suspicion of neo-colonialism in many EMP partners, most of whom experienced European colonialism in the past.[15]

Algeria eventually signed a Cooperation Agreement in 1976 and the first delegation to Algeria was opened in 1979. The first two heads of delegation were British, followed by a French delegate in 1987, at which point the status of delegate was promoted to that of ambassador. Table 8.1 outlines the history of EU diplomacy, diplomats and specific events of EU–Algeria cooperation.

In the late 1980s, Algeria entered into a period of deep reforms with the opening up of the political sphere. Following this, in the early 1990s, the EU renewed its Mediterranean Policy and substantially increased its budget for the region. The Algerian *coup d'état* of 1992, however, along with the cancellation of the electoral process and the declaration of a state of emergency, changed everything. The conflict of the 1990s and the constant threat of terrorism had profound consequences. With the direct targeting of foreigners by the Islamist insurgency, many of the embassies and international organisations withdrew. Between 1994 and 1998, the EU delegation 'technically'

Table 8.1 History of the EU delegation in Algiers.

Date	Head of the delegation	Nationality	Localisation of the delegation	Specific events
1979–83	Sir Samuel Fall	British	Cheraga	2nd Financial Protocol adopted
1983–6	Graham Kelly	British	El Biar	3rd Financial Protocol adopted
1987–90	Jean-Paul Jesse	French	El Biar	Renewed Mediterranean Policy, increase in staff, title of Ambassador for head of delegation
1990–4	Agostino Trapani	Italian	Hydra	4th Financial Protocol adopted
1994–8	Technical Closure	X		National team remains, MEDA I launched at the regional level
1999–2	Lorenzo Sanchez	Spanish	Ch.Poirson and Bvd 1960 El Biar	Return to Algeria after the violence reduces, increase in Staff, first civil society programme launched
2002–6	Lucio Guerrato	Italian	El Biar	MEDA II launched, Algeria signs Association Agreement 2002,
2006–8	Wolfgang Plasa	German	El Biar	Second civil society programme launched
2008–12	Laura Baeza	Spanish	El Biar	Strengthening of political dialogue
2012–16	Marek Skolil	Czech	El Biar	Strategic Energy Partnership signed
2016–present day	John O'Rourke	Irish	El Biar	

closed down due to the security situation. Some cooperation is said to have continued behind the scenes, with the maintenance of the national team, but relations between Algiers and European capitals were strained. Because of the closure of embassies, Europeans had great difficulty even understanding what was happening on the ground, let alone knowing what action to pursue. Europe was largely absent from the field in Algeria, except for a few contested missions from parliamentarians, which lasted a few days and were limited geographically to the capital.[16] The EU therefore had little information throughout the 1990s concerning the needs of the country in terms of security, reconstruction, institution-building or its new civil society organisations.

Returning to Algeria after the 'black decade' was challenging for the EU. Logistical structures were absent, as were diplomatic and informal mechanisms such as the presence of European associations or businesses in the country. The EU turned to consultants who could assist them but not necessarily replace programme officers and diplomats on the ground. The structure of the Commission, its bureaucracy and rigidity, did not help.[17] Constant reforms meant a high turnover of staff, leading to less-experienced personnel. As a result, there was a very slow take-up of the EU-Algeria cooperation programmes. The figures and programmes discussed below show limited expenditure, despite the significant need for Algeria to re-construct. The limitations of the EU were matched by equally challenging positions from the Algerian state. From its bilateral programmes to the Union for the Mediterranean, Algeria stood out in the region in its refusal to sign up to EU policies. In Brussels, Algeria gained the reputation of 'being the EU's most difficult partner', whereas the Algerian side attributed difficulties to the EU's failure 'to fully appreciate the interests and specificities of third countries'.[18] Accusations of European neo-colonialism certainly fit well with the narratives of the FLN, which was seeking to improve its own weak legitimacy, while at the same time Algerian diplomats negotiating with the EU certainly felt the EU's inability, due to its structures, to listen to other countries.[19] Yet, despite these challenges, the Algerians and the EU did succeed in negotiating a number of cooperation programmes, including some in more sensitive areas such as civil society and the growing associational movement.

European Union Programmes in Algeria

On achieving 30 years of cooperation, the EU delegation published information about its relationship with Algeria from 1979.[20] In addition to commercial agreements the EU had four five-year protocols between 1976 and 1995. A social component was developed but never came into force. The protocols supported target sectors, which changed with each protocol. Over time, the numbers of sectors reduced and infrastructure support became the most significant sector. Civil society, governance or political reforms were never specifically targeted.

Table 8.2 indicates the sector priorities financed by the EU over this 20-year period.

The four protocols made up 214 million euros. Given the period of 20 years over which these funds were committed, the reduced team and

Table 8.2 EU support to Algeria between 1976 and 1996.

Period	Protocol	Sector	% of the cooperation
1976–81	1	Rural development	34
		Environment	31
		Transport	24
		Training	6
		Industry	3
		Scientific co-operation	2
1981–6	2	Infrastructures	70
		Energy	18
		Scientific co-operation	9
		Infrastructures	2
		Industry	1
1986–91	3	Infrastructures	50
		Irrigation	30
		Agriculture	8
		Industry	7
		Scientific co-operation	5
1991–6	4	Infrastructures	68
		Agriculture	21
		Structural adjustment	10
		Industry	1

frequent changes of office, cooperation with Algeria was at a relatively low level.

Following on from these protocols, after 1996, the EU renewed its Mediterranean Policy and launched the Barcelona Process. This significantly increased EU ambitions in the southern Mediterranean. The Barcelona Process began in 1995 and in 1996, MEDAI (the Accompanying Measures Programme) was launched. Negotiations began with Algiers, although many meetings took place outside Algeria. Despite the early difficulties, the EU still managed to programme 164 million euros to be spent in Algeria in the late 1990s, targeting the private sector and representing 6 per cent of EU funds in the region.[21] After difficult negotiations, Algeria signed an Association Agreement with the EU in 2002 which entered into force in 2005. There was little mention of civil society. The EU reformed relations with its neighbouring countries once again in 2007, creating the European Neighbourhood and Partnership Instrument, which involved equally challenging negotiations with Algiers.

Official EU documents explain that the limited uptake of EU funding in Algeria was due to the 'security situation, the poor administrative capacity and delays in the economic reforms,'[22] clearly attributing blame to the Algerian side of the cooperation. In the early 2000s, few European officials or consultants really knew the context in Algeria. Few Algerians knew the EU, its procedures or methods of working. EU consultants struggled to design relevant programmes, to identify beneficiaries, to find and retain human resources and to handle the complex relations with national authorities. Difficulties were experienced by EU delegation staff in monitoring projects. Overwhelmed by contractual problems, they were also rarely given security clearance to leave their offices and so seldom made field visits.[23]

Increased interest in Algeria at the end of the 1990s meant that significant commitments were made in all sectors. Yet statements were not followed up by effective programmes. Even when programmes were drawn up, they were not necessarily even contracted, let alone implemented. The figures showed that many planned programme budgets were simply not spent. Of the 164 million euros programmed, under MEDA I, only 18 per cent was actually paid out. Table 8.3 indicates that the EU sought to spend 164 million euros in Algeria

Table 8.3 EU support to Algeria between 1995 and 1999 (MEDA I).

	MEDA I (1995–9)		
Year	Commitment (euro million)	Actual payment (euro million)	Payment commitment (%)
1995	0	0	0
1996	0	0	0
1997	41	0	0
1998	95	30.0	32.0
1999	28	0.2	0.7
Total	164	30.2	18.4

Source: EU Algeria country strategy paper 2007–13, p. 13.[24]

between 1995 and 1999, but in fact only spent 30 million, the lowest disbursement rate in the region.

The figures for the next programming cycle are equally low but they are an improvement on MEDA I (Table 8.4).

Overall, in the period, the EU spent only a third of its planned funding and subsequently reduced its ambitions. Table 8.4 shows that it took the EU roughly five years after re-opening its delegation in Algiers to return to relatively normal programming levels.

Table 8.4 EU support to Algeria between 2000 and 2006 (MEDA II).

	MEDA II (2000–6)		
Year	Commitment (euro million)	Actual payment (euro million)	Payment commitment (%)
2000	30.2	0.4	1.3
2001	60	5.5	9
2002	50	11	22
2003	41.6	16.8	38
2004	51	42	82.4
2005	40	39.4	98.5
2006	66		
Total	339	115.1	34

Source: EU Algeria Country strategy paper 2007–13, p. 13.

European Support to Algerian Civil Society

Despite the challenges, limits and weaknesses of past cooperation and the strained relations with the EU, Algerian civil society was growing and, with the increasing global trend towards civil society support, the EU became the most likely actor that could intervene. On re-opening its offices in Algiers in 1999, the EU sought to cover a huge number of sectors in Algeria. These included infrastructure, education, health, professional training and many others. However, as shown above, most of these commitments were unsuccessful and many programmes were simply not implemented. In 2008, Liverani described the 'plethora of civil society assistance programmes' offered by donors in the early 2000s.[25] He attributed this to euphoria at the initial increase in associations, the return to peace and stability and the role of associations in legitimising the state in Algeria. There were certainly public commitments to launch such programmes. However, the EU figures, as well as interviews with associations between 2007 and 2012, suggest that in reality only a limited number of programmes were funded in the early 2000s. However 'euphoric' international actors were about the potential of civil society, the structural difficulties identified above, the targeting of foreign actors, including the bombing of the UN offices in Algiers in 2007, restrictions on foreign actors by the government and time delays by donors, were all factors that limited donor funding in Algeria.

The 2001 EU programme for civil society was therefore one of the first cases of organised, external funding to NGOs in Algeria. Following on from that, similar programmes funded by the French, Spanish, British and the UN were set up. In financial terms, however, these were small compared to similar programmes in the region. In terms of approach, national ownership and the diversity of the actors supported, the EU's intervention in Algeria was significant. An evaluation of the programme was carried out in 2004 by a team of European and Algerian consultants. Concerning the setting up of this programme, it asserted:

> This programme was conceived in 1999 in a context of very limited information, on the nature and size of the Algerian associative movement, and in a political climate which was still uncertain concerning the relations between the state/civil society/ private sector.

[...]
This initiative from the EC had then – and still has – high stakes for Algeria, and this justified a prudent and open approach; the CE opted for a wide definition of terms such as civil society, development, poverty, excluding only religious or political organisations.[26]

As one of the first programmes launched after the re-opening of the EU offices in Algiers, the civil society programme was sensitive. It was important to the EU, to the Algerian government and also to the associations, which had high expectations. The historical backdrop and complexity of EU–Algeria relations meant the programme needed to ensure national ownership and deal with the image of the EU in Algeria. The conditions for associations and civil society in the country were also challenging, after the levels of violence much of the population had experienced. In this context, two successive programmes aiming to support civil society were financed by the EU, starting in 2001.

Programme to Support Algerian Associations, 2001–5 (ONG1)
The Algerian associations support programme (known as ONG1) was signed in 2001 for a duration of four years and had a budget of 5 million euros. Its objectives were to promote the role of Algerian civil society in development processes and more specifically to strengthen development associations. It aimed to improve the functioning of associations by providing small grants, by supporting networks, by clarifying the institutional context for associations and by training ministry staff. A programme management team was set up in a national research centre in Oran, the Centre for Social and Cultural Anthropology (CRASC). Four local coordinators were recruited to monitor projects and coach associations across the different regions of Algeria and all members of the project staff were Algerian. At the end of the project, 76 associations had received small grants and co-financed their own local development projects. This was almost double the initial target. A total of 151 associations had responded to the call for proposals launched by the project. Whilst there were a few delays, the project was successfully implemented. It respected the EU's complex contracting procedures and the calls for projects were publicised widely across Algeria. After receiving training, associations were able to present projects in a wide

field of local development, culture, social protection, heritage, human rights or environmental protection.

Projects selected included Bel Horizon in Oran, who launched their school to train heritage guides, and instigated the recuperation of the Santa Cruz area – the mountain dominating the city of Oran. This zone had been completely off-limits during the terrorism of the 1990s. With the help of the local population and authorities, the association ensured that the area was once again a secure, open, public space for the citizens of Oran. In another project, Maissa Bey, one of Algeria's most celebrated contemporary writers, equipped and launched a library for children in Sidi Bel Abbess through the women's association she presided over. *Le Petit Lecteur*, active since 1993 running mobile libraries for schools and poor areas of Oran, created a space for reading, literary creation and events based around books, including festivals, writing competitions and the publication of two children's books in Arabic. The projects covered a geographical zone from Oran in the north-west, to Tamanrasset in the deep south, to Annaba in the north-east, huge distances from any perspective. Many of the projects touched some of the most vulnerable sections of the population and raised sensitive questions related to history and cultural identity.

The final evaluation stated that the programme:

> had rendered more visible the commitments of the European Union and above all promoted the plurality of an associative movement which is inventing multiple strategies for inserting itself into a public space which is, in itself, in transformation. The European support also increased the legitimacy of associations in their institutional environment as well as within the population, and in this sense, has reinforced civil society. It would be useful to diffuse the concrete results of a programme whose very existence provoked much skepticism; the confidence of the population and associations in the national process of opening up and reinforcing the rule of law would be raised.[27]

Programme to Support Algerian Associations II, 2006–10 (ONG2)

Following on from the first support programme, a second one was signed in 2000. It was to last four years, with a budget of 10 million euros, plus a contribution of 1 million euros from the Algerian Government. The objectives of the programme were again relatively open: to promote the role of Algerian development associations, with no conditions or sectors imposed. It again aimed to improve the functioning of associations through providing small grants, supporting networks and training institutional actors.

The main difference, besides the significant increase in funds, was the role of the state in the implementation. The management team was this time set up in the Ministry of National Solidarity, within the Social Development Agency, where a programme support unit was based in Algiers. Despite significant delays in the start-up and difficulties in finding the balance between the different actors, the programme nevertheless was successfully implemented. Three calls for projects were launched and 131 projects were supported, including 13 networks of associations. Six regional coordinators assisted associations in identifying needs and beneficiaries and in designing their projects. Helping with the accounting requirements and project management, the coordinators filtered the bureaucracy and assisted the associations in considering the impact of their actions. The programme financed social, heritage, environment, gender, youth, culture and community development projects.

In Ghardaia, at the gates of the Sahara, the *Association Forum des Educateurs* set up an after school centre for reading and language support in English, French and Arabic, and IT skills for primary school learners. They easily managed to find the counterpart funding of 20 per cent, which was necessary to receive the grant, from private donors in Ghardaia and were allocated a beautiful building in the palmary of Beni Isguen by a benefactor who wished to remain anonymous. In Djelfa, the association *Assala* launched a project to help 25 vulnerable women to set up micro-businesses. Alongside training, the association provided basic equipment to set up the businesses, such as coffee grinders, sewing machines, materials, livestock and computers. It delivered training in marketing, management and communication, and coached the women for the first year of their initiative. The success of the project, through careful budgeting and through the beneficiaries giving back to the association once they were autonomous, so as to help other women, meant by the end of the project the association could exceed its targets and support 43 individual micro-businesses. In Annaba, *Hippone Sub*, an environmental organisation, managed an ambitious project to clean up the coast around the city and raise awareness about the degradation of marine life. Targeting school children, tourists and fishermen, staff themselves also cleaned 50 hectares of the coastline, gathering photographic evidence of the pollution of the seabed. The association trained other associations in running such operations and worked alongside the university and schools. *Hippone Sub* also participated in the national day to clean up the beaches, launched in 2007 by an association from Algiers, *Recif* and the national radio. By 2011, over 100 environmental associations and 28,000 people participated in cleaning up Algeria's beaches, in all 14 coastal regions of the country, on the same day.

Despite the wide range of sectors that could be targeted by the associations under the EU's programme, the vast majority of associations involved designed and implemented projects in the social sector. Table 8.5 outlines the different sectors and where the main concentration of projects was located.

The final external evaluation of the programme interviewed 115 members of associations. It acknowledged the fragility of Algerian civil society and avaialble support structures, but remarked upon the integrity of the management and implementation of projects by the majority of the associations. Out of 131 initially inexperienced associations, only three contracts were cancelled due to inability to manage, and funds were returned to the EU. The evaluation noted:

Table 8.5 Sectors of the EU's second Support to Algerian Associations Programme (ONG2).

Themes	Number of projects	Percentage
Social (including women and young people)[28]	60	46%
Culture and sport	24	18%
Environment and eco-tourism	18	14%
Heritage	15	11%
Community and sustainable development	14	11%
Total	131	100%

The associations are very satisfied with the multiform support given by the programme ONG2. The beneficiaries are now able to ensure a greater efficacy and greater rigour and transparency in their activities. A greater credibility has also been attained thanks to the programme. It has resulted in a sort of label, from the grants that the associations have been able to manage, with results which are more than satisfactory.[29]

Apart from these specific programmes to support civil society in Algeria, the EU also funded NGOs under the European Instrument for Democracy and Human Rights and other sectoral programmes. A donor group had been set up by the EU delegation to try to coordinate support for associations. Coordination was said to be complicated, as there was only limited sharing of information in any systematic way between the different actors. In 2011, a project for a common resources centre for associations was negotiated and launched with support from a number of donors, mainly the EU.

All in all, both programmes and other support to associations in Algeria allowed a fairly wide remit for the latter to present projects they wished to set up. In neighbouring countries, by contrast, calls for associations were far more targeted, national priorities were fixed and associations had to support, say, the national electoral process, women or 'youth employability', depending on the donor preference at the time. Given the difficult place of European NGOs in Algeria, there was also a far stronger presence of Algerian NGOs accessing EU funding, whereas in neighbouring countries European NGOs dominated such funding calls.[30]

Many of the donors interviewed in Algeria indicated that there had been a substantial increase in their budgets for civil society after the Arab Spring. In Tunisia, the EU financed huge NGO spending programmes in a remarkably short time frame, to support civil society after 2011. By 2012, 2 million euros had been awarded to NGOs to work on elections, amongst an abundance of other funding calls. The majority of associations selected were European.[31] This came after a period of very limited support to Tunisian civil society organisations and prior to any in-depth studies of the needs of the organisations. In contrast, there were no new prospects for a future EU programme to specifically support civil society in Algeria. Any new initiative will now depend on diplomatic relations between the EU and Algeria. The Algerian Government has nevertheless signed up to a significant programme, financed by the EU, to support the heritage sector, mainly targeting the ministries but with a component for associations.

Conclusion

At the final conference to mark the closure of the EU's support to Algerian Associations in 2010, the EU Ambassador praised Algerian associations. In a joint statement with the Minister of Solidarity, she announced, 'this programme is above all an indicator of the formidable potential in terms of energy, creativity and commitment of the associative movement'.[32] Despite the historic mistrust, as well as the diplomatic and technical challenges of working in Algeria, the EU had managed to implement a modestly funded, but geographically and technically ambitious programme to support local associations. In supporting the state to also work with associations, in the presence of a third party, the programme had created new possibilities for bridging the divide between state and society. In this way, the EU could in some way support, as Addi writes, this 'passage towards the public sphere which Algeria struggles to achieve'[33] in a context where the expectations of the state were very high. Many of the associations and the ministry staff interviewed highlighted that it was Algerian institutions that most needed assistance in order for state–society relations to improve. In interviews with the project staff in Algiers at the end of the project, it was stated that:

> Today there is a good team in the EU in Algeria. The Ambassador recognizes that it is necessary to work with the state and the national authorities to support civil society sustainably, even, and perhaps more so, in authoritarian contexts. The state and its institutions have been weakened in Algeria. Competent persons have left, or are side-lined. There is poor human resource management. We need to start with the institutions.[34]

The need to support the staff of the ministries and decentralised authorities across the country was seen as an important step in rebuilding trust and capacity.

The experience of the EU as a more modest donor in Algeria is a useful case to study. Increasing budgets for countries which appear to abide by EU-sanctioned reform processes can be counterproductive. Flooding countries with civil society funding is unsustainable and risks corrupting and deforming labour markets. It distracts local elites, who could otherwise potentially be integrated into the political and institutional life of a country. The Algerian case demonstrates that it is not the amount of funding that leads to success or failure, but the relationships, the needs, the way in which funding is managed, and who it is that receives it.

The historical context, the lack of trust and poor track record on cooperation, combined with the absence of the EU during the 1990s, meant that EU funding for civil society in Algeria has been modest. The overall EU budget for Algeria, for 2007–10, was 220 million euros. The budget for civil society was only 10 million euros, less than 5 per cent of that total. Yet the EU arguably remains the most important donor in Algeria, both symbolically and financially. Whilst the competition is weak, with few external partners deemed appropriate contenders to assist Algeria in its ongoing reforms, the EU's impact is not insignificant. Its recent programmes and work with Algerian associations appear to have had an impact both on the EU's presence and the development of civil society in Algeria. The success of EU funding, in the eyes of the associations, in part was due to the EU allowing appropriation of the programme by local actors. The Algerian associations themselves defined the priorities of their actions, rather than having them imposed. There was far less restrictive language in the negotiations, discussions and calls for projects. As a result, each association developed its activities in response to problems its members had identified in their region, rather than having priorities decided for them by the EU. How the EU identifies and directs associations, through the language of its calls for projects, impacts upon the implementation of its programmes. This impact of the language of others will be explored in more detail in the next chapter.

CHAPTER 9

LANGUAGE AND THE CONSTRUCTION OF CIVIL SOCIETY

> Dynasty and government serve as the world's market place, attracting to it the products of scholarship and craftsmanship alike [...] In this market stories are told and items of historical information are delivered [...] whenever the established dynasty avoids injustice, prejudice, weakness, and double dealing [...], the wares on its market are as pure silver and fine gold. However, when it is influenced by selfish interests and rivalries, or swayed by vendors of tyranny and dishonesty, the wares of its market place become as dross and debased metals.
> Ibn Khaldun, *The Muqaddimah an Introduction to History*[1]

Written in the fourteenth century, in the west of Algeria near modern-day Tiaret, Ibn Khaldun's *Muqaddimah* introduces the idea that governments manipulate and condition the validity and quality of historical data. Five centuries later, Ibn Khaldun's work itself was subject to the bias of translation, under a European colonial government. Hannoum writes that 'translation was a part of the whole enterprise that the early colonial administration in Algeria set in place'.[2] For example, the introduction to the De Slane translation of Ibn Khaldun in 1863 clearly widens the role of the translator to one which 'rectifies the errors of the message'. Hannoum continues that, in a colonial context, 'this means that the translator converts the original text into a colonial one'.[3] The colonial rulers found support for their *mission civilisatrice* and for the wider colonial project in their use of language and in the reinterpretation of historical texts. Thus, Ibn Khaldun was himself categorised by orientalist scholars, not as part of a long tradition of Arab learning, but as a solitary genius, standing out from an Arab civilisation which was described, using the Hobbesian phrase, as 'nasty, brutish and short'.[4]

Six centuries after the Muqaddimah was written, in the context of the Algerian war of liberation, Frantz Fanon provided a counterbalance to the European supremacist rhetoric which had defined colonialism. His use of a new performative language as well as challenging colonial injustice, contributed to shaping Algeria's foreign policy and diplomacy in the early post-colonial period. He also changed perceptions as to what development aid (or, as he saw it, reparations) should be in the aftermath of liberation. He wrote:

> So when we hear the head of a European state declare with his hand on his heart that he must come to the aid of the poor underdeveloped peoples, we do not tremble with gratitude. Quite the contrary, we say to ourselves: 'It's a just reparation which will be paid to us.'[5]

Yet, however defined, as charity or reparation, external aid and the actors who manage it remain an intrusion into the institutional and political systems of another country. Their involvement, through language or actions, affects local political life. As Abu-Sada and Challand point out, international donors, 'through their institutional or discursive implication', can cause the 'redistribution of symbolic and relational capital'.[6] Despite being well intentioned, development facilitators, as they are often considered, can, by their presence and language, impede local political autonomy in recipient countries.[7] The paradigms and priorities set by donors impact upon local actors. They can determine their paths and access to the political sphere. The language of donors is rarely neutral. Hannoum reminds us that this is even more so in former colonial contexts.

> Colonizing the imaginary also means that colonial judgments, whose birth and formulation are linked to a specific context, continue to be reproduced, passed on uncritically, even in the

postcolonial period, carrying with them their original myths, and perpetuating colonial relations.[8]

The question of how language has been used by donors, by nationalist movements or by Algerian associations has been a recurrent theme throughout this book. Chapter 1 explored the denial of the existence of an Arab-Muslim civil society, in academic writing and the language of donors. Challand investigated this issue in his study of NGOs in Palestine. He explored how, using the assumption that civil society did not exist, donors justified their attempts to construct civil society from scratch.[9] In order to do this they needed to impose a new language and new concepts on recipients. Roy analyses how this was done by the Bush administration in the Greater Middle East Project.[10] This project ignored the traditional structures and networks already in place in the Middle East. Creating civil society, as donor language required it to be, meant that the legitimate claims of the real political actors were bypassed. These actors were either ignored, or 'civilised', by 'recasting their agendas in terms compatible with Western thinking'.[11] Chapter 2 explored how the conceptual paradigms adopted by international development agencies changed over time, impacting upon the recipients of development aid. The more recent revival of the concept of civil society is an example. In Eastern Europe, the idea of civil society was used as a frame for peaceful political transitions. Because of its clear success, the civil society concept became a development paradigm and was then uncritically transposed to the Middle East and to Africa, by actors such as the European Union.

The second part of the book elaborated upon the relationship between the state and associations in Algeria. It explored how the state's language policies influenced who had access to the public sphere or which segments of society were excluded. It noted how heritage associations, for example, challenged existing discourses around historical narratives. In the final part, the Chapter 8 explored the role of the European Union as a weak actor – one which was obliged to reform its language in Algeria to become less normative and intrusive. It is now useful to bring together some of these different elements about the impact of language, as seen through the experience of Algerian associations. It is within these alternative political spheres, such as associations or alternative artistic and cultural forms, that expression is less restricted by language barriers and new voices have been able to enter into political life. The language of external donors, that of recorded history and that of national language policies, all impact on these alternative spheres. Performative language may create new realities, or, on the contrary, impede internal processes of change. Algeria can again provide a useful and timely case study, as both the state and associative actors continue to openly contest the dominance of Western narratives. This is now a position increasingly adopted in other North African countries, particularly since the uprisings of 2011. In response, the EU, which increasingly values its relations with Algiers, seems to have moderated its language, becoming more self-critical,[12] and admitting failures; its responses becoming more conservative.[13]

The Performative Effect of Language

In his book *How to do things with words*, Austin developed a theory of the performative. The performative utterance, he claimed, was different from the constative utterance, which simply described something. The performative was instead an action which in itself constituted a new reality in the external world. Austin asks, 'how many senses are there in which to say something *is* to do something, or *in* saying something, and even *by* saying something we do something'.[14] In posing this question, Austin introduces the idea of the performative effect of language, for those uttering the words and for the recipients. John Searle built on Austin's theory in his work *Mind, Language and Society, Philosophy in the Real World*. He argued that abstract social and institutional realities come into being and are accepted through language.[15] It is, in his view, the performative speech act that creates institutional and social reality. The performative effect of language can have both positive and negative implications. The work of Albert O. Hirschman analysed how negative statements concerning a policy or a reform resulted in the expectation, and then the reality, of its failure. Hirschman explored an example of this in Latin America, where he observed the repeated categorisation of reforms as 'utter failures' by external actors leading 'to real failures,' a phenomenon that he labeled 'fracasomania'.[16]

In a similar vein, donors can influence the success or failure of national reforms by their assessments of countries, through country reports, statements in the press or other publications, which are often then repeated, copied and pasted into other international reports. This could be, for example, by presupposing the existence or absence of civil society itself or the failure of a particular policy field. The assumption, for example, of an absence of democracy, that women do not have rights, or that there is gender imbalance in a given context, and that the EU can solve this, by providing money, may actually in itself, as Hirschman argued, create that very imbalance. In line with Hirschman's ideas of fracasomania and failure complex, McDougall develops the idea that external actors can themselves create the 'need for reform'. That is, they can create the state of backwardness through their own language, thereby justifying their own intervention. He writes:

> We must first avoid presuming, like the reformists, that there is a reform movement in a given society because the society is afflicted with backwardness [...] that an external action is necessary to operate change. In this schema, the backwardness (in whatever measure) would pre-exist and render necessary the reform. [...] However, it could be that the inverse is the case, that is to say, we begin by remarking the 'state of backwardness' only from the moment when there is a reform movement. It would be then the reformers which create the state of backwardness as a thought in itself.[17]

In this way, in the Algerian context, the Algerian state and associations may themselves take on negative perceptions and the expectation of failure as stated by certain external actors or academic writing about Algeria. The president of the association of psychologists, SARP, noted this internalisation in 2009 – in a Friedrich Naumann-sponsored workshop – when she publicly spoke out against 'the overly negative vision of associations'. She pointed out that there were 'active and effective associations in Algeria, for example very courageous women's movements'. She also noted, in later discussions, that 'associations work in hostile and arbitrary climates, it is necessary to recognize and value the work achieved'.[18]

Critical perceptions may create the expectation of failure, as Hirschman writes. Yet in order to be performative, language must originate from actors who matter; who have an audience and are trusted or believed. In Algeria, foreign actors are not generally trusted. Change could probably only be initiated through the language of the domestic actors or associations themselves. It is the actors within Algeria that matter most on this question and Djamel Benramdane points to the growing negative domestic discourses that had increasingly stigmatised associations throughout the 2000s. Some of these judgements were launched by Yazid Zerhouni, Minister of Interior at the time, and then widely reported in the press and online media. In 2006, the Minister spoke of a new law 'to clean up the associative movement, the big consumer of grants'. He asserted that out of 73,000 associations only 5,000 were active, the others all being 'totally useless to society'.[19] His successor, Ould Kablia, was more conciliatory in tone but the image and message of 'only 5,000 active' remained anchored in the vision of Algerians, many of whom now also felt that associations were a waste of time.

This book has argued that, generally, the performative effects of external donor language have been resisted in Algeria, where both the state and associations were highly sceptical of foreign donors. Yet donors can still have a negative influence at the micro level when terms are imposed upon recipients. At its worst, this can produce an artificial civil society, where terminology is simply used in order to access funds. The language of civil society actors becomes distorted through the need to design projects that mirror donor criteria. Donor paradigms, such as gender equality or good governance, may not be the main priority for an organisation which applies for the funds. Interviews with an Algerian association from Bordj Bou Arreridj, *El Ghaith*, for instance, highlighted this frustration of working with an international donor which imposed its own terminology. The association explained that the donor expected it to change the descriptions of almost all its planned activities, so as to be seen as entering into and complying with the category of gender equality, as defined and prioritised by the agency. The association wanted to support poor rural women of the region by promoting income-generating activities. The donor agency, however, wanted them to frame their project in broader political language, targeting women's rights in general, rather than giving practical support to women in their region. After having re-written the project several times, and translated the entire text into English each time, the association was at the point of abandoning its proposal, even though it had already been selected as one of the best submissions.

At the time of the interview, it was not clear whether the project would go ahead. The association felt that, under the conditions about to be imposed, the project would no longer be theirs.[20] As one of the leaders argued, 'they should be satisfied with good monitoring of our activities, not imposing upon us their own'.[21] In this case, the association indicated quite clearly that it would prefer to abandon the funding if it involved adopting a new language, just for the sake of ticking boxes and filling in the form. The issues were eventually resolved and the project did go ahead.

So far, the EU, one of the main donors present in Algeria, seems to have limited its tendencies to impose priorities on Algerian associations. Its language in Algeria, like its programmes, has been modest; programmes have been tentative, aimed at small-scale support to grassroots organisations. It does not appear to have imposed its language, jargon or conditionality in Algeria quite as much as in other countries. As such, Algerian associations have generally been able to avoid the rigid imposition of donor priorities and have been able to exercise a degree of flexibility. The language of the EU's calls for proposals, discussed in Chapter 8, was deliberately wide so that associations could respond as they wished in line with their own priorities. Even the restriction against religious or political organisations was loosely defined, with many funded associations being inherently religious in their motivations and others overtly political in their campaigns.

The doubts of the Algerian public and, until recently, the reticence of the Algerian state to engage with the EU have tempered the EU's language. This has in some ways protected Algeria from one-way, donor-imposed funding programmes and language. The recently improved relations and increase in funding may risk reversing this. Yet, throughout this volume it has been shown that in the Algerian context, associations are quick to challenge European impositions: they refuse to take lessons in human rights and do not submit to the EU's demands. Negative self-perceptions and the language of domestic politicians and journalists are harder to dispel, however. Criticism of the associative movement, such as those critiques which SARP challenged, has increasingly entered into public discourse in Algeria and this will be a greater challenge to overcome.

Historical Narratives

The re-writing of history under colonialism, during decolonisation and more recently in the historical narratives of heritage associations today can be seen as part of a process of recapturing power in the cultural sphere, and of reinventing the Algerian collective memory. From the annihilation of an independent Algerian identity and history during colonialism, the historical self-perceptions of Algerians were revisited in the national liberation struggle. Scheele writes that as 'colonial injustice was increasingly understood in terms of democracy, socialism, Islamic reform', attempts were made by civil society 'to rewrite Algerian history according to nationalist standards'.[22] With the revision of 'French supremacy and readings of history', Algerian history was re-drawn as a long series of foreign invasions in which 'the Eastern invaders who were seen as "civilising", were set against the Europeans who had come merely to occupy and destroy'.[23] This re-writing of Maghrebi history was part of the cultural decolonisation process and Taoufik El Madani was one of the main protagonists from the 1930s. In his overturning of the myth of 'Latin Africa,' in which France was the logical continuation of the Roman Empire in North Africa, he redefined Rome as the 'barbarian destroyer'. The post-colonial state's subsequent abandoning of the Roman, as well as the colonial, heritage in Algeria is at the core of some of the aims and desires of Algerian citizens and the heritage associations they have created since 1990. Whilst not denying colonial crimes and the historical manipulations that accompanied them, heritage associations such as Bel Horizon, Castellum and APPAT have challenged both colonial and post-colonial narratives on ancient history. In their counter-narratives, Roman ruins in Algeria were redefined as part of a national Algerian history and heritage, neither Christian nor European but, if anything, far more closely entwined with the lives of the original inhabitants of North Africa, its Berber populations, and as such worthy of preservation for all future generations. Overall they argued for an intelligent, honest and critical debate about the legacy of such buildings and artefacts and for the need to involve young people in that debate. This was particularly visible in the work of Bel Horizon and Castellum, where students and young people were at the forefront of such discussions.

Also in the historical narratives of El Madani, there was, as McDougal describes it, another 'radical departure from previous self-conceptions', in the rediscovery of the first independent Islamic kingdom, in North Africa in Tahert, Tiaret, under the Ibadi Kharajite dynasty of the Rostomids.[24] This 'rediscovery' was important in that it strengthened ideas about the existence of an Algerian nation, a question which had split the nationalist movement – Abbas and Ben Badis in particular. However, it is also important today for organisations such as APPAT, which had proudly worked on preserving its vestiges and educating young people in Tiaret about them. APPAT's conflicts with the Algerian state are perhaps in some way a sign of the limits to which opposing narratives can be accepted. Recognising the Berber Mozabite population as the descendants of the first Algerian state perhaps did not fit well with the Arab-Muslim unifying identity that the FLN had set out to create. The state's recent shift in policy to a far more inclusive approach, including Berber as a national language and recognising the Berber New Year as a national holiday, is perhaps an indication that the work of the active Berber cultural associations since the 1990s have ultimately impacted upon the narratives of Algerian identity and history. Al Madani's project to institutionalise a 'new legitimate language of history and culture' for the 'rediscovery of ourselves' was essential to forging a new Algerian identity in the post-colonial era.[25] It is equally important today, in the continuation of this process, particularly for associations seeking to widen understandings of Algerian nationhood and identity, to include the Berber heritage in the history of the country.

In the post-colonial period, the language of history was also an important means of authority. History was used to forge power relations and to control the population. The suspicion of traitors and the lack of trust which emanated from the eight years of the liberation war continued to define political life. Determining a person's status as a martyr decided their place in society. Power relations were decided in accordance with the history of the war. Historical facts were manipulated, controlled or simply hidden. In her fieldwork with the inhabitants of a village in Kabylia, Scheele describes their feelings on the theft of history and the paradox of the 'general consensus' of the villagers that 'history is all-important', and yet is 'totally absent from the village itself'.[26] For the villagers, Algerian civil society had been an unacknowledged victim of the official FLN history. Members of the

Algerian People's Party, the Berbers, and the Harkis (the native Muslim Algerians who had served in the French army and suffered great cruelty on independence) had been obscured in official histories. The misrepresentation of different groups of Algerians by the official state narratives represented a theft of history by the new elite. History was a source of power and the new elite could decide who was a martyr and who was a traitor. The privileged class claimed to have this knowledge and it would not be shared on an equal basis. History was either 'dangerous' or 'forgotten' and 'the gap between what had actually happened at village level and the "official" history was too large to be bridged'.[27] As a result, at the local level, history was felt to be totally absent. In this context, the work of those cultural organisations which did dare to work on heritage, particularly in Berber areas such as Kabylia, takes on even greater significance. It also highlights, however, that access to the privileges and resources they might need was still very much in the hands of the new elites – in the local levels of the state structures – who continued to control the narratives of history.

The absence of truth about historical events in Algeria over the last century remains a central problem, internally, and also in Algeria's foreign relations. There has been no official apology for the crimes committed under colonial rule and during the War of Independence. Although many artists, writers and film-makers have recorded them, the lack of official recognition makes their occurrence intangible and the grieving process incomplete. Associations such as SARP spoke of the need to look into the traumas of colonialism and the Independence War. However, having been created in the 1990s, their focus had to be primarily on the urgent challenges of the 1990s.[28] In 2012, during the French presidential visit to Algeria,[29] François Hollande acknowledged the suffering and the 'brutal and unfair system' of colonial rule. Speaking to the Algerian Parliament, he stated that the truth must be spoken about the circumstances in which Algeria was delivered from the colonial system, in 'this war whose name was not mentioned in France for a long time'.[30] He stopped short of fully acknowledging responsibility and issued no apology. The question of colonialism was raised again in the 2017 French elections, with the denial of the evils of colonialism from the far-right candidate Marine le Pen, in response to Emmanuel

Macron's statements that French colonialism had been 'a crime against humanity'.[31]

Equally difficult for the Algerian state and civil society is the truth about the conflict of the 1990s during which an estimated 200,000 people lost their lives, although official figures report only half of this number. The lack of information about the crimes committed by all sides, combined with the amnesty for the perpetrators, means Algeria struggles to move forward. Although the 2006 Reconciliation Charter did bring peace, the burying of history has once again meant that there is no official recognition of the suffering of the victims and their families. It is for these crimes that the Algerian population, associations, actors, writers and journalists still seek truth and reparation. Whilst there is a strained official discourse on this aspect of Algerian history, it is in the associative sector that actual words are given to the suffering of Algerians by associations such as *Djazairouna*, *SOS disparus* or the Boucebci Foundation. These organisations record and speak on behalf of the victims and campaign for a more honest approach to recent history. Members of these associations working with victims of terrorism denounced the absence of the right to speak out about the Reconciliation Charter which denied them the truth. Whilst the charter did end the violence, for the president of *Djazairouna* what was needed was justice, truth and the rule of law, without discrimination, particularly for the families of the 15,000 victims who disappeared in Algeria in the 1990s.

Associations such as *Djazairouna* and Bel Horizon have the capacity and the legitimacy to challenge the language of history, and do so in practical ways. Their actions impact nationally and even internationally, with the president of *Djazairouna* regularly invited to speak at international conferences, including at the UN. On questions of heritage, certain associations have become alternative voices, offering different visions of Algerian identity. Whilst their membership might represent a limited section of the population, their work is important and they are able to attract large audiences. Over 20,000 people participated in Bel Horizon's heritage walk in Oran in 2011. *Djazairouna* is currently training 50 associations in the Mitidja region to build their capacities and skills. Associations such as these are actively reclaiming the public sphere and in doing so appear to have the legitimacy to speak for the populations of their cities.

Language Policies and the Public Sphere

The language used within the different spheres of influence of political or social life crucially determines who has access to them and thus, feasibly, access to the democratic process itself. With this in mind, associations have played a role in seeking reforms to language policy in politics and education more widely. In 1962, Algeria faced a difficult choice as to which language to adopt for the newly independent nation. The colonial period had seen the imposition of French onto every aspect of education and onto institutions, as well as on the social and cultural life of Algeria. Modern standard Arabic was now hoped to be a unifying force, and an important part of the decolonisation process and recuperation of the cultural sphere. However, with it came barriers, confusion and the stigmatisation of Algerian Arabic, of French as the working language of many Algerians and of the Berber languages, the mother tongue of a significant part of the population. The imposition of a form of Arabic that was foreign to many in the population, the rejection of the French language, despite its dominance in many aspects of life, and the rejection of Berber, spoken by an estimated 30 per cent of Algerians,[32] meant that the post-colonial language policy would necessarily be complex and challenging.[33] Gafaiti writes that the:

> unilateral imposition of Modern Standard Arabic as the country's sole official language and its repression of Tamazight and Algerian Arabic, the vernacular languages of the country, and of French language [...] is an act of linguistic 'purification' that marginalizes significant segments of Algerian society.[34]

Despite these huge difficulties in managing the different languages of Algeria, reforms in the twenty-first century have increasingly sought to tackle these challenges, particularly concerning the status of Berber. Since the 1990s, a more tolerant and inclusive approach to language policy and education has evolved. Original hostility towards Tamazight has been replaced with a more inclusive approach, valuing Berber languages in the Algerian public sphere, political life and education system. This was at least partly in response to increasing popular mobilisation, through the Berber Cultural Movement and associations, which demanded it. Following strikes in the early 1990s, the government introduced reforms in the education system to include education in Tamazight. This was accompanied by the creation of the High Commission for Amazighté, attached to the presidency in Algiers in 1995. The revision of the Constitution in 2002 amended Article 3, enshrining Tamazight as a national language and ensuring that the state works for its promotion and development in all its varieties, within the national territory.[35] In 2016, Tamazight was elevated to the status of an official language through the new constitutional reform process.[36] This was an important step for Berber associations. With Arabic as the sole official language of the democratic process and state institutions, the Berberophone population had been significantly excluded and were often more at ease in French. Berber could now be used for official documents, but the language of government would still be Arabic.

These reforms have in many ways been a result of the active mobilisation of Berber associations and social movements, particularly in Kabylia, since the 1990s. Associations were crucial in lobbying to bring about the changes in language policy in Algeria as part of what they saw as an important process to open up the political sphere and the democratic process which excluded so many. The introduction of Tamazight into the education system from 1995 was seen by the Berber Cultural Movement as a historic event. The universities of Tizi Ouzou and Bejaia had already integrated diplomas in 1990 and 1991 but, prior to this, Berber had been kept far away from any official sectors, despite being spoken by millions of Algerians. From the 1990s onwards, the tone of negation and stigmatisation changed definitively. There was still impatience with the pace of reforms and the speed of implementation of the policy. The absence of a clear language policy and the lack of pedagogical tools remained obstacles. Impatience, however, was also balanced with realism concerning the difficulties and the ambitious nature of the policy. The clear motivation of both students and teachers gave many reasons to be optimistic about the prospects of Berber becoming a language of education in the future.

The status of Algerian Arabic and of the French language in Algeria has been more problematic. Assia Djebar, in her novel *Algerian White*, writes of the significant advances which were made in terms of literacy in the education system post-independence, but criticises the stultifying effects of the language policy, with the banishing of Algerian Arabic and exile of many Francophone writers.

The institutionalised mediocrity of the educational system since 1962 – despite a clear effort toward making the population literate: literacy has almost tripled in thirty years – was practiced on two levels: promoting the 'national language' by officially restricting the living space of the other languages; then, in addition to this sterilizing monolingualism, the diglossia peculiar to Arabic (the structure's vertical variability that can give the child who is being educated a precious agility of mind) was handled badly by comparison with other Arab countries, by banishing a dialect that was vivid in its regional iridescence, subtle in the strength of its challenge and its dream.

Thus, the denial of an entire people's genius went hand in hand with the mistrust of a minority of French-language writers whose production, in spite of or for lack of anything better, continued in exile.[37]

In line with Djebar's critique of the 'sterilizing monolingualism', for the linguist Khaoula Taleb-Ibrahimi[38] the stigmatising of the vernacular languages and of French also prevented 'the emergence of an Algerian intelligentsia' which would play a role in the public sphere. Civil society was now split between two languages: French and Arabic, neither of which were truly mastered by the majority.[39] The ongoing stigmatisation of Algerian Arabic and of French created barriers and reinforced divisive and exclusionary tendencies. Berger writes that,

> the double scarring of dialectical Arabic and French in Algeria, the mutual, albeit unequal historical cross-inscription of languages, the symbolic and literal wounding of Algerian speakers, split as they are by each utterance, may indeed reveal something about the experience of language.[40]

Yet, while the state failed to successfully deal with these language realities of post-independence Algeria, in many cases the new civil society associations embraced the country's linguistic diversity. Algerian Arabic was the language of expression in almost all associations. The cultural productions of theatrical associations such as the Fondation Alloula in Oran or Association Warchat Fonoun in Blida were in

Algerian Arabic. The poetry reviews published by the Boucebci Foundation were always in French, ignoring the prescriptions of the 1990 law which had previously sought to impose Arabic on associations and their publications.[41] The Petit Lecteur in Oran published children's books in French and in Arabic, and its activities were equally bilingual.

The place of the French language is perhaps more complex than that of dialectal Arabic. The francophone Algerian writers mentioned above, both in Algeria and abroad, as well as French writers of Algerian descent, remain part of a vibrant Algerian francophone literature. The international renown of these writers is a source of pride in Algerian cultural life and they play an important role, in the increasing number of international book fairs in Algiers and as ambassadors of Algeria abroad, despite being often highly critical. Direct targets of the Islamist violence of the 1990s, the exile of many more francophone writers, intellectuals, journalists and artists to France, where they were often actively engaged in associations, from cultural to human rights, means the bridges linking French and Algerian civil society were stronger than ever.

Unlike Morocco, French is not recognised as a national language. Algeria is not a member of the International Organisation for *La Francophonie*, despite being possibly the second-largest francophone country in the world after France. The relaxing of the Law on Associations in 2012, so that any language could be used in publications,[42] was symbolic of the state's recognition that the working language of Algerian institutional life is still often French. It is also recognition that achieving a more open language policy could be to Algeria's advantage, rather than representing a problem or a threat.

One perverse effect of the Arabisation policy had been that the children of the well-off attended schools where they would receive bilingual education in French and Arabic. Less fortunate children would receive only Arabic instruction. An unplanned tool of social selection, the Arabised education policy restricted access to the job market for those who could not fully master French.[43] Associations whose members did not master French also complained of discrimination in accessing funding, particularly from international donors. Despite the efforts of the Algerian state, French remained the working language of state institutions and the private sector, with one respondent suggesting that even the law which Arabised the Algerian state was most probably first written in French then translated.

Within associations, pragmatic solutions are often found for questions of language. As a younger member of Bel Horizon association remarked during a meeting in Oran in reference to the protection of colonial architecture which the state was reticent to approve, 'it is like French, French is our language – we speak the colonial language, but it is ours'.[44] The burgeoning number of private or charitable language schools and multilingual libraries form part of the local response for a more open approach in Algeria. The risks of denying the language diversity of Algeria are becoming increasingly acknowledged. The risk of unnecessarily dividing Algerians along ethnic or religious lines, of creating barriers to the job market or of creating generational divides, were all referred to in interviews with members of associations. All felt it was important to support young Algerians learning all languages of relevance to Algeria, including English. Even the European Union seemed willing to open up its programmes to support Arabic speaking associations accessing its grants. The potential of increased funding from the Gulf States, primarily targeting Arabic-speaking and Islamic associations, was seen as potentially divisive. The role of the state in overseeing the origins of all international funding coming into Algeria was seen as important, particularly by European donors who were keen to maintain a monopoly over funding Algerian associations from all backgrounds.[45]

There have been significant developments in terms of language policies in Algeria since 1990. Despite the previous legal restrictions, the place of Berber, and French to a certain extent, seems now to have been guaranteed in the public sphere, in the education system and in the cultural life of the country. The Algerian Government has supported greater English-language education at all levels and has signed agreements with the British Government to allow Algerian researchers to study for doctorates in the UK. Some risks of division and barriers in education, the job market or political life have been removed through a more inclusive approach from the government, from associations through their lobbying for reform and from international donors who have perhaps become more pragmatic and accommodating.

Conclusion

Different questions of language have significantly impacted on the construction of civil society in Algeria over the last century. The performative effects of colonial or neo-colonial language played a role in reinforcing negative self-perceptions and damaging local political autonomy. Yet, to a great extent, Algerian civil society and the state have proved resilient and wary of the language of others. Neo-colonial narratives and persistent prejudice, such as the denial of an Arab-Muslim civil society or the Berber myth, have been challenged. Reformist agendas justifying external interventions from donors have been tackled head on, as have overly negative perceptions of associations within Algerian society, including those coming from the highest level, the Minister of Interior.

Associations have challenged the colonial, but also the post-colonial FLN narratives of history, seeking to offer a wider, more inclusive vision of Algerian nationhood and identity – one which includes the entirety of Algerian history from Berber, Roman and Jewish roots to the Arab, Ottoman and even colonial heritage in the towns, cities and countryside. Young people have been directly engaged in these processes of reflection. The place of Berbers, Ibadis and all the diverse ethnic communities which make up Algeria, with their role in its history, is discussed in the small Algerian associations that are contributing to the work of preserving the past, from restoring Kabyle villages to protecting religious manuscripts. History, used to control Algerians in post-independence Algeria by determining who was a true martyr and who was a traitor, is now escaping from its monopolisation by the older generation. Since 1990, in principle, anyone can set up or join an association and young people are predominantly those most active in the associations I met with across Algeria. Independent associations can provide a voice for those who were previously denied one – particularly the victims of the 1990s – and alternative spheres in which to discuss difficult questions of identity and nation.

The stigmatisation of Berber, French or dialectal Arabic, through language or education policy, has been increasingly challenged, particularly by Berber cultural associations, but also by Francophone writers and in the press. Within associations and artistic expression, spaces are freer than those regulated or restricted, such as the education sector, the workplace and particularly the political institutions. Challenging the sole use of Arabic as the language of government has been an important step to widening access to the democratic process and Berber associations have played a significant role in this. Whilst most association members formerly had little trust in the democratic process, in more recent years a number of association leaders have decided to stand for local government, particularly in Kabylia and in Oran. The experience of community activism and greater awareness of the role local government plays has perhaps contributed to this. More successful and well-managed associations from all fields have played an important role in creating examples for others to follow. Through networks, associative spheres span from Beni Isguen to Tizi Ouzou, Tamanrasset to Tebessa, as civil society is gradually coming together to discuss important questions about the future of Algeria.

CHAPTER 10

IMAGINING A NEW FUTURE

Civil society in Algeria was published in 2018. Much of the data for the book was gathered between 2007 and 2017, a period during which, despite multiple challenges, Algerian civil society, in particular registered associations, was burgeoning. It was also published a year before some of the most spectacular and dramatic events in contemporary Algerian history known as the *hirak,* the movement. Five years on, this additional chapter draws on more recent scholarship and on new data gathered during a large research project focused on youth environmental activism. A network of Algerian and international researchers managed this, with participants including Algerian youth in Algeria and the UK. The chapter has included some of the evidence from our seventy interviews with young people, associations, entrepreneurs and academics. These focused on the environment and the green economy, but also sought to understand some of the implications of the mass mobilisation of the Algerian *hirak*.[1] In February 2019, huge numbers – men, women and children – joined in this revolutionary movement of mass demonstrations for democracy, the rule of law and justice. When President Abdelaziz Bouteflika announced his decision, or rather it was announced for him, that he would stand for a fifth presidential term, despite being seriously ill and this breaching the Algerian constitution, the population stood up in mass protests. First, in the east of the country, then in Algiers and across all Algerian cities on 22 February 2019, millions marched, demanding the president step down. In April 2019, following weekly marches with similar numbers he subsequently did stand down. Yet, the demands went deeper than this. With so many having mobilised tirelessly at grassroots level for over three decades in increasingly organised associations, as documented throughout this book, Algerians could no longer accept the humiliation of poor governance, mismanagement, cronyism and corruption. On their side, democratic procedures had been respected. General assemblies had been held and bureaucracy ceaselessly adhered to. Volunteering had been the mainstay of the associative movement. The desire to contribute to rebuilding Algeria, once again after conflict, motivated so many of the associations' members interviewed, but they faced an increasingly out-of-touch, uncaring, authoritarian and wasteful elite, across so many sectors. The vision of a new Algeria young people could aspire to was increasingly remote. As the corruption cases mounted, more and more youth burned their papers and took dangerous boats across the Mediterranean.

Why and how, though, did Algerians mobilise at this very point in 2019 even though the difficult aftermath of the Arab Spring was increasingly apparent? Instability persisted in neighbouring Libya; the war continued in Syria and 3,000 had been killed following the counter coup against Morsi in Egypt.[2] The painful memories of the 1990s, frequently invoked by the prime minister and other politicians, made the risks associated with mobilisation in Algeria high. The Algerian *hirak* however is very different from the other Arab Spring demonstrations. As many scholars have argued, Algeria had already had her Arab Spring in 1988. Political awareness and engagement of all Algerians, and their activism across multiple arenas, from football stadiums to local protests, associations and the press, meant that when the tipping point came in 2019, they were well prepared. They could engage with a government that no longer had solutions, or even the capacity to communicate, and they could do this in a peaceful and very different way. The memory of the Algerian liberation war of 1954–62, reinforced by the active engagement of some of those former fighters, including famous women combatants, gave protesters the courage to continue, reclaiming their revolutionary legitimacy. Demonstrations were clearly understood as the continuation of the process of liberation from colonialism and the collective struggle of the previous generation. Hamza Hamouchene underlines the profound nature of the movement, writing that,

> the events that took place in Algeria during 2019-2021 are truly historic. This movement (Hirak) is unique is its huge scale, peaceful character, national spread – including in the marginalized south, and massive participation from women and young people, who constitute the majority of Algeria's population. This kind of mobilization has not been seen since 1962, when Algerians went to the streets to celebrate their hard-won independence from French colonial rule. This revolution is like a breath of fresh air. The people have affirmed their role as agents of their own destiny.[3]

Ultimately, it was this peaceful nature of the new protest movement, the *hirak*, that profoundly marked its organisation. Along with its survival for over fifty-four months, this made it an unprecedented form of mobilisation, worthy of further study and understanding.

Asef Bayat's concept of 'refolution', focusing on reform rather than revolution, as applied to the Arab Spring, can help us understand the build-up and the true revolutionary potential of the *hirak* as a transformative moment in Algerian history.[4] Bayat writes:

> In times of revolution/insurrection, the fiercest battles take place in the streets, the locus where revolutionary breakthrough is achieved. This exceptional episode is marked by a swift transformation of consciousness, utopia, and euphoria. It is these extraordinary moments – with their unique spatial, temporal, and cognitive elements – that inspire awe, offer inspiration, and bring the promise of a novel social order.[5]

However, it is the post-revolutionary times that fundamentally affect how transition might occur and embed. Institutions matter and 'political parties, genuine civil society, voting, parliament, and above all rule of law' are all indispensable. Alone, they cannot guarantee the 'inclusive polity' that the revolutionaries aspire to, but they are nevertheless its fundamental building blocks.[6] The consequences of the three decades of civil society activism should not be underestimated. This is not only in terms of the nature of the *hirak* movement, but in the potential of the post-revolutionary period. As Bayat writes, 'Whereas the street matters most in times of revolution/insurrection, it is the political society and state that reign in the postrevolution.'[7] The impact of the *hirak* in uniting Algerians accelerated processes of structured organisation that were already underway since 1990, following the 1988 uprisings. Bayat's second book on the Arab Spring revolutions, *Revolutionary Life*, focuses more on the social side and 'grassroots' of revolutionary movements. This is the 'transformation in people's subjectivities, expectations, relations of hierarches' as well as the 'alternative practices in farms, factories, neighborhoods, schools, streets, and private realms.'[8] The civic engagement and discipline of so many Algerians during the *hirak* marches were symbolic of this and were perhaps unsurprising, given their quiet acts of solidarity, environmental protection, social work and awareness raising over many years, in a country with more registered associations than most of the region. The rebuilding of trust during the *hirak* in public squares, in artistic creation, in the physical act of being together in the public space in such great numbers was a new practice which enhanced the feelings of belonging and identity, as Algerians, shaped by their history and collective struggles. Such processes can be defined as a 'rupture', and the opportunity to imagine 'a different order of things'.[9]

The young people we interviewed throughout 2021, as part of our Youth Futures project, highlighted these feelings of unity, shared identity and purpose. When asked about environmental activism, they made connections to the public space, to caring for nature and Algeria's precious resources: concerns which had all been an integral part of the *hirak*. Challenges to the neoliberal order and to the extractivist nature of hydrocarbon companies were key messages in a number of the marches. Protesters drew on mobilisation campaigns active since the early 2010s, such as those against fracking in the Algerian south. Led by networks of the unemployed, women and middle-class environmentalists, the antifracking protests had managed to unite very diverse communities, with women playing prominent roles.[10] Other low-level protests, known locally as *protesta*, mainly over housing and basic public services at neighbourhood level, also saw a significant increase over the last decade. Similarly, strikes increased across many sectors, all this alongside a steady decline in voter participation. These micro-riots, or unauthorised highly local *protesta*, whilst disruptive, were only symbolically violent with roadblocks or burning tyres. Usually spontaneous, they always made specific claims on the state, with participants 'refraining from theft, looting or attacks on bystanders'.[11] The coming together of multiple groups and claims over the past decade may well have influenced the *hirak* demonstrations. Outside of the political sphere, these demands continued to emerge, even if claims were not always successful. To better understand the movement and how it connects to civil society developments since 1990, let us first explore the nature of the *hirak* throughout 2019, then how it developed through the pandemic in 2020 and, lastly, what new tools and political consciousness it may have provided, and the implications for the future of political life in Algeria.

The *Hirak* Revolution

After twenty years of banned demonstrations, yet an active associative life, Algerians took to the streets in the capital Algiers on 22 February 2019 and marched, often in their millions, twice a week for over a year. In Kherrata, in the east of Algeria, they had begun marching even earlier on the 16 February 2019, and marches progressively took place in every city and region of the country. The demonstrations were some of the largest and longest sustained peaceful marches for democracy in Africa, if not in the world. Whilst triggered by opposition to President Bouteflika's proposed fifth mandate, the contestation began in the football stadiums in the years before. Football songs eloquently expressed clear political messages about the frustration and disillusionment of young people and became the backdrop and anthems of the *hirak*. Tired with politics, young people sang about the corruption, their loss of hope and their desire to flee the country. In a context of limited public spheres for political debate, despite an increasingly active press and associations, stadiums remained one of the few spaces left for collective free speech critical of the government and Algerian politics.

The initial demonstrations in 2019 occurred after Bouteflika announced his decision to stand for a fifth term, despite the constitutional reform of 2016 that limited presidential mandates to two. Now in 2019, Bouteflika's decision to stand again was a constitutional infraction of the presidential limits. Furthermore, the president's poor health also meant that physically and constitutionally, he was no longer able to maintain the position of president. Article 102 of the constitution states that in the case of incapacity of the president, the head of the senate takes over for 90 days. Moreover, whilst ordinary Algerians often struggle to access good-quality healthcare and medicines, the president, like many high-ranking politicians, was receiving treatment abroad in Geneva. The humiliation of this situation drove even greater numbers of Algerians to the streets in cities across Algeria to demand change.

The first marches of 22 February 2019 were met with threats of the likely return of violence, with former prime minister Ahmed Ouyahia invoking memories of the Black Decade of the 1990s and of the Syrian conflict. Algerian scholar Faouzia Zeraoulia describes how the president had consistently been presented as 'the architect of peace' and how 'now the strategy changed to threatening the people that without him the violence would be back'. Yet, the strategy failed. Zeraoulia notes that 'the people developed a counter narrative', one which was focused on peaceful protest or '*silmiya*', a key slogan of the marches, and drew on multiple tools and strategies to challenge the regime.[12]

Frustration with corruption and the lack of governance or rule of law was at the forefront of this contestation. Algerians were tired of elite privilege, and there had been 'multiple signs of profound discontent'.[13] This included '*hogra*', the Algerian word for contempt shown towards citizens by the ruling class. Slogans on banners included '*Joumhouria machi Mamlaka*' (Algeria is a republic not a monarchy), targeting

Bouteflika's brother, who was widely accused of monopolising power for the clan, given the president's incapacity. Demonstrators also questioned the role of the army in political life, the Army Chief of Staff General Gaid Salah having been the major decision-maker within the regime, with banners declaring their demands for a civil and not a military state: *'Dawla madania, machi aaskaria'*. Every Friday throughout 2019, and every Tuesday for students, Algerians came together in the streets and public spaces and challenged the government, and progressively found their demands accepted. These included the sacking of the prime minister and other ministers, the standing down of the president, the cancellation of the contested April and the postponed July elections, and the arrest of business elites and politicians, including former prime ministers Ouyahia and Sellal, on corruption charges. In September, presidential elections were called for 12 December 2019. These were carried out, despite significant mobilisation against them and with no non-regime-linked candidates on the ballot paper. With a very low turnout, Algerians elected Abdelmajid Tebboune, a former minister under Bouteflika, as president, and the peaceful protests for democracy continued.

Repression did increase towards the end of 2019 with a number of clashes between police and protestors. Police fired rubber bullets and tear gas into the crowds, injuring civilians and arrested significant numbers of young people, former revolutionary figures and opposition politicians, a number of whom remain in prison three years on. Reasons for the arrests included threatening national unity, by holding the Amazigh flag, offending a national institution or weakening the morale of the army. Neither the arrests, understood as arbitrary forms of intimidation or attempts to divide Algerians along ethnic lines, nor the consistent huge police presence appeared however to limit the marches. Nor did they diminish the watchfulness of an increasingly politically engaged public over all political decisions. The demonstrators continued their peaceful protest until March 2020. With the global coronavirus pandemic, protesters moved online, transforming their messages to include a focus on public health, calling on Algerians to 'stay home to protect Algeria'.

Whilst there were no leaders in the *hirak* marches, collective organisation was considerable. The astute political narrative of the football stadiums, and the reclaiming of public spaces, meant that the movement took multiple forms. Cultural activities in main squares, debates on the steps of the national theatre in Algiers, collective cleaning of public spaces, particularly by young people, reinforced the collective identity, feelings of active citizenship and the political engagement that had begun in the stadiums. Such everyday resistance and activism also built upon the experience of organising that had been growing since 1990 within associational life, challenging social injustice, division and lack of public services at grassroots level. This absence of leaders or organisations in the *hirak* meant on the one hand that the movement could not be co-opted by the authorities. The co-opting of civil society organisations or movements remained a fear and consistent claim of many Algerians, who previously called out associations who took state funding and who then, supposedly, lowered their voices. The horizontal structure of the *hirak* was praised and celebrated, but it also meant there was no one to mediate in potential negotiations. Louisa Dris Aït-Hamadouche described the *hirak* as 'a movement which is organised but unstructured. Neither civil society nor political opposition parties took part.'[14] However, whilst officially registered parties and associations were absent from the demonstrations, their members marched and organised as individual Algerian citizens. What happened between and after the marches was almost as important. New networks, partnerships and forums, such as the Alternative Pact for Democracy and later Nida 22, emerged proposing alternative responses and pathways forward.[15]

The manner in which millions of Algerians collectively mobilised, without specific leaders, also draws on important historical experiences. Links to the Algerian liberation struggle, which saw similar forms of mobilisation, were explicit throughout the demonstrations. Independence figures such as Djamila Bouhired, now in her eighties, marched on the streets of Algiers, alongside young people. Youth protesters referred to the Algerian liberation struggle as well as to their current problems on their signs and banners, framing the current struggle as a continued intergenerational fight for freedom and justice. Powerful political songs expressed the pain and frustration of young people, particularly about losing family members who had burned their papers and taken boats to Europe, often losing their lives in the crossing. These messages were at the heart of the *hirak*, uniting protesters of all ages. Scholars describe the sense of empowerment felt by young people in gaining the respect of their elders. Following the success of their actions, Benalycherif quotes one young person saying that, 'we consider that we are in the process of a true revolution. We are doing what our elders have not finished. Older people who used to criticise us are now discovering that we are capable of making a difference.'[16]

This energy of young people also bolstered the *hirak's* resilience, creativity and ideas for reform. Like Bayat, Lafi argues that, on the wider scale, the North African movements were not just about contestation, but a movement of ideas, creating 'new social practices' and a 'new civic sphere'.[17] For the duration of the marches in Algeria, committees organised first aid and local residents prepared food and left bottles of water on pavements, particularly during the hot summer months. In Ramadan, Algerians continued to demonstrate, then laid out the longest table they could along the central street, Rue Didouche, in Algiers. They then broke the fast together in a symbolic reuniting of Algerian citizens, reclaiming the street in a new social practice and space. The importance of cleaning and appropriating such public spaces, highlighting the civil nature of the protests and the aspirations and commitments of the movement, came across in our interviews with Algerian youth. One associative volunteer stressed his pride in Algerian youth for having done this, demonstrating their willingness to engage and work for a better future. He pointed out,

> Young people, since the Algerian Hirak, have shown their capacity to contribute. We saw them cleaning the streets. This gave a good image of Algerian youth and their desire for a decent and clean life. During covid – again cleaning and disinfecting public spaces – young people were acting on the Algerian street.[18]

Questions of language also emerged once again in this unifying moment. The main slogans of the protests were in Algerian Arabic, the native tongue of the majority of Algerians, as yet unrecognised officially, or standardised.[19] When a journalist questioned a young man in the early stages of the *hirak*, his response in Algerian Arabic of 'yetnahaw gaa!', that 'they should all leave!', went viral and became a key slogan of the movement.[20] It also signified the importance of communicating in the Algerian language and of valuing the cultural heritage of the country. In our interviews, language was also cited as an intergenerational challenge, preventing young people from accessing certain spheres. One retired association president pointed out the difficulties for young people in accessing opportunities despite their desire to be involved. He added:

> Young people want to be involved but there is a lack of support. We are retired we have time. Our age also means the community respects us so we can act. They struggle to find work, it is hard for them. Then there is the question of language. We are more francophone, they are more Arabophone.[21]

One of the *hirak's* important achievements was to challenge certain outdated narratives, fed by colonial prejudices, of Algeria as fragmented, weak or divided over language and culture. The *hirak* showcased the highly resilient forces in a unified Algerian population, as well as the wealth of cultural traditions, including the solidarity, generosity and care integral to those traditions. The importance of uniting all for the common cause did mean that some campaigns were felt to be sidelined. Whereas women were prominent in the marches, the question of putting gender equality at the forefront of claims was contested. In her new book *Algerian Women,* Latefa Guemar explains how,

> while women and the youth played a key role in maintaining its peaceful character over the coming weeks, the question of the extent to which the Hirak was to be a movement for social justice and gender equality began to arise as early as the fourth

week of protests. The mantra of 'machiwaktism' ('It's not the time for this') was the answer that many leading figures of the Hirak gave to the feminists who organised 'les carres des feministes' (the 'feminist squares') on the edge of the protests.[22]

Whereas women's active participation challenged 'the stereotypical representation of women in the region as oppressed victims',[23] attempts to intimidate young women protesters were documented. This was 'a weak point' that could be exploited. Yet despite these challenges, many of the women Guemar interviewed did feel that the *hirak* had 'seeded hope'. It enabled Algerians to reclaim citizenship, at home as in the diaspora, and feel pride in it. Many of the divisions that had been previously stoked by the authorities were falling away.[24] Powerful images of demonstrators, particularly women, dressed in different regional costume and jewellery, symbolised the coming together of the population in their diversity, in shared aims of mutual respect, democracy and justice. Zoubir describes how '[this] strong unity of Algerians, who have put aside their ethnic, regional, or ideological differences, which the regime had used to its own purposes in the past, is reviving values that were buried for decades, especially under Bouteflika's rule'.[25] By marching together, despite their differences, the *hirak* enabled Algerians to reconcile and reunite, and to prepare for the challenge ahead of them with the global pandemic of 2020.

Pandemic Activism

In March 2020, as the world began to realise the extent of the pandemic about to arrive, Algeria introduced a strict lockdown, closing the borders and introducing curfews. The city of Blida was the first affected, with the number of cases and deaths rising rapidly. For the Friday marches, a number of Algerians went to social media to demand that people stay home in the interest of public health, and to continue to mobilise online. As many families faced destitution – losing jobs, income and social support – networks of young people were formed to provide food parcels, to clean and disinfect the cities and public spaces and to set up food kitchens. Similar to the work of many of the social associations documented throughout this book, across the country, groups organised. They produced protective and medical equipment, including masks and visors. Organisations sent food packages to Blida to support the families in confinement there.

Internationally, Algerians fundraised to purchase ventilators and support Algerian hospitals. The pandemic particularly affected certain groups within the Algerian diaspora, especially young people, such as students, who were unable to travel or extend their student grants, and undocumented migrants with limited funds and job insecurity. Abroad, Algerian charities and unofficial groups organised extensively to support vulnerable Algerians in Western capitals, to fund funerals and medical supplies. Strong networks of solidarity supported undocumented migrants in Europe, who lost their jobs and income, often overnight. Foodbanks were set up, deliveries organised and fundraisers launched. In 2021, as part of our research project, having witnessed many of these initiatives, we interviewed a number of Algerian civil society organisers in the UK. From interviews with these London-based Algerian charities, we confirmed the impressive reach of this local activism in the diaspora. Community leaders explained the fear felt by many Algerians, either on account of their immigration status or on account of the virus, and how associations were able to respond effectively. They described their pride and sense of community, but also ambitions as to what would truly strengthen their role in the diaspora, in terms of education, solidarity, cultural representation and activism after years of dislocation and mistrust, particularly in the UK context that we researched.[26] The Algerians we interviewed wanted to actively contribute to building the community locally and to strengthening links with organisations back home, working on the crisis response and on wider reflections about the future of Algeria.

As around the world, the shift to online accelerated. The public debates that emerged around the *hirak* went on Zoom. Academics and associations organised international conferences on topics such as public health, the environment and democracy. Well-connected and technologically savvy young people were able to take the lead on such initiatives. Student clubs offered online trainings, discussions and debates. Associations were able to recruit international volunteers and diaspora professionals to support them in online activities and fundraising. Such activities continue today with numerous conferences organised, such as those for the sixtieth anniversary of Algerian independence, using online technology to include Algerians and scholars in Algeria and internationally.

Online education and digital technologies in education equally made significant developments. The national curriculum was delivered via television channels and teachers were supported to develop online content. Whilst a difficult process for a system with little experience of working online, the Covid-19 crisis, and the massive demand to turn to distant learning methods, was seen by many as an opportunity. The possibility and potential to redefine and re-evaluate the education system at all levels and to benefit from universally available resources was a significant opportunity for teachers, from primary schools to universities.[27] In our interviews, associations also pointed to progress that was being made within universities to train young people in entrepreneurship. One association in the south pointed out:

> There is a *'maison de l'entreprenariat'* in every university across Algeria. Around 6 years ago, they created these. Each young person who graduates must have an entrepreneurial project. ... The best ideas win prizes and local investors come to the university to see if they will finance those ideas. There is also an entrepreneurship module in every degree now in Algeria. This is to help youth to create jobs. Individual projects and small businesses will be vital. There are more and more opportunities and support mechanisms, including the new Ministry of Start Ups.[28]

Many associations such as Injaz Aljazair whom we interviewed and then worked with to run a joint training on sustainability leadership in Oran in May 2022, specifically focus on entrepreneurship training. Injaz run programmes across different regions working with the private sector and other associations to engage young people in project design and planning.

Despite progressive change, there remain continued frustrations with public and political life, particularly among youth. Young people explained how difficult it was to launch projects, gain trust and have an educated debate, even after the progressive achievements of the *hirak*. One youth activist explained,

> Young people need guidance to channel their ambitions and desires. Many just want to leave. There is a lack of group spirit, particularly recently, they need elites to advise them and offer direction.
>
> What disappoints most, is those who leave the country and do not give back or return. They criticize, but do not invest back in Algeria. Even if only their time! Whereas here there is an enormous amount of work which is needed to be done to support young people. We need help them, guide them, give direction.[29]

The added difficulties of the pandemic have perhaps diminished the energies and creativity of some in the population, or rather highlighted areas where greater support and connection is needed. Another associative member from the south felt that young people were 'demobilised and demotivated. They want to leave and go to Morocco.' He pointed out that so many young people had university degrees, but no chance of meaningful employment. With the state unable to create those opportunities, they sought to create them within the associational sector. Critical of past failures in providing finance to young people, he stressed the need for ideas and creativity among youth, arguing, 'development is about ideas; about creating innovation'.[30]

Others were more optimistic, pointing to the innovation and adaptation taking place, particularly in the south where climate change and biodiversity were major themes in our discussions. Associations were working on product transformation, circular economies and job creation as a means to preserve precious and fragile ecosystems and livelihoods there. Speaking from Laghouat, one associational member told us that there was an increase in associational activism and an increased interest in the environment and resource management,

> In the last ten years, there has been a huge increase in the numbers of young people engaged in associations. Just recently I was discussing with a youth very concerned about environmental risks of hydrocarbon extraction on superficial water sources. They are visible, they are assertive, they know how to articulate their ideas and to explain their products. Young people are beginning to invest in associations and in start-ups. This is happening.[31]

Despite the difficulties and regional differences, the desire for real grassroots democracy and participation has continued to inspire frequent debates. Since Algerians broke the wall of fear on 22 February 2019, discussions have taken place online and in public spaces that were previously closed. Whilst this process has been challenging, Zoubir describes its contribution to future prospects for reform: 'Debates are being held in universities – which had lost their role of centers of knowledge and ideas in the last twenty years – and among some respected national figures to work out transition strategies.'[32] Our participants in the Youth Futures programme also referred to the universities as important spheres for debate and action, increasingly since the pandemic began, and particularly regarding the environment and climate change. One young person told us,

> Young Algerians are more aware of environmental issues. I see more events organised at universities ... Events such as TEDx talks are organised by young people and environmental activists are invited. I see this as a good sign of the motivation of young people to protect the environment.[33]

In cities across Algeria, artists reclaimed public spaces for concerts, and exhibitions, calling for public policies to support the arts and cultural institutions. Such calls continued online during the pandemic, and as soon as it was safe to do so, artists returned to public spaces bringing people together once again. At the same time, during the pandemic, young people have been actively engaged and invited into new spaces for political dialogue. One interviewee explained:

> Algerian youth now have new opportunities for participation. There are quotas for elections, as enshrined in the new constitution 2020, for the town hall, parliament and in the new Supreme Council for youth. Thirty percent on the electoral lists have to be under 40 and with a diploma. It seems there is a space for participation in political life now. In theory this exists, we now have to see it put into practice. We await a lot from the promised 'New Algeria'. We have to open the door for young people. These are modest developments but they are helping in structuring the confidence of youth.[34]

The political debate has been ongoing. Algerians have vocally challenged the arrests of hundreds of citizens both during the marches and afterwards, often for posts online criticising the government. They called out the very fact that Algeria should have political prisoners at all; that there were political activists dying in Algerian prisons, such as the Algerian human rights activist Kamel Eddine Fekhar who had died after a hunger strike in May 2019,[35] and they stood in solidarity with all detainees.[36]

In the crisis of the global pandemic, such calls and actions continued online. Connections between activists and with the diaspora strengthened with the sharing of information online. However, the use of online technology is not without its challenges and asymmetries of knowledge. According to the political activist Hakim Addad 'online surveillance' became a 'tool to control citizens and activists'.[37] The sharing of ideas, strategies and meetings on social media can make transparency and political activism more difficult and high risk.[38] Arrests for social media posts continued throughout the pandemic, with young people particularly affected. Some suggest that the repression now is worse than under Bouteflika, with Addad indicating,

> In the past, we used to know when we risked our freedom. The few hundred activists who denounced Bouteflika and his cronies were under threat. And even they were rarely sent to jail. Today, not only activists but also regular citizens who post the wrong message on Facebook or who record a sensitive scene without permission in a hospital or a public space with their phone can be prosecuted by what is called the 'justice system.'[39]

Whereas the risks remain high, young people continue to mobilise in different ways. Addad challenges those who suggest the *hirak* failed. Acknowledging there may have been an 'organisational deficit', the positive achievements, he argues, should be recognised, including the 'thousands of young people who strive to improve the state of their country by joining the social and political struggle' and the 'very concrete propositions that have been formulated'[40] even if, in his view, these have been so far ignored.

New Tools, Space and a Revolutionary Consciousness

Following the Marxist political theorist Antonio Gramsci, Asef Bayat describes the importance of bringing about change in the collective consciousness. This could include a transformation of civil society, as a means of revolution to transform the state, building a new 'hegemony in favour of a new social order'. Whilst Bayat's writings focus on other states and revolutionary movements in the region, Egypt and Tunisia in particular, his analysis of changes in the political consciousness are particularly relevant to Algeria, and the building of consensus for a new social order. He argues:

> Following Gramsci, it should be possible to work on such a project even under the shadow of authoritarian states and

neoliberal economies. I have suggested that the idea may begin with building an 'active citizenry' endowed with the 'art of presence'—a citizenry that possesses the courage and creativity to assert collective will in spite of all odds by circumventing constraints, utilizing what is possible, and discovering new spaces within which to make themselves heard, seen, felt, and realized.[41]

Such an 'active citizenry' was already present in the thousands of Algerians engaged in the associative movement of over one hundred thousand registered associations, more than most countries of the region, and the *hirak* multiplied these numbers. Given the history of Algeria, their quiet engagement and the difficulties of mobilisation, Zoubir, like so many commentators on the region, was surprised by the inherently political nature of the *hirak*, writing that '[no] less amazing was the progressive politicization of the movement'.[42] Similarly, Benalycherif quotes one of the participants in the marches who describes the feelings of responsibility, as a citizen, in the political future of the country. His interviewee explained how: 'We have become more aware that we have a role to play, that we will have to seek this change through our own efforts that nothing will fall from the sky.'[43] One of the key achievements of the movement was bringing people together to seek that change and believe in their own ability to bring it about. In his interview with Thomas Serres, Hakim Addad points to

> initiatives that now bring together people who didn't talk to each other, who didn't know each other. In spite of the repression, people talk to each other thanks to the Hirak. From east to west, from north to south. This is a victory. When they are taken into custody or incarcerated, Algerians from the north of the country will mobilize to defend Algerians from the south and vice versa. These are things that those who dismiss the Hirak don't want to acknowledge – as if they needed to validate a colonial mode of thinking that presents Arabs as incapable of organizing themselves and carrying out a revolution.[44]

Building on the findings discussed throughout *Civil Society in Algeria*, I argue that the actions of thousands of Algerian associations since the late 1980s in many ways anticipated the *hirak* movement. Raising awareness and popular mobilisation around community issues like heritage and social welfare, associations brought together diverse populations to challenge the status quo and provide practical solutions at grassroots level. The popular energies apparent in those associations have fed into the outburst of explicitly political demands in 2019. Their practical work at grassroots level, their patience and knowledge of how to manage local development challenges, their quiet work across so many regions and cities done peacefully and respectfully, in order to achieve their goals, I believe may have inspired the spirit of the *hirak*. If associations were not present in the marches, their members were, and their methods of peaceful, collective organisation framed how the *hirak* organised. The *hirak* did not appear out of nowhere. Rather, the latent energies and quiet daily activism of thousands of Algerians, particularly those in associations, were now transferred and multiplied to a much greater number in society, particularly young people who now carried them.

Throughout the last three decades of civil society mobilisation and the more recent demonstrations, Algerians have developed new forms of activism and engagement including art, music, poetry, online and physical protests. They have developed what Bayat describes as the 'art of presence' and the 'courage and creativity to assert collective will' despite huge constraints, whilst creating new spaces to do this. They have called out and responded to the global challenges of inequalities, extractivism, capitalist exploitation, climate change and environmental crises such as the devastating fires in 2021, as well as the injustices in international responses to the pandemic. Hamouchene clearly defines in transformational terms these developments, which themselves would engender further transformation. He writes, 'one of the greatest achievements of the current popular uprising is the change in political consciousness and the determination to fight for radical democratic change. This liberatory process unleashed an unequalled amount of energy, confidence, creativity and subversion.'[45]

This new energy, confidence and creativity certainly came across in the interviews we held with young Algerians throughout 2021 and 2022, during which our team noted the rising youth awareness and engagement. One young woman explained to us how

> the *hirak* movement really did change people's mindsets. It made them more engaged in protecting their local environments. It is not covid that did this. It is a political issue. Doing something good and positive was part of creating the 'New Algeria' that so many aspired to. The government changed in 2019. Change was possible. [46]

She went on to link this development more specifically to care for the public space explaining how, 'people began to care about and protect their environments'. Speaking at the height of the pandemic, she added, 'the situation is now more difficult. People are less optimistic. However, they do continue to care about their environment.'[47] The energies and aspirations of those many activists of the associational movement documented throughout this book were now spreading to a much wider population, and in particular, the younger generation, who through their participation in a mass movement had found new means and networks with which to engage in social and political activism.

A young entrepreneur from the east of Algeria told us about the explosion of youth activism across the country. From innovative projects, to engineering new technology and developing community infrastructure, he felt that youth were at the forefront of transformative change. He described how

> lately, there is a great community mostly made up of young people who are very active in volunteering and social activism. This also continued during the pandemic when people started donating money and whatever they had to save lives. [48]

Bayat suggests that it is the memory of the extraordinary and revolutionary events and the 'moral resources' they generate that become 'part of the popular consciousness'. He argues that this then serves 'as the normative foundation to imagine and build a "good society" of inclusive social order'. Such a new and transformed society, as clearly imagined by many of the young people we interviewed, is one based on 'solidarity, egalitarian ethos, and social justice'.[49] Across North Africa, such transformations are ongoing. Bayat describes the Arab Spring as a 'revolution as movement', or as 'monumental episodes of mobilization, solidarity and sacrifice, shift in consciousness, cognitive break from the past, and imagination of new possibilities'. As such, he writes, the results, 'may keep the transition chapter unfinished and its narrative complex'.[50]

Whilst there is still uncertainty and frustration among Algerian youth and the population more widely about the rate of political change, the narrative is indeed complex. For many, there is a renewed hope in the future and multiple examples of practical action on the ground to contribute to achieving that future. In the Conference held at SOAS University in London on the sixtieth anniversary of Algerian independence, participants were asked to express their feelings about the future of Algeria in twenty years' time: whether they felt positive, whether it would be a status quo, or if they felt negative. Over half felt the future would better, just under half thought it would be a status quo and not one participant thought the future of Algeria would be worse than the present. Such a change in political consciousness and the belief that change is possible has important implications for Algerian civil society more widely. It is such transformations 'in society's sensibilities' that represent the necessary preconditions 'for far-reaching democratic transformation'.[51]

Like Addad, Robert Parks describes one of the most important achievements of the *hirak* as the fact that 'it has invigorated a new generation of activists, who over the last ten months have learned new repertoires of placing demands on the state, not dissimilar from the localized *protesta* of the past decade'.[52] In such a new political context, the new and future governments would be obliged to grapple with this new political order and expectations, particularly of those young people who had led this impressive movement.

Conclusion

The lessons from the last five years since 2018 are profound. The *hirak* surprised Algerians, as it did international commentators, with the intensity and longevity of its peaceful marches for a meaningful and inclusive democracy. What range of futures can Algerian youth now aspire to and what future can we expect for public life in Algeria? It could be considered that the period since 1988 and Algeria's initial Arab Spring was the long revolution that has perhaps now borne fruit. New ways of working, of considering power relations and citizens' rights have emerged through the consistent hard work of associational volunteers on the ground, and now through the most impressive and vocal demonstrations the continent has seen, which multiplied and generalised this. Despite the persistent challenges, divisions and frustrations, the revolutionary moment of the *hirak* throughout 2019 was the culmination of these years of active engagement on the ground by citizens, in organised associations, in localised protests, and in the strikes and union activism. The *hirak* was also followed by a period of intense crisis with the pandemic. It was during this time that the values and ideals of the *hirak* and the associative movement, of sharing, care, and collective solidarity, were continually demonstrated. Across the country, young people and small networks across society responded to the enormous challenges facing citizens and public services.

Throughout our trainings, discussions and interviews with Algerian youth, the challenges of achieving a society informed by the ideals of caring, egalitarian ethos, and inclusive democracy were debated. Fairness, in exams, in opportunities, in access to the job market, were all major concerns for young people. How to cooperate across generations and create new opportunities and livelihoods for young people that were consistent with a sustainable future were part of their aspirations. They wanted to understand the past, including acknowledging and valuing the legacy of the independence struggle, recognising and responding to the traumas of the 1990s, whilst looking to a future which would value their creativity, skills, ambition and hard work. Across our interviews, like Muriam Haleh Davies, we felt a 'deep-seated desire to recount one's own history rather than have it recounted by someone else. To define oneself rather than being defined.'[53]

The radical reimagination of their roles and possibilities yet to come, during the fifty-four weeks of marching, gave hope that the future could be different. The continuing relentless struggle and persistent popular engagement, despite ongoing obstacles and barriers, indicate the potential for a better future than the previous generation had endured. Connecting across borders, both during the *hirak* and then even more so during the pandemic, reunited Algerians in the diaspora and the homeland. The expanding online sphere is connecting students with international opportunities, but these remain limited by the restrictive visa conditions for any foreign travel faced by the majority of Algerian and African youth more widely. The necessity of opening borders, exchanging knowledge, whilst simultaneously working locally to protect the vulnerable ecosystems, from the deserts of the south to the forests of the north, came over in our discussions. Associations from the south spoke of the potential environmental threats that would soon also affect the north. One activist in the south warned that

> the desert does not advance, it is created. Algiers, Oran, everywhere in the north this could happen. If we do not care for the vegetation, the desert will come. Trees are not the solution always, we need endemic species, and we need an emergency plan for Algeria. It can happen very quickly. In 50 years, we have seen significant change to our landscape. We are warning the northern regions, drawing on our own experience.[54]

Along with adaptation and innovation, migration will likely thus be a key component of Algeria's future, both internally from the regions increasingly suffering from climate change and desertification, and across borders as populations adapt to changing conditions such as temperatures over fifty degrees Celsius. The work of associations and civil society activists in debating and reflecting on how such transitions and change can be carefully managed will be of vital importance. The need for inclusivity, equality and solidarity, drawing on Algerian traditional values, which already include these, will be paramount.

The new forms of activism and engagement that Algerians have developed since 2019, could be fundamental to how future change will be brought about. The inclusion of art, music, poetry, and online and physical protests to their 'art of presence', demonstrating courage and creativity, has allowed them to assert their collective will despite huge constraints. Young people are at the heart of this. The *hirak* movement has created new aspirations, innovation and spaces for activism that cannot be easily closed down. Algerian civil society's challenges to the global injustices of inequality, extractivism, capitalist exploitation, climate change and environmental crises should inspire wider reflection in the Mediterranean region and beyond.

CONCLUSION

Since the 1990 reforms in Algeria, which opened up the opportunity to create associations, there have been significant developments, both in the numbers and in the nature of civil society organisations in the country. Despite the devastating conflict of the 1990s, associations continued to register and organise. Whilst Algerians remain governed by an authoritarian regime, associations have nevertheless managed to create independent spaces outside of those hierarchical structures, and have progressively facilitated debate in wide areas including history, culture, national identity, human rights, equality and social justice. Through a study of civil society associations working on the ground, and of the historical challenges and political obstacles they face, this book has questioned previous stereotypes and more cynical assumptions about Algerian civil society, namely as being no more than a conservative force legitimising and reinforcing authoritarian regimes.

Algerian civil society reflects the diversity and differences which make up the country. Whilst often deeply conservative, it is simultaneously secular, religious, Berber, Islamist, feminist and traditional. Its members master Modern Standard Arabic, Algerian Arabic, French, Berber, Spanish and now increasingly English. Different strands of civil society can, and sometimes do, come together on questions of Algerian heritage – the importance of protecting all parts of it – and on their shared despair at the state of political life. They collectively lament the failures of post-independence governments to implement the free and fair Algeria, based on equality and democratic principles, that was promised to them by the liberation struggle in the last century. Deeply attached to the Algerian nation and identity, whilst critical of the state, Algerian associations are still protective of the state against external interference, and the role of foreign donors is very much conditioned by that sentiment.

Unlike other contexts, where donors have been accused of trying to 'construct' civil society from the outside, imposing their own language and methods and thus creating an artificial civil society, Algeria has given them limited space for intervention. Donor programmes which elsewhere across the region have resulted in a lack of autonomy for local actors – or poorly managed interventions turning civil society support initiatives into 'winning the lottery' scenarios[1] and resulting in animosity, corruption, labour market distortion and ultimately even violence[2] – have been largely avoided in Algeria. Where donor budgets are excessively high, such as in Palestine, local civil society has to compete with a multitude of European NGOs. In comparison, Algeria has one of the highest densities of local associative life, and yet the lowest levels of donor funding. The position of donors is considerably weaker in Algeria and the very densest areas of associative life, the south and Kabylia, are also the furthest from donor interventions. Historically complex relations meant that a language of 'dominance' was not possible for the state to accept in Algeria. Through a more modest approach, in the 2000s, the EU did implement programmes targeting Algerian civil society and these fared better than its previous development programmes of the 1990s. The wording of EU calls for proposals was far more open than in neighbouring countries, where they obliged NGOs to claim to promote democracy, human rights or gender equality in their bids for funding. Algerian associations, such as the association Bordj Bou Arreridj described in Chapter 9, have been able to challenge donors as to their demands. In Algeria, the funding has been much lower and the language more open, with the result that organisations were able to put forward their own ideas with confidence.

In order to ascertain whether Algerian associations somehow potentially represent a counter-hegemonic force, using Gramscian terms, an in-depth exploration of their functioning at the micro-level, the activism of their members, their relations with the state, their capacity to represent citizens and their ambitions to instigate change is required.[3] According to Schmitter, associations would have to inculcate civic and democratic behaviour, provide channels for expression, steer members towards collective commitments or provide a source of resistance to tyranny if they are to be considered as contributing to democratic reform. If, conversely, they made majority formation difficult, were biased, were class-based or ethnically or culturally exclusive, they would simply reinforce divisions and be negative for democracy.[4]

In an attempt to consider this contribution made by Algerian associations to democracy, this volume has explored who these new associations in Algeria are, what they have been doing and the power they have. The members of associations in Algeria, which as Chapter 5 showed number well over a million – at least on paper – come from a wide range of backgrounds. They are young, retired, professional, seeking work, former state officials, sportspersons, Imams, former FIS politicians or parents of disabled children. Many are teachers, some are wealthy private sector industrialists and others are women entrepreneurs. Membership of associations includes all socio-economic groups, ethnic or religious identities. Within associations there might be a shared ethnic or religious identity; however, I found in my research no registered Algerian association that reinforced those divisions in society that underpinned the violence of the 1990s – as has been suggested by some scholars. From interviews and observation of associations carried out across Algeria, I found cases of cooperation across religious, ethnic or language divides. From the work of *Djazairouna* and *SOS Disparus*, to the CNCD, which brought together Islamists and secular organisations demanding political reform in 2011, it seems that the associative sphere can, although not without difficulty, provide space for people to come together.

Associations are providing social services to vulnerable populations, campaigning for human rights and actively preserving heritage. They are also forming networks at the national and sometimes international level through the PCPA or Nada networks discussed in Chapter 7. In 2012 they actively lobbied parliament to change the new Law on Associations, and, whilst they failed, their coming together collectively was significant. Whilst they have little influence over national policy, the Berber associations in Kabylia did make gains in achieving official status for the Berber language in Algeria. Mozabite associations in Ghardaia recognised the effectiveness of the Kabyle associations and lamented that they themselves had not been more actively engaged, wondering whose version of Berber would now prevail. At the local level, associations do influence politics – for example, the Boucebci Foundation's work in the education sector – and, in contrast to the negative framing of associations in the early 2000s, their narratives are now increasingly being taken up in the press, with more positive stories about their work being published.

The majority of the associations interviewed were well organised and functioned with limited budgets. Most ran democratic processes during the annual general meetings to elect their leaders and boards. These practices were adopted across the range of associations, with Cavatorta and Durac noting the 'surprisingly democratic' structures of the Islamist associations they interviewed.[5] As a cornerstone of Algerian claims against the regime – as being corrupt and non-democratic – the need for fairness, democracy and transparency in the management of public money was seen as vital. Organisations which failed on these fronts were called out and publically ostracised by the others, particularly in smaller towns where information circulates fast.

Associations interact with the Algerian state on various levels. Far from legitimising the state,[6] most associations' members were deeply critical of it. This was perhaps less so in the south, where for historical reasons President Bouteflika retained a personal vote and respect from the population. Equally, some associations did participate in election campaigns, when asked or 'encouraged' by the state to support the FLN. Yet entwinement in political life did not necessarily neutralise or co-opt those associations, as shown in Chapter 4. Echifaa association went on to run an ambitious health project without state funding, and was then attacked by the state for seemingly random reasons of jealousy and power. Across Algeria, seemingly apolitical associations in the heritage and social sectors have contested the state and its narratives. They have also been challenged or attacked by the state, and yet did not necessarily desist in their activities. Significant structural constraints persist and inhibit Algerian associations. State obstructionism, including the blocking of statutes, institutional slowness or the attacking of associations in the press or through the justice system, continues. Significant administrative and bureaucratic burdens, as well as arbitrary state responses, sometimes lead to Algerians abandoning their associations. Yet increasing numbers overcome these burdens. Through commitment to their cause, they challenge the bureaucracy, or deal with it, and find new ways to interact with the state. As discussed in Chapter 4, the boundaries between state and society are blurred; associations do not automatically see themselves as in direct confrontation with the state. The limits of the responsibilities of each side are created by a dialogical process in which both sides can frame the debate and influence processes of regulation.

In *Le Développement, une affaire d'ONG? Associations, Etats et Bailleurs dans le Monde Arabe*, Abu-Sada and Challand hypothesise that involvement of associations in public life in the Arab world has led to the 'emergence of new forms of contestation' in a process of 're-politicisation', and not de-politicisation, of associative actors.[7] I also argue this to be the case. There are clearly different forms of contestation emerging in Algeria, as new associations actively participate in public life. Heritage associations such as Bel Horizon, in questioning state narratives of the past, push for a more inclusive national identity and the protection of a wider range of cultural heritage, challenging the idea of a purely Arab-Muslim nation. Social sector associations, such as *Nour* in Oran, engage with local authorities around the provision of social care. Associations such as *Djazairouna*, SARP or the Boucebci Foundation, in dealing with trauma, challenge the national reconciliation policy but also contribute to reconciliation and the healing which is necessary for Algeria to move on. The actions of these associations have impacted on public policies. Associations do challenge the government and are sometimes successful. The integration of Berber into the education system, the 30-per cent quota for women deputies in parliament or the reaffirmation from the state that Islam must play a central role in the Algerian nation have all in part been the result of mobilising and campaigning by Algerian associations. The lifting of the Emergency Laws in 2011 was also symbolic that the public space could no longer be controlled and monopolised by the state as it had been before.

Associations do not need to directly challenge the government in order to meaningfully engage in processes of democratic reform. In *Life as Politics*, Bayat reminds us that most people do not wish to see violent revolution. As a result 'unconventional forms of agency and activism', what he calls 'non-movements', have emerged across the Arab world. These do not get the attention they deserve, as they do not fit into prevailing categories of Middle Eastern exceptionalism which are at the core of the 'western democracy promotion industry'.[8] Grassroots associations in Algeria reclaimed a voice in the public sphere, in their networks in 2011, but also in their daily activities. The cases explored have shown how associations have managed to engage with officials, challenge policy decisions, gain experience of governance and even go on to take up elected roles in municipal councils. Challenging the distinction between lobbying associations and 'depoliticised' service providers, Abu-Sada and Challand describe an associative movement across the Arab world which is now 'participating in public policies', particularly on the question of 'public services'.[9] They write that it is no longer simply control by the state over associations, but that there is also an impact of associative changes upon political life.[10]

In her discussion of the practices of Algerian converts to Christianity, a sensitive, small, yet not insignificant phenomenon in Algeria, Nadia Marzouki identifies how their 'practices and narratives' have been 'significantly influenced by an attempt to redefine the past and future of the Algerian nation'.[11] She writes that there is 'a significant interest in rewriting this national culture'[12] and in reconstructing Algeria's identity as 'a specifically Maghrebi one, or as an African one'.[13] This desire to re-write and redefine national history was seen at a number of levels throughout many of the associations – not uniquely those working on heritage, although they were the strongest voices. Bel Horizon deplored the 'lack of interest' in history from the authorities and from citizens, and sought to rediscover and value the multicultural heritage of Oran. APPAT in Tiaret sought to promote and protect the Berber, Phoenician, Roman, colonial, as well as the Arab-Muslim history of the region. This included even sites pertaining to the history of the nationalist struggle and the Emir Abd el-Kader, which had not been protected despite the alleged importance attached to that particular period of history by the state. Associations across Algeria are challenging what Langlois describes as the 'over-reductive construction of identity, limited by a postcolonial understanding of "statehood" that fails to engage with a far richer and more complex cultural reality'.[14]

The case studies throughout the book have highlighted a number of Algerian associations which challenge national narratives, from the colonial to the post-colonial interpretations of history that have constrained Algerian identities, manipulated power relations and prevented access to the public sphere over the last century. Associations have often tried to do this sensitively and constructively, rebuilding trust within communities by offering more inclusive, tolerant, transnational, spiritual and faith-based spaces in which to encourage more Algerians to actively engage in their communities and to reflect on the meaning of Algerian national identity. This development is more prominent in some regions than others. Where associations flourish, there are new spaces for public debate and this is not just in offices or community halls. In Oran, Bel Horizon takes thousands of citizens to the top of the Santa Cruz Fort to engage them in new reflections about history. Online spaces are also important. The association of modern female entrepreneurs, for example, now has 80,000 followers. Cultural associations and artistic expression transform spaces and participation. Britta Hecking describes how young people performing caipoeira or street dance 'by accessing central spaces within the Algerian capital, representing themselves globally via social media', empower themselves and 'resist socio-spatial exclusion as well as dominant representations'.[15]

Finally, given the persistent weakness of political parties in Algeria, it remains within civil society that political and social demands are articulated. Associations are spaces in which people can act, criticise and propose. Despite the fear of state controls, autonomous organisations now exist in addition to the traditional spaces of socialisation. Whilst the Algerian Government has tried to rely on civil society politically, co-opting certain organisations for support, associations are sceptical of being entwined in electoral politics, which is felt to have limited relevance. Associations prefer to work with the state on the real issues at stake, such as the provision of public services, the right to education, the right to justice and, increasingly, the history and meaning of the Algerian nation and identity.

Associations do not necessarily always challenge the state, but this does not mean they are compromised. Their legitimacy comes from their members, from how they are perceived in the public sphere and particularly by the press. As Association Echifaa in Medea indicated, the greatest success of the association was 'reaching a membership of 5,000 members after only five years.'[16] This reinforced their legitimacy, independently of their relations with the state. This, along with the fact of their now being part of a larger, informal network of associations, had effectively 'shifted the balance of power' between the authorities and the association. The ACEC Students Cultural Association in Adrar also confirmed such a shift. The significant increase in the number of their members meant that local authorities now came to the association, rather than the other way round.[17] Associations whose objectives were more in confrontation with the state, such as those questioning the Reconciliation Charter and campaigning for justice for families of the disappeared, also sought similar means – a wide membership and strong networks – to reinforce their legitimacy and to protect themselves against any arbitrary measures from the state.

There are still many challenges facing civil society in Algeria. There is fragmentation and there is frustration about the slow pace of reform. With the transformations and instability in the region, the situation in Algeria remains tense. Associations are often divided, and unsure of a common line. They can disintegrate or easily be repressed by state structures. Yet, at the same time, they are also capable of launching impressive mobilisation initiatives, as the case studies have shown. In his 2007 study on Algerian associations, Omar Derras wrote that further reforms and support were needed, to anchor such developments into Algerian political, social and cultural life. If these were found, he writes, the associative movement could then 'become a rampart against the arbitrary and against authoritarianism', allowing the emergence of 'an important part of civil society, not simply placing itself in a strategy of confrontation, but one of mediation, in essential partnerships'.[18]

Derras' words indicate the potential for a new reality lying within reach of associations and of the state. The dialogue is less confrontational now and there are cases of cooperation. Equally, the associative movement has trained significant numbers of qualified and committed personnel who have new expectations about the future. With an increasing number of successful examples, and with appropriate reforms and support under such conditions, the associative movement could become a greater force for change. Associations in Algeria are uniquely placed to engage the wider population in a more open dialogue about reconciliation, development and the construction of an inclusive civil society. Many obstacles remain, but it seems clear that associations will continue to play a central role in how Algerians imagine possible futures for their nation and for its citizens.

NOTES

Introduction

1. In 2015, Cherifa was assaulted by police in Algiers during a protest on 8 March, International Women's Day, demanding truth and justice for the women and men who had lost their lives. In 2017, she organised the protest again, defying the Algerian authorities and standing up to the violence they had inflicted and to their denial of the claims for justice (see www.djazairouna.ranahna.dz/ for more information on Djazairouna).
2. Hugh Roberts, *Berber Government: The Kabyle Polity in Pre-colonial Algeria* (London, 2014).
3. James McDougall, *A History of Algeria* (Cambridge, 2017), p. 131.
4. Malika Rebai Maamri, *The State of Algeria, The politics of a Post-Colonial legacy* (London, 2015), p. 45.
5. Abdou Filali-Ansary, 'State, society and creed, reflections on the Maghreb', in Amyn B Sajoo (ed.), *Civil society in the Muslim world, Contemporary Perspectives* (London, 2004), p. 309.
6. Sarah Ben Nefissa, *Pouvoirs et associations dans le monde Arabe* (Paris, 2002), p. 17.
7. Lahouari Addi, 'Les obstacles à la formation de la société civile', in Anna Bozzo and Jean-Pierre Luizzard (eds), *Les Sociétés Civiles dans le Monde Musulman* (Paris, 2011).
8. Omar Derras, *Le phénomène associatif* (Algiers, 2007), p. 21.
9. 1990–31 Law on Associations, now replaced by the Law on Associations 2012–06.
10. Anna Bozzo and Jean-Pierre Luizzard, *Les Sociétés Civiles dans le Monde Musulman* (Paris, 2011), p. 10. 'De tous ces mouvements, il n'a pas échappé aux observateurs avertis qu'octobre 1988 à Alger a été, malgré son échec, le premier, celui qui a ouvert la voie à cette nouvelle série de protestations.' All translations are the author's unless otherwise stated.
11. Ben Nefissa, *Pouvoirs et associations*.

12. Andrea Liverani, *Civil Society in Algeria, The political functions of associational life* (Abingdon, 2008).
13. Hugh Roberts, 'The Bouteflika Presidency and the problems of political reform in Algeria', Speech to the Forum on the Middle East and North Africa, 3 February 2005. Madrid: FRIDE; Francesco Cavatorta and Azzam Elananza, 'Political opposition in civil society: an analysis of the interactions of secular and religious associations in Algeria and Jordan', *Government and Opposition* 43/4 (2008), pp. 561–78.
14. Liverani, *Civil Society in Algeria*, p. 9.
15. Ibid.
16. Olivier Roy, *The Politics of Chaos in the Middle East* (New York, 2008), p. 41.
17. Mohamed Youcef Hadj Ali, *Lettre Ouverte aux francais qui ne comprennent décidément rien à l'Algérie* (Paris, 1998).
18. Albert O. Hirschman, *Getting Ahead Collectively Grassroots Experiences in Latin America* (New York, 1984), p. 55.
19. See John L. Austin, *How to do Things with Words* (Oxford, 1975) on performative language.
20. Francesco Cavatorta and Vincent Durac, *Civil Society and Democratization in the Arab World, The Dynamics of Activism* (Oxford, 2011).
21. Caroline Abu-Sada and Benoit Challand (eds), *Le Développement, une affaire d'ONG ? Associations, Etats et Bailleurs dans le Monde Arabe.* (Paris, 2011) p. 17. 'L'association est, selon les cas, appréhendée comme un lieu d'innovation, libre des pesanteurs bureaucratiques des administrations centrales qui ont longtemps revendiqué le monopôle du développement légitime, comme un lieu de dissidence, de contre-pouvoir, un laboratoire pour le développement d'une contre-société, pour la démocratisation des sociétés et des régimes arabes, un lieu de mobilization locale et politique. Quasiment àl'inverse, elle est aussi considérée comme un instrument privilégié au service des politiques de développement, mobilisable tant par les autorités centrales que par les bailleurs internationaux, pour promouvoir leurs politiques: comme des institutions clés, des nouvelles politiques de développement, voire comme des "Gouvernemental NGO ou GONGO". C'est cet entre-deux, et les effets de réels qu'ils produisent, qu'il s'agit d'examiner.'

Chapter 1   Civil Society in the Arab World and Algeria

1. Mohamed Arkoun, 'Locating civil society in Islamic contexts', in Amyn B. Sajoo (ed.), *Civil Society in the Muslim World, Contemporary Perspectives* (London, 2004), p. 39.
2. Filali-Ansary, 'State, society and creed, reflections on the Maghreb', in ibid., p. 309.
3. Galia Golan and Walid Salem, *Non-State Actors in the Middle East* (Abingdon, 2014), p. 1.
4. Ibid.

NOTES TO PAGES 18–28   229

5. Since 1987, registered associations went from 10,000 to 93,000 in 2012, and to 109,000 in 2017. For latest figures, see www.interieur.gov.dz/images/pdf/Thematiquedesassociations.pdf (accessed 20 July 2017).
6. Francesco Cavatorta and Vincent Durac, *Civil Society and Democratization in the Arab World, The Dynamics of Activism* (Oxford, 2011), and ICNL NGO Law monitor: www.icnl.org/research/monitor/ (accessed 20 July 2017).
7. A total of 167,000 charities are registered with the Charities Commission in 2016 for England and Wales: www.charity-commission.gov.uk (accessed 20 July 2017).
8. 'Les députés relèvent des ambigüités et des atteintes à la liberté d'association,' Nabila Amir, *El Watan*, 28 November 2011.
9. Anna Bozzo and Jean-Pierre Luizzard (eds), *Les Sociétés Civiles dans le Monde Musulman* (Paris, 2011).
10. Charity Butcher, 'Can oil-reliant countries democratize? An assessment of the role of civil society in Algeria', *Democratization* 21/4 (2014), pp. 722–42.
11. Figure 1.3 shows citing of the words civil society, or democratisation in the monthly or periodical titles of six major development policy journals: *Revue Tiers Monde, Development and Change, World Development, Third World Quarterly, Development Policy Review, International Affairs*.
12. Saad Eddin Ibrahim, 'The troubled triangle: populism, Islam and Civil Society in the Arab World', *International Political Science Review* 19/4 (1998), p. 374.
13. Butcher, 'Can oil-reliant countries democratize?', p. 724.
14. Jean Cohen and Andrew Arato, *Civil Society and Political Theory* (Massachusetts, 1994).
15. See Amaney Jamal, *Barriers to Democracy, The Other Side of Social Capital in Palestine and the Arab World* (Princeton, NJ, 2007), p. 4.
16. See Andrea Liverani, *Civil Society in Algeria, The Political Functions of Associational Life* (Abingdon, 2008).
17. Alexis de Tocqueville, *Democracy in America* (London, 1994 [1840]).
18. Malika Rebai Maamri, *The State of Algeria, The Politics of a Post-Colonial Legacy* (London, 2015), p. 30.
19. Jamal, *Barriers to Democracy*, p. 4.
20. Cavatorta and Durac, *Civil Society and Democratization*, p. 12.
21. Ibid., p. 12.
22. Asef Bayat, *Life as Politics: How Ordinary People Change the Middle East* (California, 2013).
23. Robert D. Putnam (with Robert Leonardi and Raffaella Y. Nanetti), *Making Democracy Work: Civic Traditions in Modern Italy* (Princeton, NJ, 1994).
24. Ibid.
25. Phillippe Schmitter, *Some Propositions About Civil Society and the Consolidation of Democracy* (Vienna, 1993). Available at www.ihs.ac.at/publications/pol/pw_10.pdf (accessed 20 July 2017).
26. Ibid., p. 15.
27. Liverani, *Civil Society in Algeria*.

28. Cavatorta and Durac, *Civil Society and Democratization*, p. 2.
29. Benoit Challand, The evolution of Western aid for Palestinian civil society: bypassing local knowledge and resources, *Middle Eastern Studies* 44/3 (2008), p. 399.
30. Ibrahim, 'The troubled triangle'.
31. See Challand, 'The evolution of Western aid for Palestinian civil society', p. 400.
32. Filali-Ansary, 'State, society and creed, reflections on the Maghreb', p. 309.
33. Quintan Wictorowicz 'Civil society as social control', *Comparative Politics* 33/1 (2000), pp. 43–61 and Liverani, *Civil Society in Algeria*.
34. Vickie Langhor, 'Too much civil society, too little politics: Egypt and liberalizing Arab regimes', *Comparative Politics* 36/2 (2004), pp. 181–204.
35. Cavatorta and Durac, *Civil Society and Democratization*, p. 21.
36. Ibid., p. 28.
37. Jamal, *Barriers to Democracy*, p. 6.
38. Ibid., p. 7.
39. Ibid., p. 9.
40. Cavatorta and Durac, *Civil Society and Democratization*.
41. John K. Glenn III, *Framing Democracy Civil Society and Civic Movements in Eastern Europe* (California, 2001), pp. 21–3.
42. Caroline Abu-Sada and Benoit Challand (eds), *Le développement, une affaire d'ONG? Associations, Etats et Bailleurs dans le Monde Arabe* (Paris, 2011).
43. Kazemi and Norton, quoted in Liverani, *Civil Society in Algeria*, p. 5.
44. Yahia Zoubir, quoted in Liverani, *Civil Society in Algeria*, p. 5.
45. Sarah Ben Nefissa, *Pouvoirs et associations dans le Monde Arabe* (Paris, 2002). 'L'Algérie semble être le seul pays arabe qui, sur le plan juridique, connaît la procédure de la déclaration et non celle de l'autorisation. Aujourd'hui, il est possible de parler d'une véritable explosion associative. Les catégories sociales qui se sont senti les plus menacées par l'extrémisme islamiste et l'Etat algérien ont été les premières à s'organiser. Il s'agit principalement des femmes et des Berbères. Actuellement, il est possible de dire que la forme associative, plus que le parti politique ou la presse, constitue l'une des principales voies d'expression de la société algérienne qui cherche à ne pas se laisser emprisonner dans le binôme Etat/islamistes.'
46. Martin Evans and John Philips, *Algeria; Anger of the Dispossessed* (New Haven, CT, 2007) p. 299.
47. Speech to the Forum on the Middle East and North Africa (FRIDE Madrid) 3 February 2005.
48. Francesco Cavatorta and Azzam Elananza 'Political opposition in civil society: an analysis of the interactions of secular and religious associations in Algeria and Jordan', *Government and Opposition* 43/4 (2008), pp. 561–78.
49. Cavatorta and Durac, *Civil Society and Democratization*, p. 4.
50. Ibid., p. 5.
51. Ibid., p. 33.

52. Djamel Benramdane, *Les associations algériennes, des acteurs émergents en quete de reconnaissance*, CISP (Algiers, 2015), pp. 19–20.
53. Evans and Philips, *Algeria; Anger of the Dispossessed.*
54. Axel Hadenius and Fredrik Uggla, 'Making civil society work, promoting democratic development: what can states and donors do?' *World Development* 24/10 (1996), p. 1629.
55. Albert O. Hirschman, *Getting Ahead Collectively: Grassroots Experiences in Latin America* (New York, 1984), p. 33.
56. Navaras, online blog, *angles de vu*, 20 August 2009: https://edda.hi.is/wp-content/uploads/2012/08/Pat-abstract-2.pdf (accessed 14 March 2017). Navaras writes that according to an interview with the AFP French Press Agency, Anouar Haddam, the Islamist leader qualified the assassination as the 'exécution d'une sentence par les moudjahidine'.
57. Patrick Crowley, 'Algerian traumas: the real, the chosen and the aesthetic', in *Cultural Representations of Trauma* Conference: 31 August–1 September 2012, University of Iceland.

Chapter 2   International Donors and Democracy Promotion

1. Francis Ghiles, 'A unified North Africa on the world stage: overview of Maghreb Sector Studies', in G. C. Hufbauer and C. Brunel (eds), *Maghreb Regional and Global Integration: A Dream to Be Fulfilled* (Washington, DC, 2008).
2. Sheila Carapico, 'Foreign aid for Promoting Democracy in the Arab World', *Middle East Journal* 56/3 (2002), p. 381.
3. Interview with a civil society activist in Tipasa, 29 October 2011.
4. Richard Youngs, 'The European Union and democracy promotion in the Mediterranean: A new or disingenuous strategy?' *Democratization* 9/1 (2002), pp. 40–62.
5. Federica Bicchi, '"Our size fits all": normative power Europe and the Mediterranean', *Journal of European Public Policy* 13/2 (2006), p. 287.
6. Benoit Challand, 'The evolution of Western aid for Palestinian civil society: bypassing local knowledge and resources,' *Middle Eastern Studies* 44/3 (2008) p. 410.
7. Carapico, 'Foreign aid for promoting democracy', p. 383.
8. See Westminister Foundation for Democracy: www.wfd.org/about (accessed 14 March 2017).
9. Stefan Mair, *The Role of the German 'Stiftungen' in the Process of Democratization*, quoted in Carapico, 'Foreign aid for Promoting Democracy', p. 285.
10. S. Grimm and J. Leininger, 'Not all good things go together: conflicting objectives in democracy promotion', *Democratization* 19/3 (2012), pp. 391–414.
11. Andrea Liverani, *Civil Society in Algeria, The Political Functions of Associational Life* (Abingdon, 2008); Quintan Wictorowicz, 'Civil society as social control', *Comparative Politics* 33/1 (2000), pp. 43–61.

12. Sarah Henderson, 'Selling civil society, Western aid and the nongovernmental organization sector in Russia' *Comparative Political Studies* 35/2 (2002), pp. 139–67.
13. Ibid., p. 152.
14. Julia Elyachar *Markets of Dispossession: NGOs, Economic Development, and the State in Cairo* (Duke University Press, 2005), p. 29.
15. Olivier Roy, *The Politics of Chaos in the Middle East* (New York, 2008), p. 41.
16. Liverani, *Civil Society in Algeria*.
17. Thomas Carothers, 'Civil Society', *Foreign Policy* 117 (1999–2000), p. 18.
18. Challand, 'The Evolution of Western Aid', p. 411.
19. Ernest Gellner, *Conditions of Liberty: Civil Society and Its Rivals* (London, 1994).
20. The EU's commitment to promote democracy was made explicit in the 1991 Development Council resolution and incorporated subsequently into the foreign policy objectives of the EU in the Maastricht Treaty. See A. Güney and A. Çelenk, 'European Union's democracy promotion policies in Algeria: success or failure?', *Journal of North African Studies* 12/1 (2007), p. 115.
21. Güney and Çelenk, 'European Union's Democracy Promotion Policies', p. 115.
22. Kristi Raik, *Promoting Democracy through civil society: How to step up the EU's policy towards the Eastern Neighbourhood*, CEPS Working Documents No. 237, 1 February 2006.
23. Article 6, Cotonou Agreement.
24. Interview with Pierre Nicolas Meido, EU consultant, Paris, 2 January 2013.
25. Maurizio Floridi, Beatriz Sanz-Corella and Stephano Verdecchia, 'Capitalisation study on capacity building support programmes for non state actors under the 9th EDF', European Commission Report (2009), p. 20.
26. Barcelona Declaration, 1995.
27. Hakim Darbouche, 'Decoding Algeria's ENP policy: differentiation by other means?', *Mediterranean Politics* 13/3 (2008), p. 377.
28. Ibid.
29. Ibid.
30. John Entelis, 'Civil Society and the authoritarian temptation in Algerian Politics. Islamic democracy versus the centralized state', in Augustus R. Norton (ed.), *Civil Society in the Middle East*, vol. 1 (Leiden, 1994), p. 53.
31. See Youcef Hadj Ali, *Les élites françaises et la crise Algérienne (1991–1998): Perceptions, Positions, Prédictions*, doctoral thesis (University of Toulouse, 2003), p. 278. 'Imprégnant profondément les esprits, le franco centrisme a été un obstacle à la production d'analyses novatrices, audacieuses et donc susceptibles de rendre compte des processus socio-politiques complexes et des voies inédites par lesquelles une société peut cheminer vers la démocratie et ce faisant asseoir les éléments constitutifs de la nation moderne avec son propre rythme et ses spécificités historiques.'
32. Darbouche, 'Decoding Algeria's ENP Policy', p. 380.

33. Quoted in E. Barbé and A. Herranz-Surrales, *The Challenge of Differentiation in Euro-Mediterranean Relations. Flexible Regional Co-operation or Fragmentation* (Abingdon, 2012), p. 1.
34. This was confirmed by interviews with EU and Embassy officials in October 2011, June 2012 and September 2016 in Algiers.
35. *Programme d'appui aux associations algériennes de développement* 1 and 2, implemented respectively from 2001 to 2006 and from 2006 to 2010.
36. The details of these programmes will be explored in greater detail in Chapter 8.
37. Interviews with the EU delegation and with Ministry officials, October 2011.
38. Interviews with the British Embassy, 18 June 2012.
39. Ibid.
40. Final Evaluation of the Programme to support Algerian Associations, EU, 2010.
41. The UN retained only a limited presence in Algeria after the bombings of the HQ in 2007.
42. Benoit Challand, *Palestinian Civil Society. Foreign Donors and the Power to Promote and Exclude* (London, 2009), p. 93.
43. Benoit Challand, 'Coming too late? The EU's mixed approaches to transforming the Israeli–Palestinian conflict', *MICROCON Policy Working Paper* 12, MICROCON (Brighton, 2010) p. 3.
44. Ibid., p. 4.
45. Sibille Merz, '"Missionaries of a new era': neoliberalism and NGOs in Palestine', *Race & Class*, July–September 54/1 (2012), p. 51.
46. Benoit Challand, *Palestinian Civil Society*, p. 91.
47. Francesco Cavatorta and Vincent Durac, *Civil Society and Democratization in the Arab World, The Dynamics of Activism* (Oxford, 2011), pp. 138–9.
48. Ibid., p. 139.
49. Afkar Programme. Available at http://ec.europa.eu/europeaid/documents/case-studies/lebanon_intitutional-reform_afkar_en.pdf (accessed 20 July 2017).
50. Figures given in an interview with the EU delegation programme manager in Beirut, 22 December 2011.
51. Interview with the EU delegation programme manager in Beirut, 22 December 2011.
52. EU Final Evaluation of the Projet d'Appui aux Associations Algériennes de Développement, ONGII, Z. Ould Amar and E. Taib, January–February 2010.

Chapter 3   Historical Perspectives on Civil Society in Algeria

1. Martin Evans and John Philips, *Algeria: Anger of the Dispossessed* (New Haven, CT, 2007), p. xv.
2. Hugh Roberts, *Berber Government: The Kabyle Polity in Pre-colonial Algeria* (London, 2014).
3. Ibid., p. 26.

4. James McDougall, *A History of Algeria* (Cambridge, 2017), p. 41.
5. Ibid., p. 46.
6. Ibid; Alistair Horne, *A Savage War of Peace, Algeria 1954–1962* (New York, 2006).
7. Roberts, *Berber Government*, p. 8.
8. Ibid., p. 32.
9. After taking power from Ahmed Ben Bella through the coup in 1965, Boumediene recognised the importance of having an egalitarian, consensual type of leadership which Roberts links to the traditional village council form of governance and to the necessity of avoiding the cult of personality of his predecessor. Roberts, quoted in Evans and Philips, *Algeria: Anger of the Dispossessed*, p. 82.
10. McDougall, *A History of Algeria*, p. 44.
11. Evans and Philips, *Algeria: Anger of the Dispossessed*; Luis Martinez *The Algerian Civil War, 1990–1998* (London, 2000).
12. Malika Rebai Maamri, *The State of Algeria: The Politics of a Post-Colonial Legacy* (London, 2015), p. 67.
13. Ibid., p. 31.
14. Ibid., p. 28.
15. Ibid., p. 34.
16. Horne, *A Savage War of Peace*, p. 37.
17. McDougall, *A History of Algeria*, p. 4.
18. Ibid., p. 141.
19. Andrea Liverani, *Civil Society in Algeria: The Political Functions of Associational Life* (Abingdon, 2008), p. 15.
20. Ibid., p. 15.
21. McDougall, *A History of Algeria*, p. 133.
22. Horne, *A Savage War of Peace*, p. 38.
23. McDougall, *A History of Algeria*, p. 158.
24. Rebai Maamri, *The State of Algeria*, p. 42.
25. McDougall, *A History of Algeria*, p. 173.
26. Ibid., p. 175.
27. Omar Carlier, *Entre nation et djihad. Histoire Sociale des Radicalismes Algériens* (Paris, 1995).
28. Asef Bayat, *Life as Politics: How Ordinary People Change the Middle East* (California, 2013), p. 5.
29. Ibid., p. 6.
30. McDougall, *A History of Algeria*, p. 261.
31. Emmanuelle Berger, *Algeria in Others' Languages* (Ithaca, NY, 2002), p. 2.
32. Omar Derras, *Le Phénomène associatif en Algérie* (Algiers, 2007).
33. Lahouari Addi, 'Les obstacles à la formation de la société civile', in Anna Bozzo and Jean-Pierre Luizzard, *Les Sociétés Civiles dans le Monde Musulman* (Paris, 2011), p. 376: 'Le projet populiste ne voulait pas que l'Algérie soit une société civile avec ses conflits et ses divergences d'intérêts individuels ou de groupes,

NOTES TO PAGES 75–86   235

souhaitant que l'Algérie soit une famille nationale unie par la mémoire des ancêtres et des martyrs.'
34. Derras, *Le Phénomène associatif en Algérie*, p. 8.
35. Circular of the Interior Ministry no. 40/DGAPG/AG 2/03.1964, quoted in Derras, ibid., p. 10.
36. Michael Collyer, 'Transnational political participation of Algerians in France. Extra-territorial civil society versus transnational governmentality', *Political Geography* 25/7 (2006), p. 840.
37. Derras, *Le Phénomène associatif*, p. 10: 'Parallèlement au processus d'assainissement des espaces de sociabilité (...) l'Etat entame progressivement la création et la propagation, à travers le pays et à différents niveaux institutionnels, d'un ensemble d'associations étatiques et partisanes qui auront pour rôle la création des structures de soutien inconditionnel, et aussi un moyen efficace d'encadrement, de contrôle et de quadrillage de la société.'
38. Liverani, *Civil Society in Algeria*, p. 18.
39. Rebai Mamri, *The State of Algeria*, p. 46.
40. Constitution of 1989 and the Law 90–31 of 1990 on the Freedom of Association.
41. Mohamed Brahim Salhi, *L'Algérie: citoyenneté et Identité* (Alger, 2010).

Chapter 4   Civil Society and the State

1. James McDougall, *A History of Algeria* (Cambridge, 2017), p. 3.
2. Mohamed Brahim Salhi, *L'Algérie: citoyenneté et Identité* (Alger, 2010).
3. Andrea Liverani, *Civil Society in Algeria: the Political Functions of Associational Life* (Abingdon, 2008).
4. Timothy Mitchell, 'The limits of the state: beyond statist approaches and their critics', *The American Political Science Review* 85/1 (1991) pp. 77–96.
5. Lahouari Addi, 'Les obstacles à la formation de la société civile', in Anna Bozzo and Jean-Pierre Luizzard (eds), *Les Sociétés Civiles dans le Monde Musulman* (Paris, 2011), p. 375: 'c'est le refus du politique et de sa conflictualité qui caractérise le projet populiste niant la pluralité pour ne pas avoir à l'institutionnaliser'.
6. McDougall, *A History of Algeria*, p. 295.
7. Ibid.
8. Ibid., p. 296.
9. Frédéric Volpi, *Islam and Democracy: The Failure of Dialogue in Algeria* (London, 2003), p. 99.
10. Salhi, *L'Algérie: citoyenneté et Identité*, p. 288.
11. Ibid., p. 99.
12. Omar Derras, *Le Phénomène associatif en Algérie* (Algiers, 2007), p. 26.
13. McDougall, *A History of Algeria*, p. 294.
14. Ibid.
15. Volpi, *Islam and Democracy*.
16. Interviews with associations in Blida, September 2016.

17. McDougall, *A History of Algeria*, p. 295.
18. Ibid.
19. Volpi, *Islam and Democracy*, p. 105.
20. Ibid., pp. 101–35.
21. Blog of the FFS, February 2011: http://ffs1963.unblog.fr/2011/01/22/le-ffs-estime-que-la-concertation-doit-sapprofondir-et-eventuellement-selargir-a-lavenir/ (accessed 19 July 2017).
22. James McDougall, 'In the shadow of revolution', in Patrick Crowley, *Algeria: Nation, Culture and Transnationalism, 1988–2015* (Liverpool, 2017), p. 36.
23. Anna Bozzo and Luizzard, Jean-Pierre (eds), *Les Sociétés Civiles dans le Monde Musulman* (Paris, 2011), p. 10: *'Atomisée, divisée, traumatisée, la société algérienne s'est montrée apparemment en retraite par rapport à la vague.'*
24. See www.lrb.co.uk/v33/n22/hugh-roberts/who-said-gaddafi-had-to-go (accessed 18 March 2017).
25. Interview with EU delegation officials, October 2011.
26. Interview with ministry officials, November 2011.
27. Interview with a regional social sector association, Algiers, November 2011.
28. Interview with regional associations in Oran, October 2011.
29. 'Assises régionales sur le développement local', organised and facilitated by the CNES, November 2011.
30. Interview with the former regional animator of the EU support programme, November 2011.
31. Interview with associations in Algiers, October 2011.
32. Amel Boubekeur, *Countries at the Crossroads 2011 Algeria*, available at: www.refworld.org/docid/4ecba654c.html, Freedom House Report (accessed 20 July 2017).
33. *Loi 12–06 of 12 January 2012*, Official Journal of the Algerian Republic, 2012, no. 2, 15 January 2012, p. 28.
34. Interviews with a number of associations including the FAPH, in Algiers, November 2011.
35. Preamble to the draft Law on Associations, 2011, 'En vérité, la législation actuelle a fini, et cela est un fait admis, par être perçue, à tort ou à raison, comme l'expression d'une volonté de (brider) les initiatives et de "verrouiller" les espaces de prédilection du mouvement associatif.'
36. Draft Law on Associations, September 2011, p. 3.
37. Minutes of the inter-associative meeting concerning the new Draft Law on Associations, 29 October 2011, Oran: 'Dans ce nouveau projet de loi, il y'a une transgression fondamentale qui apparaît dès les premiers articles, notamment l'article 9. En effet, c'est l'administration (Wilaya) qui se donne le droit de décider si une association peut exister ou pas. Or, l'administration est un pouvoir exécutif au service du citoyen, c'est à la justice de prendre ce genre de décisions. Dans un état démocratique, ce n'est pas le pouvoir exécutif qui juge ou qui décide de la non-existence d'une association. La procédure normale, serait

d'informer l'administration, et c'est à elle de saisir la justice en cas de non-conformité.'
38. See www.petitionpublique.fr/?pi=P2011N17181 (accessed 20 July 2017).
39. See www.elwatan.com/actualite/les-deputes-relevent-des-ambiguites-et-des-atteintes-a-la-liberte-d-association-28-11-2011-148916_109.php (accessed 20 July 2017).
40. See www.liberte-algerie.com/actualite/les-deputes-redoutent-le-complot-de-l-etranger-financement-des-associations-166883 (accessed 20 July 2017).
41. Boubekeur, *Countries at the Crossroads*, p. 4.
42. See www.petitionpublique.fr/PeticaoVer.aspx?pi=loiasso (accessed 20 July 2017).
43. Ibid.: 'Elle remet en cause le système déclaratif en cours dans tous pays démocratiques et crée de multiples obstacles à l'action associative bénévole.'
44. Preamble to the Draft Law on Associations 2011, quoted in the Petition for the withdrawal of the new law on associations: www.petitionpublique.fr/PeticaoVer.aspx?pi=loiasso (accessed 20 July 2017). 'Malgré toutes les difficultés rencontrées dans la gestion de leurs activités, elles ont tout de même réussi à donner à la vie associative un sens, un élan et une dimension dont la réalité quelle qu'elle soit est incontestable [...] Reconnu dans sa vocation, rétabli dans sa mission et son rôle, soutenu dans ses buts et ses objectifs au profit de l'intérêt général, le mouvement associatif contribuera par sa vitalité et sa vigueur à donner à la démocratie participative dont il est l'un des ferments essentiels plus de sens et de réalité.'
45. Interviews with associations in Blida, September 2016.
46. Presentation document, ADS Conference Algiers, October 2011: 'de créer un espace pour s'y rencontrer et réfléchir les voies et moyens à mettre en œuvre pour accompagner les malades atteints de différentes pathologies de la colonne vertébrale dans leur quête de soins et aussi et surtout d'intervenir dans le domaine de la prévention de ces maladies qui peuvent être évitées grâce à une hygiène de vie et à des pratiques quotidiennes aisément accessibles à tout un chacun'.
47. Exchange with the Association Echifaa 4 October 2011, 'Dans le séminaire national qui a eu lieu octobre 2011 à Tipaza, sous le haut patronage de Monsieur le ministre de la solidarité nationale et de la famille sous le thème développement social entre vécu, enjeux et défis, nous étions invités à participé avec une intervention pour expliquer comment notre projet a réussi à s'autofinancer et maintenir sa périnatalité et durabilité, et ce grâce à la participation de ses adhérant qui se multiple de jour à jour, à ce jour leur nombre est de 4942. De plus on a pu donc faire cet été un aménagement à notre centre avec une extension.'
48. Contrary to a number of articles of the Algerian Law on Associations, which enshrines the freedom of association through a declaratory regime.
49. Exchange with the Association 6 December 2011: 'nous sommes déçus que nos faux problèmes ne soient pas encore résolus, on a reçu jeudi passé une visite d'un

inspecteur envoyé par Mr le Ministre de la santé, mais il n'a rien pu faire car l'affaire est entre les mains de la justice. Il a même parlé avec Mr le Wali, mais toujours la même chanson. Par conséquent la direction de la santé nous a rompue la convention qui permet le détachement des deux médecins à notre association. On est en train d'essayer de recruter un médecin rééducateur pour qu'il soit directeur médical spécialement pour notre centre et qu'il soit payé par l'association. On a déjà contacté deux médecins et on attend toujours la réponse, espérant qu'on trouvera un Médecin le plutôt possible'.
50. Réseau d'Associations du Développement Durable des Oases, http://raddo.org (accessed 20 July 2017).

Chapter 5   Associations in Algeria

1. Such as Andrea Liverani, *Civil Society in Algeria the Functional Politics of Associational Life* (Abingdon, 2008); Ammar Belhilmer, Belhilmer, Amar, 'Le Pluralisme Politique, Syndical et Associatif', in *L'Algérie de demain: Relever les défis pour gagner l'avenir* Electronic edition, Friedrich-Ebert-Stiftung (ed.) (Alger, 2009). Available at: http://library.fes.de/pdf-files/bueros/algerien/06420-etude.pdf; http://library.fes.de/pdf-files/bueros/algerien/06420-etude.pdf (accessed 20 July 2017); Omar Derras, *Le Phénomène associatif en Algérie* (Algiers, 2007).
2. Phillipe C. Schmitter, *Some Propositions about Civil Society and the Consolidation of Democracy* (Vienna, 1993).
3. Anders Hardig, 'Beyond the Arab revolts: conceptualising civil society in the Middle East and North Africa', *Democratization* 22/6 (2015), p. 1133.
4. See Ammar Belhilmer, 'Le Pluralisme Politique, Syndical et Associatif', in Friedrich-Ebert-Stiftung (ed.), *L'Algérie de demain: Relever les défis pour gagner l'avenir*, electronic edition (Alger, 2009). Available at: http://library.fes.de/pdf-files/bueros/algerien/06420-etude.pdf (accessed 20 July 2017), p. 41.
5. Frédéric Volpi, *Islam and Democracy: The Failure of Dialogue in Algeria* (London, 2003); Omar Derras, *Le phénòmene Associatif en Algérie* (Algiers, 2007); and Francesco Cavatorta and Vincent Durac, *Civil Society and Democratization in the Arab World, The Dynamics of Activism* (Oxford, 2011).
6. Interview with *Djazairouna*, 19 September 2016.
7. Volpi, *Islam and Democracy*, p. 134.
8. Cavatorta and Durac, *Civil Society and Democratization in the Arab World*.
9. Figures taken from the Ministry of Interior website dated 31 December 2011 (last consulted on 29 October 2015). For most recent figures, see www.interieur.gov.dz/images/pdf/Thematiquedesassociations.pdf (accessed 18 March 2018).
10. This was the requirement under the 1990 law, 90–31, the 2012 law has different requirements depending on the type of association created.
11. Interview in Ghardaia, 24 September 2016.
12. Derras, *Le Phénomène associatif en Algérie*, p. 82.

13. For example, Mohamed Brahim Salhi, *L'Algérie: citoyenneté et Identité* (Alger, 2011) and Derras, *Le phénoèmene Associatif*.
14. Derras, *Le phénoèmene Associatif*, p. 9.
15. Ibid., p. 34.
16. Interview with associative members in Tiaret, 31 October 2011.
17. Hardig, 'Beyond the Arab revolts', p. 1147.
18. Omar Carlier, *Entre nation et djihad, Histoire Sociale des Radicalismes Algériens* (Paris, 1995).
19. Julia Elyachar, *Markets of Dispossession: NGOs, Economic Development and the State in Cairo* (Duke University Press, 2005).

Chapter 6   Algerian Associations Protecting the Past

1. Anne-Emmanuelle Berger (ed.), *Algeria in Others' Languages* (Ithaca, NY, 2002), p. 2.
2. Omar Derras, *Le Phénomène associatif en Algérie* (Algiers, 2007), p. 41.
3. Ibid., p. 85.
4. Djamel Benramdane, *Les associations algériennes, des acteurs émergents en quête de reconnaissance*, CISP (Algiers, 2015), p. 60: 'de nombreuses OSC se mobilisent pour la protection du patrimoine, à l'image de (Bariq 21) qui a travaillé avec l'association (Les amis de Skikda) sur la réhabilitation du vieux quartier napolitain de la ville et s'est opposé à la mainmise de promoteurs immobiliers'.
5. Ibid., pp. 82–3.
6. Aharon Layish, 'The Qadi's role in the Islamization of Sedentary Society', in Miriam Hoexter, Shmuel Eisenstadt and Nehemia Levitzion (eds), *The Public Sphere in Muslim Societies* (Albany, NY, 2002), p. 84.
7. See Association Internationale Soufie Alawiyya. Available at: http://aisa-net.com/la_voie_soufie_alawiyya/cheikh-khaled-bentounes/ (accessed 20 July 2017).
8. The following article indicates the different associations (including cultural ones) of the CNCD: www.lesoirdalgerie.com/articles/2011/02/24/article.php?sid=113362&cid=2 (accessed 20 July 2017).
9. Benramdane, *Les associations algériennes*, p. 60.
10. Diana Wylie, 'The importance of being at-home: a defense of historic preservation in Algeria', *Change Over Time* 2/2 (2012), p. 174.
11. https://youtu.be/Am0tltpjhxU (accessed 18 March 2018) records the Heritage Walk of 2013. Given such significant numbers, since 2011 the association has had to review the group walk and to combine this with cultural events across the city, now involving artists from around the Mediterranean. Each year the events are filmed and made available at: www.facebook.com/oranbelhorizon/ (accessed 19 March 2018).
12. Interview with the President of Bel Horizon, 23 October 2011.
13. Taken from an interview with *El Watan* newspaper, 14 April 2005, quoted in the special edition of Bel Horizon's bulletin *10 ans au service du patrimoine*:

p. 12, available at: www.oran-belhorizon.com/revue-belhorizon.pdf (accessed 20 July 2017).
14. Ibid., 'Dans l'imaginaire d'un pouvoir conservateur dans le domaine culturel, Oran était le mauvais exemple. La ville est taxée tantôt d'espagnole, tantôt de ville coloniale: n'était-ce pas la ville la plus européenne d'Algérie? Par conséquent une ville qui charrie des valeurs qui dérangent. Depuis, une politique de culpabilisation fut mise en œuvre, prétextant une participation tiède à la guerre de libération et une prétendue large permissivité morale. Les élites locales et autres notabilités oranaises ont été complexées et, dans une large mesure, neutralisées.'
15. Association APPAT in Tiaret (promoting archeological history), Association Santé Sidi El Houari in Oran (protection of the Sidi El Houari quarter), Association Castellum in Chleff (archiving of Roman ruins) and Association Archeologique of Tenes (protection of Phoenician heritage) all reported this to be one of the motivations for their activism – to protect their local heritage, whether it be Phoenician, Roman or European monuments, which state institutions had allowed to fall into ruins.
16. Article 19 of the 1990 Law states 'Le bulletin principal doit être édité en langue arabe.' ('The main bulletin must be written in Arabic.')
17. Interviewed 30 October 2011 and 31 October 2011, respectively.
18. Djamel Benramdane, *Les associations algériennes, des acteurs émergents en quête de reconnaissance*, CISP (Algiers, 2015), p. 60.
19. Wylie, 'The importance of being at-home', p. 174.
20. James McDougall, *History and the Culture of Nationalism in Algeria* (Cambridge, 2006), p. 238.
21. Patricia Lorcin, 'Rome and France in Africa: recovering colonial Algeria's Latin past', *French Historical Studies*, 25/2 (2002), p. 307.
22. Ibid., p. 319.
23. Ibid., p. 329.
24. McDougall, *History and the Culture of Nationalism*, p. 157.
25. See www.castellum-tingitanum.org (accessed 20 July 2017).
26. John W. Kiser, 2008. *Commander of the faithful: the life and times of Emir Abd el-Kader* (New York, 2008).
27. See www.djazairess.com/fr/lqo/5144675 and www.djazairess.com/fr/elwatan/ 299284 (accessed 20 July 2017).
28. Interview with the President of APPAT, 31 October 2011.
29. See www.lesoirdalgerie.com/articles/2015/10/11/article.php?sid=185478& cid=4 (accessed 20 July 2017).
30. Scheele quotes newspaper figures of 35,000 manuscripts, of which 4,000 are held by the National Library in Judith Scheele, 'Coming to terms with tradition: manuscript conservation in contemporary Algeria', in Graziano Krätli and Ghislaine Lydon (eds), *The Trans-Saharan Book Trade: Manuscript Culture, Arabic Literacy and Intellectual History in Muslim Africa* (Leiden, 2010), p. 294.
31. Hoexter, Eisenstadt and Levtzion, *The Public Sphere in Muslim Societies*, p. 115.

NOTES TO PAGES 134–147   241

32. Scheele, 'Coming to terms with Tradition', p. 300.
33. Ibid., p. 292.
34. See www.djazairess.com/fr/latribune/18269 (accessed 20 July 2017).
35. Catherine Lloyd, 'Organising across borders: Algerian women's associations in a period of conflict', *Review of African Political Economy* 82 (1999), p. 82.
36. Ibid., p. 488.
37. McDougall, *History and the Culture of Nationalism in Algeria*, p. 18.
38. Lloyd, 'Organising Across Borders', p. 488.
39. Michael Collyer, 'Transnational political participation of Algerians in France. Extra-territorial civil society versus transnational governmentality', *Political Geography* 25/7 (2006), pp. 836–49.

Chapter 7   Algerian Associations and Social Welfare

1. Helen Chapan Metz (ed.), *Algeria: A Country Study* (Washington, DC: GPO for the Library of Congress, 1994). Available at http://countrystudies.us/algeria/68.htm (accessed 20 July 2017).
2. Interview with a disability association from Constantine, 28 October 2011.
3. Interview with the President of *Nour*, 24 October 2011, Oran: 'On gère aujourd'hui deux centres à Oran avec 39 enfants et 46 adolescents dans des ateliers journaliers. Chaque centre a un Chef de centre et un psychologue et des animateurs. On commence le travail à 7h30 pour ouvrir le premier centre, puis on se déplace vers le deuxième. On fait de bénévolat pour tout ce qui est administrative. Les autres membres de l'équipe sont des professionnels qui sont rémunérés. Il y a une liste d'attente de 50 enfants aujourd'hui. La prise en charge de l'enfant IMC est gratuite au centre. Les parents n'ont peu de moyens.'
4. Ibid. 'L'IMC est un problème de suivi médical de la grossesse. Il est donc lié au système de santé. Il est donc lié à la responsabilité de l'état. Ces enfants sont de la responsabilité de l'état et il faut que l'état fait de son mieux pour les prendre en charge, et nous appuyer dans cette démarche.'
5. Ibid. 'Les formations nous ont mis en réseau du secteur local et national. On a des liens aujourd'hui. Pour un débat sur la loi on peut le faire parce qu'on connait les autres associations.'
6. Ibid.
7. Ibid., 'On se rend compte qu'on accède à de financements, des connaissances, des formations et des idées. Pour le réseau, il faut une véritable envie de travailler ensemble.'
8. Interview with the President, Tizi Ouzou, 13 November 2012, 'C'est difficile de fonctionner avec les moyens, nous ne sommes pas reconnus en tant que centre, juste en tant qu'association. Nous recevons le prix journalier, mais ça ne couvre pas les coûts récurrents, on a besoin de personnes spécialisées pour les enfants. Nous nous sommes déplacés vers la Direction de l'Action Sociale mais les promesses ne se concrétisent pas. Personne n'est venu ici voir le travail que nous faisons.'

9. Ibid., 'Notre centre fonctionne aussi bien que, sinon mieux que les centres étatiques, avec moins de moyens. Ceci est dû au fait que nous sommes une famille pour ces enfants. Je suis ici par ma conviction en tant que parent d'un enfant handicapé. Je ne suis pas spécialisé dans le domaine social, mais je voudrais apprendre.'
10. Ranked 15 out of 108 associations which applied for grants in the first call for projects.
11. See www.solimed.net/tous-nos-projets-realises/70-les-journees-de-formation-a-la-prise-en-charge-precoce-des-enfants-autistes (accessed 20 July 2017). This was confirmed by discussions with representative of SoliMed, 29 October 2010, and separate discussions with members of the association *Tej*, 28 October 2010 in Tipasa, during the PCPA mid-term review.
12. Interview with EU regional adviser, January 2010, Algiers
13. Interview with a member of *Tej*, 30 October 2011, Tipasa.
14. See Fransesco Cavatorta and Azzam Elananza's discussion of *Djazairouna* and *SOS Disparus*, in 'Political opposition in civil society: an analysis of the interactions of secular and religious associations in Algeria and Jordan', *Government and Opposition* 43/4 (2008), pp. 561–78.
15. *Djazairouna*, *SOS Disparus* and the Algerian Human Rights League in particular.
16. Interview with the Boucebci Foundation, Project leader, 16 October 2011.
17. See www.djazairess.com/fr/liberte/36137 (accessed 20 July 2017).
18. Ibid., 'Quand mon mari a été assassiné, j'avais dit qu'ils avaient réussi à le faire taire. Mais, je me suis rendue compte assez vite que je m'étais trompée, car jamais un mort n'a autant parlé par la voix des autres.'
19. James McDougall, *A History of Algeria* (Cambridge, 2017), p. 310.
20. Interview with a psychologist in the Boucebci Foundation, Algiers, 16 October 2011.
21. Ibid.
22. Ibid.
23. Interview with the Boucebci Foundation, Project leader, 16 October 2011.
24. Interview with the President of the FAPH, 29 October 2011.
25. Such as https://ajouadmemoire.wordpress.com/qui-sommes-nous-2/ collective for families of the victims of terrorism of the 1990s (accessed 20 July 2017).

Chapter 8   Europe, Civil Society and Democracy in Algeria

1. Yahia Zoubir, 'The resurgence of Algeria's foreign policy in the twenty-first century', *The Journal of North African Studies* (2004) 9/2, p. 169 and Hakim Darbouche, 'Decoding Algeria's European neighborhood policy: differentiation by other means?', *Mediterranean Politics* 13/3, November (2008), pp. 371–89.

NOTES TO PAGES 160–165   243

2. See Zoubir, 'The resurgence of Algeria's foreign policy' and Raffaella Del Sarto and Tobias Schumacher, 'From Brussels with love: leverage, benchmarking, and the action plans with Jordan and Tunisia in the EU's democratization policy', *Democratization* 18/4 (2011), pp. 932–55.
3. Roberto Aliboni, 'Societal change and political responses in Euro-Med relations', draft paper for the *Conference on the Mediterranean Microcosm between the West and the Arab Muslim World*, Paris, 3–4 November 2011.
4. Ibid., p. 6.
5. Interviews with associations in Tipasa, 28 October 2011.
6. Interviews with EU and Algerian officials October 2011.
7. Laredj Sekkou, *L'Algérie et la Communauté Economique Européenne*, Doctoral thesis, Law Faculty, University of Lausanne (1971), 'discordances qui, à la longue, ont conduit à situation juridiquement anarchique.'
8. John Entelis in A. R. Norton, 'Civil Society and the Authoritarian Temptation in Algerian Politics. Islamic Democracy Versus the Centralized State', in A. R. Norton (ed.), *Civil society in the Middle East*, Vol. 1 (Leiden, 1994), pp. 52–3.
9. Jean-François Daguzan, 'Les relations Franco-Algériennes ou la poursuite des amicales incompréhensions', *Annuaire Français des Relations Internationales* II (2001, p. 444. Available at www.afri-ct.org/wp-content/uploads/2006/03/daguzan2001.pdf (accessed 18 March 2018).
10. Mirjam Van Reisen, 'The enlarged European Union and the developing world: What future?', in Andrew Mold, *EU Development Policy in a Changing World* (Amsterdam, 2007), p. 35.
11. Daguzan, 'Les relations Franco-Algériennes': 'l'exemplarité que la France se faisait de ses rapports avec l'Algérie transforma ceux-ci en une relation exclusive. Cela conduisit donc les autorités françaises à tenir l'Union européenne à l'écart de toute intervention politique à l'égard de ce pays'.
12. James Heartfield, Algeria and the Defeat of French Humanism, in *The Death of the Subject Explained* (Sheffield, 2002), Chapter 6.
13. Such as Henri Alleg's book, *The Question* (1958) and Gillo Pontecorvo's film of *The Battle of Algiers* (1966).
14. Van Reisen, 'The enlarged European Union', p. 38.
15. Raffaella A. Del Sarto, *Contested State Identities and Regional Security in the Euro-Mediterranean Area* (Basingstoke, 2006), p. 230.
16. Claire Spencer, 'The end of international enquiries? The UN eminent persons' mission to Algeria, July–August 1998', *Mediterranean Politics* 3/3 (1998), pp. 125–33, and Hugh Roberts, 'Dancing in the dark: the European Union and the Algerian drama', *Democratization* 9/1 (2002), pp. 106–34.
17. Aliboni, 'Societal change and political responses', p. 7.
18. Hakim Darbouche and Susi Dennisson, 'A "Reset" with Algeria: the Russia to the EU's south', in *European Council on Foreign Relations*, *Policy Brief* ECFR/46, December 2011. Available at: www.ecfr.eu/page/-/ECFR46_ALGERIA_BRIEF_AW.pdf (accessed 20 July 2017).
19. Ibid.

20. Bulletin de la Délégation de l'UE en Algérie: 30 ans de coopération, 1979–1999, http://eeas.europa.eu/delegations/algeria/documents/ue_algeria_30years_cooperation_fr.pdf (accessed 20 July 2017).
21. EU Country Strategy Paper for Algeria 2007–13, p. 13.
22. Ibid.
23. Interiew with an EU delegation official in Algiers, 18 October 2011.
24. Available at https://ec.europa.eu/europeaid/sites/devco/files/csp-nip-algeria-2007-2013_en.pdf last (accessed 20 July 2017).
25. Andrea Liverani, *Civil society in Algeria the political functions of associational life* (Abingdon, 2008), p. 153.
26. Evaluation of the EU support project to associations, 2004, Final Report, p. 51: 'Ce programme a été conçu en 1999 dans un contexte de rareté de l'information, tant sur la nature que sur l'étendue du monde associatif algérien, et dans un climat politique encore incertain sur les rapports Etat/société civile/ secteur privé. Cette initiative de la CE avait donc- et a toujours-des enjeux importants pour l'Algérie, ceci justifiant une approche prudente et ouverte; la CE a opté pour une définition très large de termes comme société civile, développement, pauvreté, n'excluant que les organizations à caractère religieux ou politique' (Evaluation du projet d'appui aux associations, 2004, Rapport Final).
27. Evaluation report, p. 51, 'Ceci a permis de rendre plus visible l'engagement de l'Union Européenne et surtout de favoriser l'expression de la pluralité d'un "mouvement"associatif qui invente de multiples stratégies d'inscription dans un espace public lui-même en transformation. Le soutien européen a aussi accru la légitimité des associations dans leur environnement institutionnel comme auprès des populations, et en ce sens, renforcé le rôle de la société civile. Il serait utile de faire connaître les résultats concrets d'un programme dont l'existence même a suscité beaucoup de scepticisme; la confiance des populations et des associations dans le processus national d'ouverture et de renforcement de l'Etat de droit en sortirait grandie.'
28. Of these, 24 exclusively target women, 18 are for disabled persons (mainly children) and 18 mainly target youth.
29. Final Evaluation of the Support to Algerian Associations Programme, Dr Zakaria Ould Amar (2010), p. 9.
30. Of ten grant contracts published on the EuropeAid website in 2011 for Algeria, six were attributed to Algerian organisations, three to French organisations and one to an Italian organisation. In Tunisia for the same year, six contracts were attributed to French organisations, one to an Austrian, one to a Dutch NGO and only two to Tunisian ones – Data available on the EuropeAid database: http://ec.europa.eu/europeaid/work/funding/beneficiaries/index.cfm?lang=fr&mode=SM&type=grant (accessed 18 March 2018).
31. Figures taken from *Rapport de diagnostic sur la société civile tunisienne* (2012) p. 34: http://eeas.europa.eu/archives/delegations/tunisia/documents/projets/rapportdiagnostic_stecivile_mars2012_fr.pdf (accessed 20 July 2017).

NOTES TO PAGES 175–180   245

32. Laura Baeza, head of delegation and Said Barkat, Minister of Solidarity, Avant Propos, *Receuil du Programme d'Appui aux Associations Algériennes de Développement (ONGII)* (2012).
33. Lahouari Addi, 'Les obstacles à la formation de la société civile', in Anna Bozzo and Jean-Pierre Luizzard (eds), *Les Sociétés Civiles dans le Monde Musulman* (Paris, 2011), p. 374, 'C'est ce passage vers la sphère publique que l'Algérie peine à réaliser.'
34. Interview with a member of the technical assistance team of the EU programme, based in Algiers, October 2011.

Chapter 9 Language and the Construction of Civil Society

1. Ibn Khaldun, *The Muqaddimah, an introduction to History*, translated by Franz Rosenthal, Vol. 1. (New York, [1377] 1967), p. 47.
2. Abdelmadjid Hannoum, 'Translation and the Colonial Imaginary: Ibn Khaldûn Orientalist', *History and Theory* 42/1 (2003), p. 61.
3. Ibid., p. 69.
4. Ibid., p. 69.
5. Frantz Fanon, *The Wretched of the Earth* (New York, 1963), p. 102. The re-edition of Fanon's *Wretched of the Earth* with a preface by the Algerian President Abdelaziz Bouteflika in 2006 shows the continued significance of Fanon's words to Algerian political life.
6. Caroline Abu-Sada and Benoit Challand (eds), *Le Développement, une affaire d'ONG ? Associations, Etats et Bailleurs dans le Monde Arabe* (Paris, 2011), p. 26, 'en effet sont souvent tout simplement considérés comme des acteurs bienveillants ou comme des facilitateurs de développement, alors qu'en réalité leur implication institutionnelle ou discursive induit une redistribution des capitaux symboliques et relationnels, ou peut empêcher l'éclosion d'une véritable autonomie politique locale'.
7. Ibid.
8. Hannoum, 'Translation and the Colonial Imaginary', p. 69.
9. Benoit Challand, *Palestinian Civil Society. Foreign Donors and the Power to Promote and Exclude* (London, 2009).
10. Olivier Roy, 'The predicament of 'civil society' in Central Asia and the Greater Middle East', *International Affairs* 81/5 (2005), pp. 1101–12.
11. Ibid., p. 1003.
12. European Commissioner Fule himself publicly stated the failure of the EU to support democratic change and promote human rights, see E. Barbé and A. Herranz-Surrales, *The Challenge of Differentiation in Euro-Mediterranean Relations. Flexible Regional Co-operation or Fragmentation* (Abingdon, 2012), p. 1.
13. The Secretary General of the European External Action Service (EEAS), David O'Sullivan, pointed out that 'during the Arab Spring, we understood that the last thing which was wanted was interference, or outside advice. We stood back

and tried to respect that'. Debating Europe Series conference at the European University Institute, Florence, 'Setting up the European External Action Service (EEAS): Experiences and Perspectives', 28 November 2012.
14. John L. Austin, *How to do Things with Words*, 2nd ed. (Oxford, 1975), p. 94.
15. John, R. Searle, *Mind, Language and Society: Philosophy in the Real World* (New York, 1998), p. 113.
16. Albert O. Hirschman, *Getting Ahead Collectively: Grassroots Experiences in Latin America* (New York, 1984), p. 55.
17. James McDougall, 'État, société et culture chez les intellectuels de l'islāh maghrébin (Algérie et Tunisie, c.1890–1940), ou, la réforme comme apprentissage de l'arriération', in Odile Moreau (ed.), *La réforme de l'état dans le monde islamo-méditerranéen aux XIXème-XXème siècles* (Paris, 2009), p. 283:

> 'Il faut, tout d'abord, éviter de présumer, avec les réformistes eux-mêmes, qu'il existe un mouvement de réforme dans une société donnée parce que cette société serait affligée d'arriération [...] qu'il devrait y avoir une action externe ou d'en haut pour opérer ce changement nécessaire. Dans ce schéma, le retard (quelle qu'en soit la mesure) préexisterait et rendrait nécessaire la réforme. [...] Or il se peut que l'inverse se produise, c'est-à-dire que l'on commence par constater un "état d'arriération" seulement à partir du moment où il y a un mouvement réformiste. Ce serait donc le réformisme qui crée l'arriération, pensée en tant que telle.'

18. Discussions with the Association SARP, 18 September 2016, Algiers.
19. Djamel Benramdane, *Les associations algériennes, des acteurs émergents en quête de reconnaissance*, CISP (Algiers, 2015), p. 20.
20. Interview with the president of the Association *El Ghaith* of Bordj Bou Arreridj, 29 December 2012.
21. Ibid.
22. Judith Scheele, *Village Matters: Knowledge, Politics and Community in Kabylia, Algeria* (Oxford, 2009), p. 32.
23. Ibid., p. 33 and James McDougall, *History and the Culture of Nationalism* (Cambridge, 2006).
24. McDougall, *History and the Culture of Nationalism in Algeria*, p. 166.
25. Ibid., p. 230.
26. Scheele, *Village Matters*, p. 75.
27. Ibid., p. 86.
28. Discussions with the Association SARP, 18 November 2016.
29. See 'France's Hollande: no apologies for Algerian past', Reuters, 19 December 2012, on the French President Francois Holland's first state visit to Algiers. Available at http://uk.reuters.com/article/2012/12/19/uk-algeria-france-idUKBRE8BI17M20121219 (accessed 20 July 2017).
30. See 'France recognises Algeria colonial suffering', Al Jazeera, 20 December 2012. Available at http://www.aljazeera.com/news/africa/2012/12/201212209928683335.html (accessed 20 July 2017).

31. See 'Emmanuel Macron, the French presidency and a colonial controversy'. Available at http://theconversation.com/emmanuel-macron-the-french-presidency-and-a-colonial-controversy-73396 (accessed 20 July 2017).
32. Taleb Ibrahimi points out that the last census including the language question was carried out in 1966. See the conference given at the Ecole Normale Supérieure in Lyon. Available at www.canal-u.tv/video/ecole_normale_superieure_de_lyon/26_les_algeriens_et_leur_s_langue_s_de_la_periode_coloniale_a_nos_jours.4351 (accessed 20 July 2017).
33. Scheele, *Village Matters*, p. 40.
34. Hafid Gafaiti 'The monotheism of the other: language and de/construction of national identity in postcolonial Algeria', in Anne-Emmanuelle Berger (ed.), *Algeria in Others' Languages* (Ithaca, NY, 2002), p. 29.
35. Law no. 02–03 of 10 April 2002 modifying the Constitution.
36. See www.bbc.co.uk/news/world-africa-35515769 (accessed 20 July 2017).
37. Assia Djebar, *Algerian White* (New York, 2003). Originally published by Albin Michel S. A., Paris, France, in 1995, under the title *Le Blanc de l'Algérie*, p. 228.
38. The title of her book indicates the plurality of Algerian language: *Les Algériens et leur(s) langue(s). Éléments pour une approche sociolinguistique de la société algérienne* (Alger, 1995).
39. Khaoula Taleb Ibrahimi, 'L'opposition du français et de l'arabe a cassé l'intelligentsia algérienne', *El Watan*, 9 June 2012.
40. Anne-Emmanuelle Berger (ed.), *Algeria in Others' Languages* (Ithaca, NY, 2002), p. 15.
41. Law on Associations no. 12–06 of 12 January 2012. The reform of the Law on Associations in 2012 resulted in the changing of the article which previously imposed Arabic as the reporting language of Algerian associations (Article 19 of the Law no. 90–31). This appeared to indicate recognition of the cultural diversity of Algeria and a softening of the state's approach in this respect.
42. Removing Article 19 of the Law on Associations no. 90–31, which imposed Arabic, from the new law in 2012.
43. James McDougall, 'Dream of exile, promise of home: language, education, and Arabism in Algeria', *International Journal of Middle East Studies* 43/02 (2011), p. 261.
44. Discussions with members of Bel Horizon, 23 October 2011.
45. In an interview with the British Embassy on 18 June 2012, it was suggested that it was important to avoid a split between Europeans funding francophone secular associations and the Gulf States supporting Islamic Arabic-speaking organisations, and that increased funding from the Gulf States was one of the reasons that the Algerian Government sought to monitor external funding to associations in the new Law on Associations.

Chapter 10 Imagining a New Future

1. For more information on this research project, see https://youthalgeria.coventry.ac.uk/.
2. Asef Bayat, *Revolution without Revolutionaries: Making Sense of the Arab Spring* (Stanford, 2017), p. 205.
3. Hamza Hamouchene, 'Generals to the Dustbin, Algeria Will Be Independent: The New Algerian Revolution as a Fanonian Moment', in Nigel C. Gibson (ed.), *Fanon Today: Revolt and Reason of the Wretched of the Earth* (Wakefield, QC 2021), p. 422.
4. Bayat, *Revolution without Revolutionaries*.
5. Ibid., p. 215.
6. Ibid., p. 217.
7. Ibid., p. 216.
8. Asef Bayat, *Revolutionary Life: The Everyday of the Arab Spring* (Harvard, 2021), p. 14.
9. Ibid.
10. Naoual Belakhdar, 'When Unemployment Meets Environment. The Case of the Anti-fracking Coalition in Ouargla', *Mediterranean Politics* 24/4 (2019), pp. 420–42.
11. Robert Parks, 'Voter Participation and Loud Claim Making in Algeria', *Middle East Report* 281 (2016), pp. 23–7, p. 23.
12. Faouzia Zeraoulia, 'The Memory of the Civil War in Algeria: Lessons from the Past with Reference to the Algerian Hirak', *Contemporary Review of the Middle East* 7/1 (2020), pp. 1–29, p. 2.
13. Muriam Haleh Davis and Thomas Serres, 'Political Contestation in Algeria: Between Postcolonial Legacies and the Arab Spring', *Middle East Critique* 22/2 (2013), pp. 99–112.
14. Louisa Dris Aït-Hamadouche & Dris, 'Le face à face hirak-pouvoir: La crise de la représentation', *L'Année Du Maghreb* 21 (2019), pp. 57–68, p. 57.
15. Networks included the Pact for an Alternative Democracy launched in June 2019, and later Nida 22 launched in October 2020, see Thomas Serres, 'The Algerian Hirak between Mobilization and Imprisonment – An Interview with Hakim Addad', *Middle East Report Online*, 16 February 2021.
16. Sabri Benalycherif, '"Nothing Will Fall from the Sky": Algeria's Revolution Marches On' – Photo Essay (18 December 2019), *African Arguments*, 2019.
17. Nora Lafi, 'The "Arab Spring" in Global Perspective: Social Movements, Changing Contexts and Political Transitions in the Arab World (2010–2014)', in S. Berger and H. Nehring (eds.), *The History of Social Movements in Global Perspective* (London, 2017), p. 702.
18. Interview with a male volunteer from a youth environmental association in Tipaza, 3 June 2021.

19. Ziad Bentahar, '"Yetnahaw fa'!": Algeria's Cultural Revolution and the Role of Language in the Early Stages of the Spring 2019 Hirak', *Journal of African Cultural Studies* 33/4 (2021), pp. 471–88, p. 472.
20. Muriam Haleh Davies '"This Is the Voice of Algeria": Radio Corona International Carries the Torch of the Hirak'. *Jadaliyya*, 20 August 2020.
21. Interview with a male activist from the south, 23 June 2021.
22. Latefa Guemar, *Algerian Women: Experiences of Exile from the Black Decade to the Hirak* (Exeter, forthcoming in 2023), p. 163.
23. Ibid., p. 170.
24. Haleh Davies, 'This Is the Voice of Algeria'.
25. Yahia Zoubir, *The Algerian Crisis: Origins and Prospects for a 'Second Republic'*, Aljazeera Centre for Studies Report, 21 May 2019, p. 14
26. Latefa Guemar, Jessica Northey and Elias Boukrami, 'Diaspora Activism and Citizenship: Algerian Community Responses during the Global Pandemic', *Journal of Ethnic and Migration Studies* 48/9 (2022), pp. 1980–97.
27. Hanane Zermane and Samia Aitouche, 'Digital Learning with Covid-19 in Algeria', *International Journal of 3D Printing Technologies and Digital Industry* 4/2 (2020), pp. 161–70.
28. Interview with a male associational project lead from the south, 29 June 2021.
29. Interview with a male youth activist from the west, 20 May 2021.
30. Interview with a male activist from the south, 23 June 2021.
31. Interview with a male associational project lead from the south, 29 June 2021.
32. Zoubir, 'The Algerian Crisis', p. 15.
33. Interview with H, youth male ambassador for the environment, Batna, 6 August 2021.
34. Interview with a male volunteer from a youth environmental association in Tipaza, 3 June 2021.
35. Malia Bouattia, 'Death of an Activist: A Shame on Algeria's State', *The New Arab*, 31 May 2019, available at: https://english.alaraby.co.uk/opinion/death-activist-shame-algerias-state.
36. Jessica Northey and Latefa Guemar, 'Hirak Anniversary: Political Prisoners Freed as Algerians Continue to Protest', in *Open Democracy* (2021).
37. Thomas Serres, 'The Algerian Hirak between Mobilization and Imprisonment – An Interview with Hakim Addad', *Middle East Report Online*, 16 February 2021.
38. Bayat, *Revolutionary Life*, p. 246.
39. Serres, 'The Algerian Hirak'.
40. Ibid.
41. Bayat, *Revolution without Revolutionaries*, p. 224.
42. Zoubir, 'The Algerian Crisis', p. 12.
43. Benalycherif, 'Nothing Will Fall from the Sky'.
44. Serres, 'The Algerian Hirak'.

45. Hamza Hamouchene, 'Generals to the Dustbin, Algeria Will Be Independent: The New Algerian Revolution as a Fanonian Moment', in Nigel C. Gibson (ed.), *Fanon Today: Revolt and Reason of the Wretched of the Earth* (Wakefield, QC 2021), p. 422.
46. Interview with a female youth researcher from Setif, 4 June 2021.
47. Ibid.
48. Interview with a male youth entrepreneur from Batna, 6 August 2021.
49. Bayat, *Revolution without Revolutionaries*, p. 224.
50. Ibid., p. 218.
51. Ibid., p. 224.
52. Robert Parks, 'From Protesta to Hirak to Algeria's New Revolutionary Moment', *Middle East Research and Information Project* 292/3 (Fall/Winter 2019) available at https://merip.org/2019/12/from-protesta-to-hirak-to-algerias-new-revolutionary-moment/.
53. Haleh Davies, 'This Is the Voice of Algeria'.
54. Interview with a male activist from the south, 23 June 2021.

Conclusion

1. Sarah Henderson, 'Selling civil society, Western aid and the nongovernmental organization sector in Russia', *Comparative Political Studies* 35/2(2002), pp. 139–67.
2. Benoit Challand, 'Coming Too Late? The EU's Mixed Approaches to Transforming the Israeli-Palestinian Conflict', *MICROCON Policy Working Paper* 12 (Brighton, 2010).
3. Phillippe Schmitter, *Some Propositions about Civil Society and the Consolidation of Democracy* (Vienna, 1993).
4. Ibid., p. 15.
5. Francesco Cavatorta and Vincent Durac, *Civil Society and Democratization in the Arab World, The Dynamics of Activism* (Oxford, 2011), p. 27.
6. Andrea Liverani, *Civil Society in Algeria, The Political Functions of Associational Life* (Abingdon, 2008), p. 169.
7. Caroline Abu-Sada and Benoit Challand (eds), *Le Développement, une affaire d'ONG, Associations, Etats et Bailleurs dans le Monde Arabe* (Paris, 2011), pp. 12–13.
8. Asef Bayat, *Life as Politics: How Ordinary People Change the Middle East* (California, 2013), p. 53.
9. Abu-Sada and Challand, *Le Développement, une affaire d'ONG*, p. 22, 'Les etudes auparavant séparent 'les associations de plaidoyer, faisant partie d'une société civile de contestation, comme opposée aux associations de "services"associations caritatives peu dissidentes'. Cette étude montre l'inverse: 'un monde associatif participant (sur des modes d'action très divers) aux politiques publiques,

en coopération avec les agences internationales et avec les administrations, notamment dans le domaine de la production de services publics.'
10. Ibid., p. 23.'Nous n'avons pas à faire non plus "simplement" à un contrôle de l'Etat sur les associations, mais aussi à un impact des changements associatifs sur le tissu politique national.'
11. Nadia Marzouki, 'Conversions as statelessness: a study of contemporary Algerian conversions to evangelical Christianity', *Middle East Law and Governance* 4 (2012), p. 73.
12. Ibid., p. 102.
13. Ibid., p. 100.
14. Tony Langlois, 'Music, borders and nationhood in Algeria', in Patrick Crowley (ed.), *Algeria: Nation, Culture and Transnationalism 1988–2015* (Liverpool, 2017).
15. Britta Hecking, 'Algerian youth on the move. Capoeira, street dance and parkour: between integration and contestation', in Patrick Crowley (ed.), *Algeria: Nation, Culture and Transnationalism 1988–2015* (Liverpool, 2017), p. 200.
16. Interview with Echiffaa Association, 27 October 2011.
17. Interview with the President of ACEC, 30 December 2009.
18. Omar Derras, interview with Hafida Ameyar, *Liberté* (6 June 2007), reported by Algeria Watch. Available at: www.algeria-watch.de/fr/article/div/mvt_associatif.htm (accessed 20 July 2017). 'À ce stade, le tissu associatif va devenir un rempart à l'arbitraire et à l'autoritarisme, et faire émerger un segment important de la société civile, non pas pour s'inscrire dans une stratégie de confrontation, mais de médiation et de partenariat indispensables.'

BIBLIOGRAPHY

Abdelrahman, Maha M., *Civil Society Exposed: The Politics of NGOs in Egypt* (London, 2004).
Abu-Sada, Caroline and Benoit Challand (eds), *Le Développement, une affaire d'ONG? Associations, Etats et Bailleurs dans le Monde Arabe* (Paris, 2011).
Addi, Lahouari, *L'Algérie et la démocratie* (Paris, 1994).
———, *Les Mutations de la Société Algérienne* (Paris, 1999).
———, 'Les obstacles à la formation de la société civile en Algérie', in Azza Bozzo and Jean-Pierre Luizzard (eds), *Les sociétés Civiles dans le Monde Musulman* (Paris, 2011).
Adler, E., F. Bicchi, B. Crawford and R. Del Sarto, *Convergence of Civilisations* (Toronto, 2006).
Aghrout, Ahmed, 'The EU–Algeria Partnership Agreement: a preliminary assessment', in *Working papers in contemporary history and politics/European Studies Research Institute*, no. 31, University of Salford (2005).
Aghrout, Ahmed and M. Bougherira (eds), *Algeria in Transition: Reforms and Development Prospects* (London, 2004).
Akacem, Mohamed, 'The role of external actors in Algeria's transition', *The Journal of North Africa Studies* 9/2 (2006), pp. 153–68.
Aliboni, Roberto, 'Societal change and political responses in Euro-Med relations', draft paper for the *Conference on the Mediterranean Microcosm between the West and the Arab Muslim World*, Paris, 3–4 November 2011.
Amir, Nabila, 'Les députés relèvent des ambigüités et des atteintes à la liberté d'association', *El Watan*, 28 November 2011.
Arkoun, Mohamed, 'Locating civil society in Islamic contexts', in Amyn B. Sajoo (ed.), *Civil Society in the Muslim world, Contemporary Perspectives* (London, 2004).
Atlani-Duault, Laetitia, *Au Bonheur des Autres Anthropologie de l'aide Humanitaire* (Paris, 2009).
Austin, John L., *How To Do Things with Words*, 2nd ed. (Oxford, 1975).
Barbé, E. and A. Herranz-Surrales, *The Challenge of Differentiation in Euro-Mediterranean Relations. Flexible Regional Co-operation or Fragmentation* (Abingdon, 2012).

Barcelona Declaration adopted at the Euro-Mediterranean Conference: 27 – 28 November 1995. Available at: www.eeas.europa.eu/archives/docs/euromed/docs/ bd_en.pdf (accessed 14 March 2017).

Bayat, Asef, *Life as Politics: How Ordinary People Change the Middle East* (California, 2013).

Bayat, Asef, *Revolution without Revolutionaries* (Stanford, CA, 2017).

———, *Revolutionariy Life: The Everyday of the Arab Spring* (Cambridge, MA, 2021).

Beaugé, Florence, *L'Algérie des années 2000: Vie Politique, Vie Sociale et Droits de l'homme* (Paris, 2008).

Belakhdar, Naoual. 'When Unemployment Meets Environment. The Case of the Anti-fracking Coalition in Ouargla'. *Mediterranean Politics* 24/4 (2019), pp. 420–42.

Belhilmer, Amar, 'Le Pluralisme Politique, Syndical et Associatif', in Friedrich-Ebert-Stiftung (ed.), *L'Algérie de demain: Relever les défis pour gagner l'avenir*, electronic edition (Alger, 2009). Available at: http://library.fes.de/pdf-files/bueros/algerien/06420-etude.pdf (accessed 20 July 2017).

Benalycherif, Sabri, '"Nothing Will Fall from the Sky": Algeria's Revolution Marches On' – Photo Essay, *African Arguments*, 18 December 2019. Available at: https://africanarguments.org/2019/12/18/nothing-will-fall-from-the-sky-algeria-revolution-hirak-marches-on-photo-essay/ (accessed 30 July 2022).

Benmalek, Anouar, *Chroniques de l'Algérie Amère, Algérie 1985 – 2011* (Alger, 2011).

Ben Nefissa, Sarah, *Pouvoirs et Associations dans le Monde Arabe* (Paris, 2002).

Benramdane, Djamel, *Les associations algériennes, des acteurs émergents en quˆete de reconnaissance*, CISP (Algiers, 2015).

Bentahar, Ziad, '"Ytnahaw ga'!": Algeria's Cultural Revolution and the Role of Language in the Early Stages of the Spring 2019 Hirak', *Journal of African Cultural Studies* 33/4 (2021), pp. 471–88.

Berger, Anne-Emmanuelle (ed.), *Algeria in Others' Languages* (Ithaca, NY, 2002).

Bicchi, Federica, '"Our size fits all": Normative power Europe and the Mediterranean', *Journal of European Public Policy* 13/2 (2006), pp. 286 – 303.

Boubekeur, Amel, *Political Islam in Algeria*, CEPS working document no. 268, May 2007.

———, *Countries at the Crossroads 2011 Algeria*. Freedom House Report (2011). Available at: www.refworld.org/docid/4ecba654c.html (accessed 20 July 2017).

Bouattia, Malia, 'Death of an Activist: A Shame on Algeria's State', *The New Arab*, 31 May 2019. Available at: https://english.alaraby.co.uk/opinion/death-activist-shame-algerias-state (accessed 30 July 2022).

Bozzo, Anna and Jean-Pierre Luizzard (eds), *Les sociétés Civiles dans le Monde Musulman* (Paris, 2011).

Boutros-Ghali, Boutros, *An Agenda for Democratization* (New York, 1996). Available at: www.un.org/fr/events/democracyday/pdf/An_agenda_for_democratization.pdf (accessed 14 March 2017).

Butcher, Charity, 'Can Oil-reliant countries democratize? An assessment of the role of civil society in Algeria', *Democratization* 21/4 (2014), pp. 722 – 42.

Byrne, B., R. Marcus and T. Powers-Stevens, *Gender, Conflict and Development. Vol. 2, Case Studies – Cambodia, Rwanda, Kosova, Somalia, Algeria, Guatemala and Eritrea.* IDS, Bridge, briefings on Development and Gender report, No. 35 (Brighton, 1995).

Carapico, Sheila, *Civil Society in Yemen: The Political Economy of Activism in Modern Arabia* (Cambridge, 1998).

———, 'Foreign aid for promoting democracy in the Arab World', *Middle East Journal* 56/3 (2002), pp. 379 – 95.

Carlier Omar, *Entre nation et djihad. Histoire Sociale des Radicalismes Algériens* (Paris, 1995).

Carothers, Thomas, 'Civil Society', *Foreign Policy* 117 (1999 – 2000), pp. 18 – 29.

Cavatorta, Francesco and Vincent Durac, *Civil Society and Democratization in the Arab World, The Dynamics of Activism* (Oxford, 2011).

Cavatorta, Francesco and Azzam Elananza, 'Political Opposition in civil society: an analysis of the interactions of secular and religious associations in Algeria and Jordan', *Government and Opposition* 43/4 (2008), pp. 561 – 78.

Çelenk, Ayse Aslihan, 'Promoting democracy in Algeria: the EU Factor and the preferences of the political elite', *Democratization* 16/1 (2009) pp. 176 – 92.

Challand, Benoit, *The Power to Promote and To Exclude: External Support for Palestinian Civil Society.* PhD Thesis, Florence: European University Institute (2005).

———, 'A nahda of charitable organizations? Health service provision and the politics of aid in Palestine', *Middle Eastern Studies* 40/2 (2008), pp. 227 – 47.

———, 'The evolution of Western aid for Palestinian civil society: bypassing local knowledge and resources', *Middle Eastern Studies* 44/3 (2008), pp. 397 – 417.

———, *Palestinian Civil Society. Foreign Donors and the Power to Promote and Exclude* (London, 2009).

———, 'Coming too late? The EU's mixed approaches to transforming the Israeli– Palestinian conflict', *MICROCON Policy Working Paper* 12, Brighton, MICROCON (2010).

Chapan Metz, Helen (ed.), *Algeria: A Country Study* (Washington, DC: GPO for the Library of Congress, 1994). Available at: http://countrystudies.us/algeria/68.htm (accessed 20 July 2017).

Chenoweth, Erica, and Stephan, Maria, *Why Civil Resistance Works: The Strategic Logic of Nonviolent Conflict* (New York, 2011).

Chiheb, Adel, Latefa Guemar and Jessica Northey, The Algerian Hirak: Young People and Non-violent Revolution. *Open Democracy* (2019). Available at: https://www.opendemocracy.net/en/north-africa-west-asia/algerian-hirak-young-people-and-non-violent-revolution/ (accessed 30 July 2022).

Ciftci, Sabri and Ethan M. Bernick, 'Utilitarian and modern: clientelism, citizen empowerment, and civic engagement in the Arab world', *Democratization* 22/7 (2015), pp. 1161 – 82.

Cohen, Jean, L. and Andrew Arato, *Civil Society and Political Theory* (Massachusetts, 1994).

Collyer, Michael, 'Transnational political participation of Algerians in France. Extraterritorial civil society versus transnational governmentality', *Political Geography* 25/7 (2006), pp. 836 – 49.

Crowley, Patrick, 'The Etat/Civil: postcolonial identities and genre', *French Forum* 29/3 (2004), pp. 79 – 94.

———, *Algeria: Nation, Culture and Transnationalism* (Liverpool, 2017).

———, 'Algerian traumas: the real, the chosen and the aesthetic', in *Cultural Representations of Trauma Conference*, 31 August – 1 September 2012, University of Iceland. Available at: https://edda.hi.is/?p¼3696 (accessed 31 March 2018).

Daguzan, Jean-Fran,cois, 'Les relations Franco-Algériennes ou la poursuite des amicales incompréhensions', *Annuaire Fran,cais des Relations Internationales* II (2001).

Dahak, Bachir, *Rapport final, La liberté d'association en Algérie*, 13 September 2007. Available at: http://bachirdahak.blogspot.co.uk/2014/02/la-liberte-dassociation- en-algerie-par.html (accessed 20 July 2017).

Darbouche, Hakim, 'Decoding Algeria's ENP policy: differentiation by other means?' *Mediterranean Politics* 13/3 (2008), pp. 371 – 89.

Darbouche, Hakim and Susi Dennison, 'A "Reset" with Algeria: the Russia to the EU's south', in *European Council on Foreign Relations, Policy Brief ECFR/46 December 2011*. Available at: www.ecfr.eu/page/-/ECFR46_ALGERIA_ BRIEF_ AW.pdf (accessed 20 July 2017).

Della Porta and M.J. Keating (eds), *Approaches and Methodologies in the Social Sciences, A Pluralist Perspective* (Cambridge, 2008).

Del Sarto, Raffaella A., *Contested State Identities and Regional Security in the Euro-Mediterranean Area* (Basingstoke, 2006).

———, 'Wording and meaning(s): EU – Israeli political co-operation according to the ENP action plan', *Mediterranean Politics* 12/1 (2006), pp. 59 – 75.

Del Sarto, Raffaella A. and Tobias Schumacher, 'From Brussels with love: leverage, benchmarking, and the action plans with Jordan and Tunisia in the EU's democratization policy', *Democratization*, 18/4 (2011), pp. 932 – 55.

Dennison, Susi, 'The EU, Algeria and the Northern Mali question', *ECFR policy memo* 69 (December 2012). Available at: http://ecfr.eu/page/-/ECFR69_ ALGERIA_ MEMO_AW.pdf (accessed 20 July 2017).

Derras, Omar, 'Le fait associatif en Algérie. Le cas d'Oran', *Insaniyat* 8 (1999), pp. 95 – 117.

———, *Le Phénomène associatif en Algérie* (Algiers, 2007).

———, 'Interview with Liberté', *L'espace associatif est producteur d'élites politiques et sociales*. Available at: www.algeria-watch.org/fr/article/div/mvt_associatif.htm (accessed 20 July 2017).

Diamond, Larry, 'Toward democratic consolidation', *Journal of Democracy* 5/3 (1994), pp. 4 – 17.

Dine, Philip, 'Sport in Algeria – from national self-assertion to anti-state contestation', in Patrick Crowley (ed.), *Algeria: Nation, Culture and Transnationalism 1988 – 2015* (Liverpool, 2017).

Djebar, Assia, *Algerian White* (New York, 2003). Originally published by Albin Michel S.A., Paris, France, in 1995, under the title *Le Blanc de l'Algérie*.
Driessen, Michael Daniel, *Religion and Democratization: Framing Religious and Political Identities in Muslim and Catholic societies* (Oxford, 2014).
Dris Ait Hamadouche, Louisa, 'Women in the Maghreb: civil society's actors or political instruments?' *Middle East Policy* 14/4 (2007), pp. 115 – 33.
Dris Aït-Hamadouche, L. and C. Dris, Le face à face hirak-pouvoir: La crise de la représentation. *L'Année Du Maghreb* 21 (2019), pp. 57–68. Available at: https://journals.openedition.org/anneemaghreb/5129 (accessed 30 July 2022).
Edwards, Michael, *Civil Society* (Cambridge, 2004 [1957]).
Elyachar, Julia, *Markets of Dispossession: NGOs, Economic Development, and the State in Cairo* (Durham, 2005).
Entelis, John P., 'Civil society and the authoritarian temptation in Algerian politics. Islamic democracy versus the centralized state', in A.R. Norton (ed.), *Civil society in the Middle East*, Vol. 1 (Leiden, 1994).
Evans, Martin and John Philips, *Algeria: Anger of the Dispossessed* (New Haven, CT, 2007).
Emerson, Michael, *Democratization in the European Neighbourhood* (Brussels: Centre for European Policy Studies, 2005).
Emerson, Michael and Richard Youngs, *Democracy's Plight in the European Neighbourhood* (Brussels: Centre for European Policy Studies, 2009).
Fanon, Frantz, *The Wretched of the Earth* (New York, 1965).
———, *A Dying Colonialism* (New York, 1965).
Fanon, Frantz, *Toward the African revolution: Political essays* (London, 1988).
Filali-Ansary, Abdou, 'State, society and creed, reflections on the Maghreb', in Amyn B. Sajoo (ed.), *Civil Society in the Muslim World, Contemporary Perspectives* (London, 2004).
Fioramonti, Lorenzo and V.F. Heinrich, 'How civil society influences policy: a comparative analysis of the *CIVICUS Civil Society Index* in post-Communist Europe', CIVICUS/ODI Research Report (2007). Available at: https://papers.ssrn.com/sol3/papers.cfm?abstract_id¼2100418 (accessed 20 July 2017).
Floridi, Maurizio, Beatriz Sanz-Corella and Stephano Verdecchia, 'Capitalisation study on capacity building support programmes for non state actors under the 9th EDF', European Commission report (2009).
Flyvbjerg, Bent, 'Case study', in Norman K. Denzin and Yvonna S. Lincoln (eds), *The Sage Handbook of Qualitative Research, 4th Edition* (California, 2011), pp. 301 – 16.
Fraser, Nancy, 'Rethinking the public sphere: a contribution to the critique of actually existing democracy', *Social Text* 25/26 (1990), pp. 56 – 80.
Fuller, Graham E., *Algeria: The Next Fundamentalist State?* (California, 1996).
Gafaiti, Hafid, 'The Monotheism of the other: language and de/construction of national identity in postcolonial Algeria', in Anne-Emmanuelle Berger (ed.), *Algeria in Others' Languages* (Ithaca, NY, 2002).
Gellner, Ernest, *Conditions of Liberty: Civil Society and Its Rivals* (London, 1994).

Gera, Gideon, *An Islamic republic of Algeria?: Implications for the Middle East and the West*. Research memorandum; no. 29, Washington Institute for Near East Policy (Washington, DC, 1995).

Ghilés, Francis, 'A unified North Africa on the world stage: overview of Maghreb sector studies', in G.C. Hufbauer and C. Brunel (eds), *Maghreb Regional and Global Integration: A Dream to Be Fulfilled* (Washington, DC, 2008).

———, 'France left a cruel legacy to Algeria', *Wall Street Journal*, 16 September 1999.

Glenn III, John K., *Framing Democracy Civil Society and Civic Movements in Eastern Europe* (California, 2001).

Golen, Galia and Walid Salem, *Non-State Actors in the Middle East, Factors for Peace and Democracy* (Abingdon, 2014).

Gramsci, Antonio, Q. Hoare and G. Nowell-Smoth (translation and eds), *Selections from the Prison Notebooks of Antonio Gramsci* (London, 1971).

Grimm, S. and J. Leininger, 'Not all good things go together: conflicting objectives in democracy promotion', *Democratization* 19/3 (2012), pp. 391 – 414.

Guemar, Latefa, *Algerian Women: Experiences of Exile from the Black Decade to the Hirak* (Exeter, forthcoming in 2023).

Guemar, Latefa, Jessica Northey and Elias Boukrami, 'Diaspora Activism and Citizenship: Algerian Community Responses during the Global Pandemic', *Journal of Ethnic and Migration Studies* 48/9 (2022), pp. 1980–97.

Guney, A. and A. Çelenk, 'European Union's democracy promotion policies in Algeria: success or failure?' *Journal of North African Studies* 12/1 (2007), pp. 109 – 28.

Habermas, Jurgen, *The Structural Transformation of the Public Sphere: An Inquiry into a Category of Bourgeois Society* (Massachusetts, 1989). Originally published 1962 and translated into English in 1989 by T. Burger and F. Lawrence.

Hachemaoui, Mohamed, ' La queˆte de la représentation d'un "notable du cru"', *Alfa. Maghreb et Sciences Sociales*, IRMC, Maisonneuve & Larose (2008).

Hadenius, Axel and Frederik Uggla, 'Making civil society work, promoting democratic development: what can states and donors do?', *World Development* 24/10 (1996), pp. 1621 – 39.

Hadj Ali, Mohamed Youcef, *Lettre Ouverte aux francais qui ne comprennent décidément rien à l'Algérie* (Paris, 1998).

———, *Les élites fran,caises et la crise Algérienne (1991 – 1998): Perceptions, Positions, Prédictions*, PhD thesis (University of Toulouse, 2003).

Haleh Davies, Muriam '"This Is the Voice of Algeria": Radio Corona International Carries the Torch of the Hirak', *Jadaliyya*, 20 August 2020. Available at: https://www.jadaliyya.com/Details/41575/%E2%80%9CThis-is-the-Voice-of-Algeria%E2%80%9D-Radio-Corona-International-Carries-the-Torch-of-the-Hirak (accessed 30 July 2022).

Haleh Davis, Muriam and Thomas Serres, 'Political Contestation in Algeria: between Postcolonial Legacies and the Arab Spring', *Middle East Critique* 22/2 (2013), pp. 99–112.

Hall, John and Frank Trentmann, *Civil Society: A Reader in History, Theory and Global Politics* (London, 2005).
Hamouchene, Hamza, 'Generals to the Dustbin, Algeria Will Be Independent: The New Algerian Revolution as a Fanonian Moment', in Nigel C. Gibson (ed.), *Fanon Today: Revolt and Reason of the Wretched of the Earth* (Wakefield, QC 2021), pp. 415–34.
Human Rights Watch, *World Report. Algeria Country Report*, January 2020. Available at: https://www.hrw.org/world-report/2020/country-chapters/algeria (accessed 30 July 2022).
Hannoum, Abdelmadjid, 'Translation and the colonial imaginary: Ibn Khaldu^n orientalist', *History and Theory* 42/1 (2003) 61 – 81.
Harbeson, John W., Donald Rothchild and Naomi Chazan, *Civil Society and the State in Africa* (London, 1994).
Hardig, Anders, 'Beyond the Arab revolts: conceptualising civil society in the Middle East and North Africa', *Democratization* 22/6 (2015), pp. 1131 – 53.
Hawthorne, Amy, *Middle Eastern Democracy. Is Civil Society the Answer?* Carnegie Papers, 1 March 2004, Carnegie Endowment for International Peace.
Heartfield, James, 'Algeria and the defeat of French humanism', Chapter 6 of *The Death of the Subject Explained* (Sheffield, 2002), pp. 111 – 28.
Hecking, Britta, 'Algerian youth on the move. Capoeira, street dance and parkour: between integration and contestation', in Patrick Crowley (ed.), *Algeria: Nation, Culture and Transnationalism 1988 – 2015* (Liverpool, 2017).
Henderson, Sarah, 'Selling civil society, Western aid and the nongovernmental organization sector in Russia', *Comparative Political Studies* 35/2 (2002), pp. 139 – 67.
Hill, J.N.C., *Identity in Algerian Politics, The Legacy of Colonial Rule* (London, 2009).
Hirschman, Albert O., *Getting Ahead Collectively: Grassroots Experiences in Latin America* (New York, 1984).
———, *Rival Views of Market Society and Other Recent Essays* (Cambridge, MA, 1992).
Hoexter, Meriem, S.N. Eisenstadt and Nehemia Levtzion, *The Public Sphere in Muslim Societies* (New York, 2002).
Hoffman, Michael and Amaney Jamal, 'The youth and the Arab spring: cohort differences and similarities', *Middle East Law and Governance* 4 (2012), pp. 168 – 88.
Horne, Alistair, *A Savage War of Peace: Algeria 1954 – 1962* (New York, 2006).
Hulme, David and Michael Edwards, *NGOs, States and Donors Too Close for Comfort?* (London, 1997).
Ibn Khaldun, *The Muqaddimah, an Introduction to History*, translated by Franz Rosenthal, Vol. 1. (New York, 1967 [1377]).
Ibrahim, Saad Eddin, 'The troubled triangle: populism, Islam and civil society in the Arab world', *International Political Science Review* 19/4 (1998), pp. 373 – 85.
Jamal, Amaney, *Barriers to Democracy, The Other Side of Social Capital in Palestine and the Arab World* (Princeton, NJ, 2007).

———, 'When is social trust a desirable outcome? Examining levels of trust in the Arab world', *Comparative Political Studies* 40/11 (2007), pp. 1328 – 49.
Jourde, Cédric, 'The president is coming to visit! Dramas and the hijack of democratization in the Islamic republic of Mauritania', *Comparative Politics* 37/4 (2005), pp. 421 – 40.
Kaddache Mahfoud, *L'Algérie des Algériens. Histoire de l'Algérie 1830 – 1954* (Alger, 1998).
Keane, John, *Democracy and Civil Society* (London, 1988).
Kessab, Amar, 'Med culture: country profile for the cultural sector in Algeria' (2014). Available at www.medculture.eu/country/report-structure/algeria (accessed 20 July 2017).
Kiser, John W., *Commander of the Faithful: The Life and Times of Emir Abd el-Kader* (New York, 2008).
Kubba, Laith, 'The awakening of civil society', *Journal of Democracy* 11/3 (2000), pp. 84 – 90.
Langhor, Vickie, 'Too much civil society, too little politics: Egypt and liberalizing Arab regimes', *Comparative Politics* 36 /2 (2004), pp. 181 – 204.
Langlois, Tony, 'Music, borders and nationhood in Algeria', in Patrick Crowley (ed.), *Algeria: Nation, Culture and Transnationalism 1988 – 2015* (Liverpool, 2017).
Lafi, Nora, 'The "Arab Spring" in Global Perspective: Social Movements, Changing Contexts and Political Transitions in the Arab World (2010–2014)', in S. Berger and H. Nehring (eds), *The History of Social Movements in Global Perspective* (London, 2017).
Layish, Aharon, 'The Qadi's role in the Islamization of Sedentary Society', in Miriam Hoexter, Shmuel Eisenstadt and Nehemia Levitzion (eds), *The Public Sphere in Muslim Societies* (Albany, NY, 2002), pp. 83 – 107.
Lazreg, Marnia, *The Eloquence of Silence: Algerian Women in Question* (London, 1994).
Lepenies, Phillip, 'Possibilism: an approach to problem solving derived from the life and work of Albert O. Hirschman', *Development and Change* 39/3 (2008), pp. 437 – 59.
Levtzion, Nehemia, 'The dynamics of Sufi brotherhoods', in Miriam Hoexter, Shmuel Eisenstadt and Nehemia Levitzion (eds), *The Public Sphere in Muslim Societies* (Albany, NY, 2002), pp. 109 – 18.
Liverani, Andrea, *Civil Society in Algeria the Functional Politics of Associational Life* (Abingdon, 2008).
Lloyd, Catherine, 'Organising across borders: Algerian women's associations in a period of conflict', *Review of African Political Economy* 82 (1999), pp. 479 – 90.
Lorcin, Patricia, 'Rome and France in Africa: recovering colonial Algeria's Latin past', *French Historical Studies* 25/2 (2002), pp. 295 – 329.
Lust-Okar, Ellen, 'Divided they rule: the management and manipulation of political opposition', *Comparative Politics* 36/2 (2004), pp. 159 – 79.
———, *Structuring Conflict in the Arab World: Incumbents, Opponents, and Institutions* (Cambridge, 2005).

McAllister, Edward, 'Postsocialist Algeria and the politics of the future', *Revista de Estudios Internacionales Mediterraneos* 18 (2015), pp. 137 – 63.

———, 'Algeria's "Belle Epoque": memories of the 1970s as a window on the Present', in Patrick Crowley (ed.), *Algeria: Nation, Culture and Transnationalism 1988 – 2015* (Liverpool, 2017).

McDougall, James, *History and the Culture of Nationalism in Algeria* (Cambridge, 2006).

———, 'Islam(s) and politics: post-traumatic states in Algeria', in *Open Democracy* (10 July 2007) Available at: www.opendemocracy.net/democracy_power/africa_islam/algeria_politics (accessed 20 July 2017).

———, 'After the war: Algeria's transition to uncertainty', *Middle East Report*, 245 (2007), pp. 34 – 41.

———, 'État, société et culture chez les intellectuels de l'islaʾh maghrébin (Algérie et Tunisie, c.1890 – 1940), ou, la réforme comme apprentissage de l'arriération', in Moreau, Odile (ed.), *La réforme de l'état dans le monde islamo-méditerranéen aux XIXéme-XXéme siécles* (Paris, 2009).

———, 'Dream of exile, promise of home: language, education, and Arabism in Algeria', *International Journal of Middle East Studies* 43/02 (2011), pp. 251 – 70.

———, *A History of Algeria* (Cambridge, 2017).

———, 'In the shadow of revolution', in Patrick Crowley (ed.), *Algeria: Nation, Culture and Transnationalism 1988 – 2015* (Liverpool, 2017).

Maddy-Weitzmann, Bruce and Daniel Zisenwine, *The Maghrib in the New Century, Identity Religion and Politics* (Gainesville, 2007).

Magaloni, Beatriz, 'Credible power sharing and the longevity of authoritarian rule', *Comparative Political Studies* 41 (2008), pp. 715 – 41.

Malley, Robert, *The Call from Algeria: Third Worldism, Revolution, and the Turn to Islam* (Berkeley, CA, 1996).

Martinez, Luis, *The Algerian Civil War, 1990 – 1998* (London, 2000).

———, 'Algeria: The Illusion of Oil Wealth.' *Les Etudes du CERI* 168 (2010).

———, *The Violence of Petro-Dollar Regimes* (New York, 2012).

Martinez, Luis and Rasmussen Alenius Boserup, *Algeria Modern: From Opacity to Complexity* (London, 2016).

Marzouki, Nadia, 'Conversions as statelessness: a study of contemporary Algerian conversions to evangelical Christianity', *Middle East Law and Governance* 4 (2012), pp. 69 – 105.

Merz, Sibille, '"Missionaries of a new era": neoliberalism and NGOs in Palestine', *Races Class*, July – September 54/1 (2012), pp. 50 – 66.

Miller, Laurel E., Jeffery Martini and F. Stephen Larrabee, *Democratization in the Arab World: Prospects and Lessons from Around the Globe* (Santa Monica, CA, 2012).

Mitchell, Timothy, 'The limits of the state: beyond statist approaches and their critics', *The American Political Science Review* 85/1 (1991), pp. 77 – 96.

Naciri, Rabea, *Les organizations de la société civile en Afrique du Nord Algérie, Maroc et Tunisie* (Rabat, 2009).

Navaras, 'L'extermination de l'intelligentsia algérienne (1993 – 98)', in the online blog, *Angles de Vu*, 20 August 2009.Available at http://anglesdevue.canalblog.com/archives/2009/08/20/14799361.html (accessed 20 July 2017).

Northey, Jessica A., 'Associations and Democracy in Algeria', *Democratization* 24/2 (2017), pp. 209 – 25.

———, 'Algerian heritage associations: national identity and rediscovering the past', in Patrick Crowley (ed.), *Algeria: Nation, Culture and Transnationalism 1988 – 2015* (Liverpool, 2017).

Northey, Jessica, 'The Algerian Hirak: Citizenship, Non-Violence and the New Movement for Democracy', in Wolf Mackert and Turner (eds), *The Condition of Democracy: Volume 3: Postcolonial and Settler Colonial Contexts* (Abingdon, 2021).

———, 'Imagining a New Political Space: The Power of Youth and Peaceful Protest in Algeria', *Revista Idees* (2020). Available at https://revistaidees.cat/en/imagining-a-new-political-space-the-power-of-youth-and-peaceful-protest-in-algeria/ (accessed 30 July 2022).

Northey, Jessica, and Latefa Guemar, 'Algeria Breaks the Wall of Fear', *Open Democracy* (2019). Available at: https://www.opendemocracy.net/en/north-africa-west-asia/algeria-breaks-wall-of-fear/ (accessed 30 July 2022).

———, 'The Algerian Hirak: Youth Mobilisation, Elections and Prospects for Reform', *Orient. German Journal for Politics, Economics and Culture of the Middle East* 2 (2020), pp. 14–21.

———, 'Hirak Anniversary: Political Prisoners Freed as Algerians Continue to Protest,' *Open Democracy* (2021). Available at: https://www.opendemocracy.net/en/north-africa-west-asia/hirak-anniversary-political-prisoners-freed-algerians-continue-protest/ (accessed 30 July 2022).

Norton, Augustus, R. (ed.), *Civil society in the Middle East*, Vol. 1 (Leiden, 1994).

O'Sullivan, David, *Setting up the European External Action Service (EEAS): Experiences and Perspectives*, Debating Europe Series conferences at the European University Institute, Florence, 28 November 2012.

Ottoway, M.T. and T. Carothers, *Funding Virtue, Civil Society Aid and Democracy Promotion*, Carnegie Foundation (Washington, DC, 2000).

Ould Amar, Zakaria, Final Evaluation of the Support to Algerian Associations Programme (2010).

Ould Amar, Zakaria, Jean Bossuyt and Caroline Valette, *Etude d'identification d'un programme d'appui à la société civile en Mauritanie* (ECDPM, 2005). Available at: http://base.afrique-gouvernance.net/en/corpus_bipint/fiche-bipint-383.html (accessed 20 July 2017).

Ould T'Feil, Hamoud, 'Number of civil society associations in Mauritania' (20 April 2017). Available at hamoud1t@yahoo.fr (accessed 20 July 2017).

———, *Etude d'Evaluation du programme d'appui aux associations algériennes de développement, ONG2, en Algérie* (ECDPM, 2010).

Parks, Robert, 'From Protesta to Hirak to Algeria's New Revolutionary Moment', *Middle East Research and Information Project* 292/3 (Fall/Winter 2019).

Available at: https://merip.org/2019/12/from-protesta-to-hirak-to-algerias-new-revolutionary-moment/ (accessed 30 July 2022).

———, 'Voter Participation and Loud Claim Making in Algeria', *Middle East Report* 281 (2016), pp. 23–7.

Pearce, Jenny, Rosemary McGee and Joanna Wheeler, *Violence, Security and Democracy: Perverse Interfaces and their Implications for States and Citizens in the Global South*. IDS Working Paper 357 (Brighton, 2011).

Philippart, Eric, *The Euro-Mediterranean Partnership: Unique Features, First Results and Future Challenges*, CEPS Working Paper No. 10, April, Middle East & Euro-Med Project (2003).

Putnam, Robert D., 'The prosperous community: social capital and public life', *The American Prospect* 4/13 (1993), pp. 35 – 42.

Putnam, Robert D. 'Bowling alone: America's declining social capital', *Journal of Democracy* 6/1 (1995), pp. 65 – 78.

Putnam, Robert D., R. Leonardi and R. Nanetti, *Making Democracy Work: Civic Traditions in Modern Italy* (Princeton, NJ, 1994).

Putzel, James, 'The politics of "participation": civil society, the state and development assistance', in *Crisis States Research Centre Discussion Papers* 1 (London, 2004).

Rahal, Malika, '1988 – 1992: Multipartism, Islamism and the descent into civil war, past', in Patrick Crowley (ed.), *Algeria: Nation, Culture and Transnationalism 1988 – 2015* (Liverpool, 2017).

Raik, Kristi, *Promoting Democracy through Civil Society: How to Step up the EU's Policy towards the Eastern Neighbourhood*, CEPS Working Documents No. 237, 2006.

Rebai Maamri, Malika, *The State of Algeria, The Politics of a Post-Colonial Legacy* (London, 2015).

Roberts, Hugh, 'Dancing in the dark: the European Union and the Algerian drama', *Democratization*, 9/1 (2002), pp. 106 – 34.

———, *The Battlefield Algeria 1988 – 2002, Studies in a Broken Polity* (London, 2003).

———, *The Bouteflika presidency and the problems of political reform in Algeria*, Speech to the Forum on the Middle East and North Africa, 3 February, 2005. Madrid, FRIDE.

———, 'Who said Gaddafi had to go?', *London Review of Books* 33/22, 17 November (2011), pp. 8 – 18. Available at: www.lrb.co.uk/v33/n22/hugh-roberts/who-said-gaddafi-had-to-go (accessed 10 July 2013).

———, *Berber Government: The Kabyle Polity in Pre-colonial Algeria* (London, 2014).

Robinson, Mark and Steven Friedman, *Civil society, Democratization and Foreign Aid in Africa*. IDS Discussion Paper 383 (Brighton, 2005).

Roy, Olivier, 'The predicament of "civil society" in Central Asia and the Greater Middle East', *International Affairs* 81/5 (2005), pp. 1001 – 12.

———, *The Politics of Chaos in the Middle East* (New York, 2008).

———, 'The transformation of the Arab world', *Journal of Democracy* 23/3 (2012), pp. 5 – 18.

Saï, Fatima Zohra, 'Les Associations Féminines en Algérie Entre le Politique et le Socio-culturel. Chapter 11', in T. Chentouf, Les Etats *face à la mondialisation*: Le cas de l'*Algérie* (CODESRIA, 2005).

Salhi, Mohamed Brahim, *L'Algérie: citoyenneté et Identité* (Alger, 2010).

Sall, Amadou, *Mécanismes de renforcement de la professionnalisation des Organizations de la Société Civile Mauritanienne et du dialogue entre partenaires*. CMAP, December 2009.

Sajoo, Amyn B. (ed.), *Civil Society in the Muslim World, Contemporary Perspectives* (London, 2009).

Sandbakken, Camilla, 'The limits to democracy posed by oil rentier states: the cases of Algeria, Nigeria and Libya', *Democratization* 13/1 (2006), pp. 135 – 52.

Saral, Melek, *Civil Society and Human Rights Protection in Irak since 2003*. Paper prepared for the Final Shur Conference Human Rights in Conflict the role of civil society, Rome, 4 – 6 June 2009.

Scheele, Judith, *Village Matters: Knowledge, Politics and Community in Kabylia, Algeria* (Oxford, 2009).

———, 'Coming to terms with tradition: manuscript conservation in contemporary Algeria', in Graziano Kra"tli and Ghislaine Lydon (eds), *The Trans-Saharan Book Trade: Manuscript Culture, Arabic Literacy and Intellectual History in Muslim Africa* (Leiden, 2010).

Schlumberger, Oliver, 'Transition in the Arab world: guidelines for comparison', *EUI Working Papers, Mediterranean Programme Series* (2002), EUI: RSC 2002/22.

Schmitter, Phillipe C., *Some Propositions about Civil Society and the Consolidation of Democracy* (Imprint Vienna: Institut fu"r Ho"here Studien, 1993). Available at www.ihs.ac.at/publications/pol/pw_10.pdf (accessed 20 July 2017).

———, 'Conceptualizing, researching and evaluating democracy promotion and protection', *EUI Working Papers*, EUI: SPS 1999/09. Available at: http://cadmus.eui.eu/dspace/bitstream/1814/309/1/sps99_9.pdf (accessed 20 July 2017).

Schwedler, Jillian, *Faith in Moderation: Islamist Parties in Jordan and Yemen* (Cambridge, 2006).

Searle, John R., *Mind, Language and Society*: *Philosophy in the Real World* (New York, 1998).

Sekkou, Laredj, *L'Algérie et la Communauté Economique Européenne*, Doctoral thesis, Law Faculty, University of Lausanne (1971).

Serres, Thomas, 'The Algerian Hirak between Mobilization and Imprisonment – An Interview with Hakim Addad', *Middle East Report Online*, 16 February 2021. Available at: https://merip.org/2021/02/the-algerian-hirak-between-mobilization-and-imprisonment-an-interview-with-hakim-addad/) (accessed 30 July 2022).

Spencer, Claire, 'The end of international enquiries? The UN eminent persons' mission to Algeria', *Mediterranean Politics* 3/3 (1998), pp. 125 – 33.

Stone, Martin, *The Agony of Algeria* (London, 1997).

Taleb-Ibrahimi, Khaoula, *Les Algériens et leur(s) langue(s). Éléments pour une Approche Sociolinguistique de la Société Algérienne* (Alger, 1995).

———, 'Toponymie et langage, à Alger', *Insaniyat, Revue Algérienne d'Anthropologie et de Sciences Sociales* I/17 – 18 (2002), pp. 132 – 5.

———, 'L'opposition du fran‚cais et de l'arabe a cassé l'intelligentsia algérienne', *El Watan*, 9 July 2012.

Temlali, Yassine, *La Genése de la Kabylie aux origins de l'affirmation Berbére en Algérie (1830 – 1962)* (Paris, 2016).

Tocqueville, Alexis de, *Democracy in America* (London, 1994 [1840]).

Triscritti, Fiorella, *Promoting Democracy Abroad: The EU and Latin America, 1995 – 2005*, PhD thesis, European University Institute, July 2008.

Van Reisen, Mirjam, 'The enlarged European Union and the developing world: what future?' in Andrew Mold, *EU Development Policy in a Changing World* (Amsterdam, 2007).

Van Rooy, Alison (ed.), *Civil Society and the Aid Industry* (London, 1998).

Venesson, Pascal, 'Case studies and process tracing: theories and practices', in Donatella Della Porta and Michael Keating (eds), *Approaches and Methodologies in the Social Sciences A Pluralist Perspective* (Cambridge, 2008).

———, 'Coping with insecurity in fragile situations', *ERD Report*, European University Institute (2009).

Volpi, Frédéric, *Islam and Democracy: The Failure of Dialogue in Algeria* (London, 2003).

Wedeen, Lisa, 'The politics of deliberation: Qat Chews as public spheres in Yemen', *Public Culture* 19/1 (2007), pp. 59 – 84.

Werenfels, Isabelle, *Managing Instability in Algeria: Elites and Political Change since 1995* (London, 2007).

———, *Who is in Charge? Algerian Power Structures and their Resilience to Change*, CNRS working paper, CERI (Paris, 2010).

Wictorowicz, Quintan, 'Civil Society as Social Control', *Comparative Politics* 33/1 (2000), pp. 43 – 61.

Willis, Michael, *The Islamist Challenge in Algeria: A Political History* (Berkshire, 1996).

———, 'Containing radicalism through political process in North Africa', *Mediterranean Politics* 11/2 (2006), pp. 137 – 50.

Wylie, Diana, 'The Importance of being at-home: a defense of historic preservation in Algeria', *Change over Time* 2/2 (2012), pp. 172 – 87.

Youngs, Richard, *The European Union and the Promotion of Democracy* (Oxford, 2001).

———, 'The European Union and Democracy Promotion in the Mediterranean: A New or Disingenuous Strategy?' *Democratization* 9/1 (2002), pp. 40 – 62.

Zeraoulia, Faouzia, 'The Memory of the Civil War in Algeria: Lessons from the Past with Reference to the Algerian Hirak', *Contemporary Review of the Middle East* 7/1 (2020), pp. 1–29.

Zermane, Hanane, and Samia Aitouche, 'Digital Learning with Covid-19 in Algeria', *International Journal of 3D printing technologies and digital industry* 4/2 (2020), pp. 161–70.

Zoubir, Yahia H., 'The Stalled democratisation of an authoritarian regime: the case of Algeria', *Democratization* 2/2 (1995), pp. 109 – 39.

———, 'The Algerian crisis in world affairs', *The Journal of North African Studies* 4/3 (1999), pp. 15 – 29.

———, 'The resurgence of Algeria's foreign policy in the twenty-first century', *The Journal of North African Studies* 9/2 (2004), p. 169.

Zoubir, Yahia, 'The Algerian Crisis: Origins and Prospects for a "Second Republic"', *Aljazeera Centre for Studies Report* (21 May 2019). Available at: https://studies.aljazeera.net/en/reports/2019/05/algerian-crisis-origins-prospects-republic-190520100257161.html (accessed 30 July 2022).

INDEX

aarouch councils, 65
active citizenry, 212
Abbas, Ferhat, 70–1, 73, 185
Abd el-Kader, the Emir, 64, 130, 132, 200
Addad, Hakim, 210, 211–12, 215
African civil society, 46
Africa, the Caribbean and the Pacific (ACP), 41, 46–8
AIS (Islamic Salvation Army), 79
Algeria
    colonisation, 66–8, 119, 126, 128
    decolonisation, 128, 184, 188
    early history of, 63, 64
    fundraising, 206–207
    independence, 72–6
    liberation war of 1954–62, 196
    lockdown, 205
    marches/slogans in, 203–4
Algerian Communist Party, 74, 84
Algerian League for the Defence of Human Rights (LADDH), 94, 138, 152
Algerian Muslim Scouts, 68
Algerian People's Party (PPA), 69, 71, 73

Algerian Women (Guemar), 204
Alleg, Henri, 162
Alloula foundation, 190
ALN (National Liberation Army), 69
Amicale, 76
Amusnaw association, 94
Antifracking, 199
APEB (*Association pour la protection de l'Environnement de Beni Isguen*), 99–100
APPAT (*Association pour la préservation du Patrimoine de Tiaret*), 127, 130–3, 184–5
Arab Spring, 3, 24, 31, 38, 87–8, 100, 196–7, 216
    donor support following, 50, 174
arabisation, 74, 119, 191
Arabophone, 204
Armed Islamic Group (GIA), 117, 153
Assala Association, 172
Association of Algerian Muslim Ulama (AUMA), 69, 70, 73
authoritarianism, and civil society, 38, 83, 202

Barcelona Process, 47, 167
Bayat, Asef, 197, 198, 203, 211, 215
Bel Horizon association, 124–7, 137, 171, 184, 187, 192, 199–201
Ben Badis, Abdelhamid, 69, 70, 73, 185
Ben Bella, Ahmed, 74
Bendjelloul, Mohamed, 70
Benalycherif, Sabri, 203, 212
Benhaj, Ali, 88
Bentounes, Sheikh Khaled, 123
Berbers, 32, 63, 65–6, 74, 76–8, 86–7, 105–6, 119, 128, 135, 185–6, 188–9
Berber Cultural Movement, 77, 188–9
Berber Spring, 77
Bey, Maissa, 171
black decade, 1, 78, 83, 86, 91, 165
Blida, 1, 2, 142, 190
Blum-Violette plan, 70
Boucebci, Mahfoud, 36
Boucebci foundation, 37, 139, 152–6, 187, 191, 198, 199
Bouhired, Djamila, 202
Boumediene, Houari, 66, 74, 75, 76
Bouteflika, Abdelaziz, 5, 89, 123, 195, 199–201, 211

Cafes, 4, 68, 72
Castellum Tingitanum association, 127–9, 184
Central Asia, 4, 43–4
Chadli, Benjedid, 77–9, 85
Christianity, conversion to, 200
civic engagement, 198

civil society, 195, 197–9, 202, 206, 211, 213, 215, 218
Civil society in Algeria, 195, 213
climate change, 208–9
CNCD (National Coordination for Democratic Change), 24, 87–8, 101, 123, 197
Conseil National Economique et Sociale (CNES), 89–90
colonisation, 66–8, 119, 126, 128
Constitution, 4, 77, 78, 89 of 2016, 4–5, 189
and new law on associations 2012, 93–5
and Tamazight, 189
Cotonou Agreement, 46
CRUA (Revolutionary Committee for Unity and Action), 72

Davies, Muriam Haleh, 217
Democracy brokers, 41
democratisation, 4, 24, 26, 43
in Algeria, 3, 78, 80–1, 85
in Arab world, 29, 42
and donors, 44, 50, 56
demonstrations
Arab Spring, 3, 87–8, 100
Setif uprising, 72
zawiyas, historical uprisings, 64
destitution, 205
digital technologies in education, 207
diglossia, 190
Disparus, *SOS*, 36, 187, 197
Djazairouna association, 1, 2, 6, 36, 105, 139, 155–6, 187
Djebar, Assia, 189–90

donors
  in Algeria, 52
  development paradigms, 41
  funding associations, 5, 6, 39, 40
  impeding autonomy, 4, 28, 38
  language policies, 192

Eastern Europe, 31, 41, 44–5, 179
Echifaa Association, 96–8, 198, 201
education
  Arabisation, 73–4, 119
  civic, 131, 136, 137
  under colonialism, 119
Egypt, 22, 88, 196, 211
El Ghaith association, 182
environmental activism, 198
Etoile Nord Africaine (ENA), 69, 71, 72
Euro-Mediterranean Partnership, 47
Europeans, euro-centric approaches, 163, 165
European Neighbourhood Policy, 47, 50
European Instrument for Democracy and Human Rights (EIDHR), 50, 52, 55, 174
European Union, 5, 6, 161, 162, 166

family code, 33, 77
Fanon, Frantz, 178
Fédération de France, 76
Fédération des élus, 70
Fédération Algérienne des Personnes Handicapées, 92, 154
Fekhar, Kamel Eddine, 210
FFS (Socialist Forces Front), 87
FIS (Islamic Salvation Front), 79, 84, 88, 153, 197

FLN (*Front de Libération Nationale*), 34, 69, 72–9, 83, 84, 88
  and national identity, 128, 165, 185
Forum des Educateurs, 172
France
  associations in, 72, 76, 137, 144
  relations with, 17–8, 161–2
freedom of association, 2, 3, 40, 48, 65, 75, 78, 85, 93–4, 152

GEHIMAB association, 134–5
Gellner, Ernest, 44, 63
Geneva, 200
GIA (Armed Islamic Group), 117, 153
global coronavirus pandemic, 201, 210
Gramsci, Antonio, 7, 26, 83, 116, 196, 211
Greater Middle East project, 44, 179
GSPC (Salafist Group for Preaching and Combat), 80
Guemar, Latefa, 204–5

Hamouchene, Hamza, 197, 213
Harkis, 186
High Commission for Amazighté, 189
Hippone Sub association, 172–3
hirak (the movement), 195–8, 199–206, 208, 212–18
Hirschman, Albert O, 6, 35, 180–1
Hollande, Francois, 186
hogra, 78, 86
human rights
  and Europeans, 49, 50–1, 159, 161–2, 171, 174, 183
  organisations, 2, 34, 57, 86, 138, 152, 191, 195

Ibadism, 123, 135–6, 185, 193
Ibn Khaldun, 130, 177–8
ICNL (the International Center for not-for-profit Law), 20–1, 23
Independence, War of, 72, 162, 186
Injaz Aljazair (association), 207–8
Islam, 69, 71, 73
Islamic associations, 33, 43, 55, 57, 74, 76–7
Islamic State, 4
Italy, 27

janviéristes, 85
Jordan, 23

Kheddar, Cherifa, 1, 3

Lafi, Nora, 203
language
 arabisation, 73–4, 119
 Berber, 74, 77, 119, 185, 188–9
 Darija, Algerian Arabic, 134–5, 188–9
 education, 73–4, 119, 188
 French, 73, 109, 126, 188–92
 multilingual, 66
 national identity, 73, 179, 188
Law on Associations
 1901 Law, 3, 4, 68, 75
 1990 Law, 3, 19, 78, 79
 2011 Law, 91–5, 126
Lebanon, 22, 35, 54–8
le Pen, Marine, 186
Le Petit Lecteur association, 171, 191
Libya, 4, 88, 100, 163, 196

Macron, Emmanuel, 186–7
El Madani, Taoufik, 128, 184–5

Mauritania, 10, 23, 99
Messali Hadj, 69–71, 73, 76
military coup, 3, 79–80, 163
Ministry of National Solidarity, 8, 10, 89, 151, 172
mirror effect, 4, 43, 59
mobilisation campaigns, 198
Mouvement pour le Triomphe des Libertés Démocratiques (MTLD), 69, 71, 73
Morocco, 18–19, 21, 65, 99, 161
MSP (Movement of Society and Peace), 94
Muqaddimah, 130, 177–8

nadis, 68, 70, 72
non-movements, 27, 199
Nour association, 143–7

OAS (Secret Army Organisation), 73
online education, 207
online surveillance, 210
Oran, 89, 93–5, 109, 124–7
organisational deficit, 211
Organisation spéciale (OS), 71
Ottoman regency, 64–6
Ouyahia, Ahmed, 200, 201

PAGS (*Parti de l'Avant Garde Socialiste*), 74, 84
Palestine, 23, 31, 53–4, 58, 179, 196
pandemic activism, 205–11
Parks, Robert, 215
Parliament, 5, 94–5, 101, 199
PCPA (French Support programme for Associations), 127, 146
protesta (low-level protests), 199, 215
political parties, 5, 6, 24–5, 32, 65, 74, 77–9, 85, 89, 201

public spaces, 210
public sphere, 2, 5, 13, 20, 30, 38, 44, 69, 74, 78, 101, 108, 130, 133, 136
Putnam, Robert, 26–7, 38

RADDO network (*Réseaud' Associations du Développement Durable des Oases*), 99
Rebai Maamri, Malika, 67, 70, 76
Récif association, 173
refolution, 197
repression, 201
riots, 2–3, 32, 77, 78
Reconciliation Charter, 33–4, 105, 152, 156, 187, 202
resource management, 209
revolutionary consciousness, 211–16
Revolutionary Life (Bayat), 198
Roberts, Hugh, 2, 32 , 63 , 65–6, 88
Roman heritage, 127–30, 184
Roy, Olivier, 4, 43
Russia, 42, 49

Salah, Gaid, 201
SantéSidi El Houari, 126–7
SARP association, 36, 155, 181, 183, 186, 199
Schmitter, Phillipe, 27, 38, 104–6, 196
Security services, 91, 139
Sellal, Abdelmalek, 201
Serres, Thomas, 212
sharia, 77, 79
silmiya (peaceful protest), 200
social capital, 26, 27, 31, 104
Social Development Agency, 8, 10, 89, 106, 143, 147, 151, 154, 172

Sonatrach, 96, 129
space, 72, 75–8, 80, 84, 87–8, 92, 116, 124, 127, 156, 171, 195–6, 201, 211–16
state of emergency, 34, 80, 85, 89, 163
stigmatisation
    of associations, 34, 182–3
    of languages, 14, 188–90, 193
student clubs, 207
sufism, 64, 66, 123, 134–5
Syria, 196

TACIS (Technical Aid to the Commonwealth of Independent States),
Tebboune, Abdelmajid, 201
thajmaaths, 65
Tamazight, 188–9
Tefayech, Sheikh (association), 123, 135–6
Tej association, 149–151
Tibhirine Monastery, 1
de Tocqueville, Alexis, 7, 26, 67
trade unions, 74, 113
transnational civil society, 72, 101, 137, 201
trauma
    associations tackling, 107, 139, 151–6, 199
    historical, 65 , 96, 117, 162, 186
Tunisia, 65, 161, 211
    associations, 22
    networks of associations, 99
    uprisings, 87–8, 174

Union for the Mediterranean, 47, 165
USAID, 41, 43

veil, 1–2
volunteering, 196

women, 1–2, 32–4, 113
　feminist movement, 76–9
　network WASSILA, 146
　protesters, 205
　quota in parliament, 199
　support associations, 172, 181–2
World War II, 71

Yemen, 20, 22
Youth
　activism, 214
　associations, 103, 113, 139–41
　dissent, 84
　NADA network, 146
　Youth Futures project, 198, 209

zawiyas, 64, 87, 123, 134–5
Zeraoulia, Faouzia, 200
Zerhouni, Yazid, 182
Zoubir, Yahia, 205, 209, 212

www.ingramcontent.com/pod-product-compliance
Lightning Source LLC
Chambersburg PA
CBHW051630230426
43669CB00013B/2249